A Guide to

THE
PRESENT MOMENT

How to Stop Believing the Thoughts that Keep You from Feeling Free, Whole, and Happy

Noah Elkrief

Noah Elkrief

www.liveinthemoment.org

ISBN: 978-0-9859534-0-9

Contents

Introduction

Do you want to stop holding on to anger, sadness, or guilt about something that happened in your past?

Do you want to stop worrying about what others think or stop feeling the need to seek others' love, approval, and appreciation?

Do you want to stop judging others, getting angry at people, or blaming others for your unhappiness?

Do you want to stop judging yourself, feeling unworthy, or sensing that something is missing from your life?

Do you want to stop struggling with anxiety, stress, or fear about the future?

All these emotions seem inevitable and even inescapable while you're in their grip. But if you're willing to look at your life with real honesty, it is possible to discover that they are all created by thoughts in your mind—thoughts about yourself, your relationships, your situations, your past, your future—and each of them can vanish in an instant if you just stop believing these thoughts to be true.

If a random person tells you, "The world is going to end tomorrow", *and you believe them,* how would you feel? You will likely experience fear. But if *you didn't believe them,* then how would their comment make you feel? You almost certainly wouldn't feel any fear. If a co-worker tells you, "I deleted all of your emails!", *and you believe them*, how do you think you would feel? You would probably get angry. But if your co-worker told you this, *and you didn't believe them at all* because they are always joking around, then how do you think you would feel? You almost surely wouldn't experience anger because there would be nothing to be angry about. If you are watching a tragic scene in a movie, *and you believe the actors*, how would you feel? You would likely experience the sadness of the movie. But if *you didn't believe the actors at all*, then how would you feel? You almost certainly wouldn't feel sad.

These scenarios demonstrate that when you believe someone's words to be true, they create emotions. But when you don't believe someone's words, their words don't have the power to create emotions.

The same is true of the thoughts (words) in your mind. If you believe a negative thought about yourself or your life, that thought will create an unwanted emotion. However, if you don't believe that thought, it quite simply won't create the unwanted emotion.

This book will help you to experience the peace and happiness you want in life by providing you with 5 steps that will enable you to identify and disbelieve the thoughts that create all of your unwanted emotions. As soon as you disbelieve a thought, you stop experiencing the emotion it created, and you automatically stop giving attention to that thought.

I've seen this process bring peace to the lives of people facing every conceivable kind of challenge. I have watched a man break free from anger towards his parents for the way they treated him as a child. I have watched a woman shed her sadness about her divorce from her husband of two decades. I have watched people stop worrying about what others think and experience the freedom to act how they want for the first time. I've watched dozens of men and women get rid of the anxiety about what may happen in their jobs, finally allowing them to enjoy their time at work. I've watched countless people come to feel whole, loved, and worthy as never before, solely because they were able to disbelieve the thoughts that made them feel unloved, unworthy, and incomplete in some way. I've watched people finally stop beating themselves up about the way their lives are, simply by disbelieving their beliefs about the way life should be.

In the pages ahead, you'll discover for yourself how to dissolve your unwanted emotions and experience the peace of the present moment through engaging with the 5-step process. First, though, I'll tell you how I discovered this in my own life.

About me

I was born and raised in Hastings-on-Hudson, a small town just north of New York City. From the time I was born, my father would bring me to meditation retreats on almost every vacation. While at these retreats, I learned many different types of meditation practices and really just enjoyed myself. These meditation practices quickly became a very important part of my life, as I started to do these practices on my own every day when I was six years old. Since I was a young child, and already very happy, I didn't choose to meditate to try to make myself happy. I don't know why, but somehow I had a really strong longing to know the truth about life. I knew that what I was seeing and experiencing wasn't the whole story. So I did these meditative practices because I believed that they would eventually expose this ultimate truth that I was looking for, a concept I often referred to as "spiritual enlightenment".

The idea of enlightenment became the most important thing to me from a very young age, so much so that every wish I ever made was only to know this truth (except one time when I wished to kiss my teenage crush). I started to have glimpses (experiences) of this truth beginning when I was 12 years old, but it never lasted for more than an hour. In order to progress towards my goal, after college, in addition to my daily meditative practices, I decided to minimize my distractions and spend as much time in silence as I could. I stopped watching TV and movies, stopped listening to music, kept my apartment internet-free, spent most of my leisure time alone by choice, and spent three months mostly in silence on a meditation retreat. Seemingly as a result of all this, my daily meditative practices began creating such intense experiences of happiness that they frequently made me cry. Eventually, I began to also have these experiences whenever I encountered beautiful sights and sounds.

Besides my goal of enlightenment, I also had many other goals, which often took up a good deal of my time, energy, and effort. I wanted success, wealth, and a job I enjoyed; I wanted to go to amazing parties, to date beautiful women, to prove I was smart, and to see the most beautiful places in the world, and I wanted people to love me. That was what I wanted in life, so that was what I pursued. Somehow, at a relatively young age, I managed to get everything I ever wanted. I was working in a prestigious and high-paying job that I loved as a corporate strategy consultant in London after a stint working on the trading floor at Goldman Sachs. I traveled around the world, saw more incredible scenes of nature than I could have imagined, enjoyed unbelievable parties in exotic places (always sober), dated beautiful women from all around Europe, was later accepted into Mensa, and everyone always seemed to love me. All of this led me to have an incredibly high opinion of myself, and I honestly believed I was the happiest guy in the world.

Yet I still wasn't content. I had an endless drive to keep improving myself and my situation. I constantly needed to keep myself busy. I was always spending my time, money, and energy searching for more fun moments. I frequently judged others in order to maintain my relative opinion of myself (as smarter, funnier, cooler, and happier than others). I forced myself to play soccer and to go to nightclubs (among other things), even when I didn't feel like it, just so that I could keep thinking of myself as a soccer player and as someone who is fun. Even though I already believed everyone loved me, I still worried about their opinions of me, because I needed to make sure I maintained or even further improved their opinions of me. I often didn't do or say what I wanted to because I was worried about what others would think. *All of this prevented me from feeling relaxed, free, whole, loving, happy, or peaceful.*

Then, while at a meditation retreat in India, I was somehow hit with the feeling that I needed to stop my meditation practice and try something new in order to progress towards discovering the truth I was looking for. This was a big shock to me, since I had been on the same path my whole life and it had seemingly given me so much, but I had no choice but to listen. So I spent about five months following my intuition, spending the vast majority of my free time alone and in silence, and often watching videos of different teachers. Then, in the summer of 2009, I ended up at a silent meditation retreat in southern England with one of the teachers I had seen in the videos.

I thought that I wanted enlightenment more than anything else. But what I realized during this retreat was that there was a big fear keeping me from it. I had created this idea in my mind that if I discovered the truth about life, I could lose everything great that I had, as well as the possibility of ever getting anything else that I wanted. Since I wasn't willing to give up everything I had and still wanted, I kept saying to myself, "I just need to go to a few more countries, date a few more girls, and save up a little more money— then I'll be ready to give it all up".

One day during this retreat, I was walking by myself in a wheat field when I suddenly realized that I had gotten enough of what I wanted in life to truly know that getting more wasn't going to give me the happiness I wanted. I was done procrastinating. Then a thought popped up in my mind, and it said, "There may not be another moment to give up everything". In this very moment, when I truly realized that knowing the truth was the absolute most important thing to me and that nothing else mattered, all of my thoughts seemed to disappear. My mind seemed completely empty.

Without my thoughts, what remained was a feeling of incredible peace, freedom, relaxation, and openness. It seemed as if I was opening my eyes and looking at the world for the very first time. It was as if I had gone through life wearing glasses with opaque black lenses with only a tiny little hole in the middle to see through—and even that part of the lens had a strange tint that altered my vision. When I lost my thoughts, these glasses came off, and everything was vast, expansive, and spacious. Also, it was as though I had never seen a tree, the sky, or a person before. I had always been paying attention to my *thoughts* about a tree or the sky, such as what type of tree it was or how the sky then compared to the sky at other times and whether I liked it or not, rather than truly witnessing the tree or the sky itself. I was always paying attention to my thoughts about whether people were smart or stupid, attractive or ugly, nice or mean—or about what I wanted from them and how they were seeing me—rather than just purely seeing them.

Now it seemed as if all of my thoughts were just blown away, nowhere to be found. My mind was open, free, and peaceful. *This* was everything I had ever wanted.

Then, a few hours later, a strange thing happened. All of a sudden I began to experience an intense new fear that I wasn't going to be able to function or do anything at all now that I had no thoughts. Luckily, I was at a retreat where I had access to a teacher who was already enlightened. At the next group session, I raised my hand, and the teacher called on me to come up and sit with her. Half ecstatic, and half incredibly fearful, I said to her, "I have lost all my thoughts! I have nothing left! I am not going to be able to do anything! It is going to be funny at work on Monday!" She responded, very calmly and compassionately, "You have nothing left except for one little story that you're telling yourself -- 'oops, this is too big, I'm scared'. Who knows? All your thoughts may be back on Monday". As soon as she said this to me, my fear instantly left me, and my mind was back in silence.

That night, as I lay in my bed, I reflected on what had happened. I realized that my fear had been created by the thought "I am not going to be able to do anything with no thoughts". I had believed this thought to be true—but now it became clear to me that the thought was actually based on two big assumptions. The first assumption was, "My mind will remain silent in the future", while the second assumption was, "I will not be able to perform tasks with a silent mind". However, the fact was that I had absolutely no idea whether either of these two assumptions was true. So I really had no idea whether my thought was true.

As it turned out, this wasn't just a passing experience. The vast majority of my recurring psychological thoughts vanished in that wheat field, and have rarely attempted to return. These psychological thoughts included almost all of my thoughts about myself, my situation, others, and what others thought about me, as well as my thoughts about the past, the future, and who I might become. Without these thoughts, my mind was left predominantly silent, and I was left in the peace I had always been searching for. That moment in the wheat field marked the end of my search for enlightenment, and the end of my pursuit of happiness.

Since peace and contentment were now my normal experience, any time I felt a degree of discontent, I knew something was off. I now knew that a silent mind left me in peace, so naturally the first place I would look to find the cause of my unwanted emotion was in my own mind. Each time I took a look at my mind while experiencing an unwanted emotion, I could see that I had been thinking a thought or telling myself a story that was creating my unwanted emotion. It turned out that some old psychological thoughts did remain after the initial loss of thoughts, and new psychological thoughts sometimes arose. However, it was usually easy to identify the thought creating my unwanted emotion, because my mind was largely empty, and there were not that many thoughts to choose from.

Once I found the instigating thought, I would ask myself, "Do I know this thought is true?" To my surprise, every time I asked myself this question, either I would immediately recognize that I did *not* know whether the thought was true, or several reasons would present themselves to show me that I couldn't possibly know for sure that it was. It seemed this recognition would occur mostly because I had no thoughts about my thought. Since I no longer had thoughts about myself, I was able to look at my thoughts objectively, without any hidden incentives (e.g., wanting to be "right"). As soon as I realized that I didn't know for sure whether my thought was true, my unwanted emotion would instantly dissolve and I would come right back to my natural state of contentment. On top of that, each time I stopped believing one of my thoughts to be true, that thought would rarely ever return. This has resulted in almost uninterrupted peace and happiness.

I wasn't unable to function, as I had briefly feared; my mind actually functioned better than ever. Without my psychological thoughts, when the situation called for it, I was able to give my complete attention to the functional thoughts that helped me to solve practical issues such as "How do I construct this chair?" or "What is the quickest way to get to the restaurant?" Because of this, I continued to perform well in my job, using my mind as a tool to analyze numbers, for another year before resigning. In addition, I didn't have to give up anything that I thought I might have had to. I still traveled, dated, played sports, and went to clubs when I wanted to. I had previously thought that my constant drive to improve myself, my situation, and the people around me arose because nothing was good enough the way it was. But what I realized was that there was actually nothing wrong with me, my situation, or others. *It was only my thoughts about everything that made things seem insufficient, making me feel discontent and incomplete.* I was only trying to improve everything in order to make myself happy. So, once I was happy, I no longer had this endless need to improve everything about my life. I could finally relax.

Since the thoughts that would normally create suffering and discontent either didn't arise in my mind or weren't believed when they did show up, all of my attention remained on the present moment. At work, I never experienced stress or pressure, even when I was behind on a project that had a strict deadline. When my intuition told me that it was time to leave my job, there was no fear, despite not knowing what I would do next. When I left London, there was no sadness, even though I was leaving all my friends behind. After knee surgery, I couldn't stand or walk for a year without being in pain, yet I didn't have any self-pity or frustration about it. When I waited with my father in the emergency room for MRIs and CT scans of his brain, I felt no worry about what might happen to him. And when I got the feeling that I needed to write a book, I had no self-doubt, even though I had never liked writing and it had been my worst subject in school.

After losing most of my thoughts, I have been left with the recognition that I don't know whether the thoughts that arise in my mind are true. What remains when we don't have, or don't believe, our thoughts is quite simply, the present moment, with nothing added.

Because I am present, no matter what my circumstances are, I remain in peace.

Guiding you to the present moment

For the first year of living like this, I spoke about my experience with only a few people. But over time, my friends spontaneously started to open up to me about their suffering and discontent. They would tell me about their anxiety, worries, resentment, sadness, and guilt, about how they didn't feel good enough or complete, and about how they frequently judged themselves and others.

Each time someone would tell me about an emotion they didn't want to have, I was able to help them identify the thought that was creating their emotion and then offer them questions to help them challenge their thought. Sure enough, they almost always discovered that they didn't actually know whether their thought was true. Each time they disbelieved their thought, their unwanted emotion would immediately dissolve, bringing them back to the peace of the present moment.

My friends were amazed that they could go from suffering to happiness in an instant simply by disbelieving whatever thought was creating their suffering in that moment. As my friends told their friends, allowing me to go through this process with more and more people, I realized that anyone could disbelieve the thoughts that create their suffering, and become present. It didn't make any difference whether a person had a spiritual background or was an atheist, whether they'd had an easy life or a seemingly horrific childhood, whether they had been hurtful in the past or had lived as a "model citizen", or whether they considered themselves to be happy or depressed. No matter what their circumstances were, no matter what emotion they were experiencing, and no matter how intense it was, their emotion would dissolve as soon as they disbelieved the thought that created it.

I thought that people would be able to disbelieve their thoughts by themselves, but everyone seemed to have a hard time finding the thoughts that were creating their emotions, and they couldn't discover why their thoughts might not be true without my showing them the different reasons. So I created a 5-step process that people can use on their own to stop believing the thoughts that keep them from living in peace and acting with love. This book was written to share that process with you.

These 5 steps, and all of the questions within each step, will help you to experience the peace and happiness of the present moment at *any* moment and will make you happier in more and more situations throughout your daily life.

The 5 Steps to The Present Moment are:

1) Pick an unwanted emotion
2) Identify the thoughts behind your unwanted emotion
3) Recognize that your emotion has been created by your thoughts and not your circumstances
4) Discover that you don't know whether your thought is true
5) Question the validity of any reason to continue suffering (if relevant)

So what would it be like to experience the present moment? Can you remember the happiness you felt in the very moment that you achieved an important goal? This may be the moment someone proposed marriage to you, the moment you gave birth to a healthy child, the moment you got the job or promotion you wanted, or the moment you found out that you had passed an important exam. Before that moment, you may have had complaints that life wasn't good enough the way it was, it may have seemed as though something was missing from your life, or you may have had a lot of anxiety about whether or not you would achieve your goal. But in the moment that you achieved your goal, all these thoughts were gone. There were no complaints about the way life is and no worries about what might happen. When you got what you wanted, you experienced a brief absence of thoughts, and that is what made you feel happy. In that moment of wonderful peace, joy, or happiness, you experienced the present moment.

This book will take you through The 5 Steps to The Present Moment, giving you clear instructions on what to do at each step along the way in order to directly experience the present moment—while you're reading the book as well as at any moment in the future. But before we dive into The 5 Steps, the first three chapters will help you to understand how our thoughts create our emotions, what it means to experience the present moment, and why the traditional pursuit of happiness isn't enough to give us the happiness we want.

Everything in this book is meant to be directly discovered and experienced. For this reason, most of the sections contain a few quick questions or an exercise. For example, there are five to nine questions to help you identify the thoughts behind each of your emotions, five questions to help you recognize that your emotion was actually created by your thoughts, and 34 questions to help you directly discover that you don't know whether your thought is true. While many of the questions can be answered mentally, you may find it helpful to designate a notebook that you will use for writing down insights and answers to questions while reading.

The content in this book is not theory, it is not philosophy, and it is not meant to be believed. Therefore, this book is not meant to be read in the same way as other types of books. If we read this book by comparing the content to what we think we already know, or by trying to see if we think the content is logical and makes sense theoretically, then it is unlikely that we will get much value from this book even if we agree with everything we read.

All of the content in this book has been *directly discovered* through watching and dealing with the thoughts in my own mind, and has been confirmed to be relevant and applicable to others through my *direct experience* of working with countless students. In order to get the most value out of this book, it's important to engage with all of the questions and exercises, and test everything against your own experience, constantly asking yourself, "Does this match my own experience in life?", or "How does this concept play itself out in my life?" This will enable you to directly experience the truth of what is written, help you to see thoughts and emotions that you may not have been aware of, allow new insights to present themselves, guide you back to the present moment, and ultimately help you to live a more fulfilling life.

This book isn't meant to provide you with a strategy that may make you happy one day once you have practiced it for years, mastered it, and sacrificed for it. This isn't a process that requires you to trust in it, having faith that you will eventually reap the rewards. This isn't about getting rid of all your emotions, or getting to some future point when you lose all of the thoughts that create your suffering in one moment, all at once.

This book is about disbelieving a thought that is causing you to suffer *right now*, thereby freeing you to enjoy the happiness of the present moment *right now,* and enabling you to feel happy in any situation where that thought would otherwise have created suffering.

Chapter One

How Our Thoughts Create Our Emotions

We all want to be happy. But in order to succeed in our pursuit of happiness, we first need to identify and understand the cause of our unhappiness. Most of us have gone through life believing that the circumstances and events in our lives are the cause of our sadness, anger, anxiety, and feeling of incompleteness. This is what we were taught. This is how we see our family and friends pursue happiness, and this is how characters in movies seem to pursue happiness. Therefore, naturally, we try to change our circumstances in order to find happiness.

Virtually everything in our lives tends to reaffirm the belief that circumstances are the cause of our happiness and suffering. For most of us, this belief is so strong and widespread that we go through much of our lives without even questioning it. But eventually, some of us reach a point when we come to realize that the way we have been pursuing happiness isn't working or just isn't enough.

The reason we don't feel free, whole, and happy isn't because we aren't good enough, it isn't because we are missing something, and it isn't because we haven't achieved the perfect circumstances. It is simply because we have been pursuing happiness in the wrong place. Our pursuit of happiness hasn't been addressing the actual cause of our unhappiness.

If you allow yourself to read this book with genuine openness and honesty, you may discover that it's not the circumstances in your life that create all of your unwanted emotions—it's actually your *thoughts* about your circumstances that cause you to suffer and prevent you from feeling free, whole, and happy.

How thoughts create our emotions

As young children, most of us are happy the majority of the time. As adults, most of us aren't. So what happened to us? Why aren't we content anymore? Quite simply, we have learned many concepts about what is "perfect". Our concept of "perfect" can also be referred to as our ideas of the "right" way, how we think things "should be", and what we think is "best", "good", "cool", or "appropriate". We were taught these concepts both formally and informally by our parents, teachers, and friends; we absorbed them from TV, movies, and collective societal views; they are shaped by our memories of pleasure, genetics, and all of our experiences in life.

When we were young children (under six years old), before we learned most of our concepts of what is "perfect", we had nothing to compare our life against. Without a concept of "perfect" to compare things against, we rarely decided that any aspect of ourselves, others, or our situation was "bad" or "not good enough". Everything was just what it was. Without these thoughts about what isn't "good enough" in our life, we felt free, whole, and happy.

As we developed more and more of our concepts of what is "perfect" over the years, we began to increasingly compare everything in our life to these concepts. Naturally, life has come up short quite a bit, and we frequently ended up labeling things in our lives—

actions, words, events, situations, feelings, personality traits, physical appearances—as "bad" or "not good enough".

As soon as a thought pops up in our mind that decides "something isn't good enough", we begin to experience a subtle sense of sadness or lack, as if something is missing from our lives. If we look to blame someone for some "bad" aspect of our life, then we experience anger towards whoever we believe is to blame.

Imagine you are happy with your current relationship. Then, when you are out with a few friends, you discover that they all go out on dates with their partners more than twice as often as you do with your partner. If you then compare your relationship to your friends' relationships, you may unconsciously decide that your relationship isn't "good enough" the way it is. The thought "my relationship isn't good enough the way it is" would then create a sense of sadness and a feeling that something is lacking in your relationship. If you then decide that your partner is to blame for the apparent insufficiencies of your relationship, this thought would create a feeling of resentment towards him or her. All it would take to go from being happy to unhappy with your relationship is believing one thought about how something isn't quite "good enough" the way it is.

Instead of realizing that our feelings of disappointment, deficiency, and anger are created by our thoughts, we believe that these emotions are directly created by our circumstances (e.g., our relationship) being factually "bad" or "not good enough". This misunderstanding causes us to try to change our circumstances from being "not good enough" to being "perfect" in order to become happy. This is how our pursuit of happiness gets started. We don't recognize that this is really just an attempt to change our thoughts about our circumstances from "this isn't good enough" to "this is perfect".

Once we believe that the "perfect" circumstances would make us happiest, we unconsciously conclude that failure to achieve the "perfect" circumstances would result in suffering, or at least less happiness. This possible result is then labeled to be a "bad" or "worse" outcome. As soon as we have formed the idea of a "bad" or "worse" outcome, we begin to fear that outcome.

For example, if we think the "perfect" relationship would make us happy, then we would inherently decide that "it would be bad if I don't ever get the perfect relationship". This thought would then create our anxiety and stress. This may also cause us to start projecting mental images in our mind (worrying) about how "bad" life would be if we never got this "perfect" relationship. We may ask ourselves over and over again, "What if this bad outcome ends up happening?" or "What if this doesn't work out?"

The intensity of our emotions is determined by several factors. Most notably, the "worse" we consider a circumstance in our life to be, and the more important we think that circumstance is to our happiness, the stronger our suffering will be. For example, we would likely get more upset about our friend getting robbed than our friend getting insulted because we are likely to think that robberies are "worse" than insults. Similarly, we would likely to get more upset if we got robbed than if our friend got robbed because we would likely think that our robbery is more important to our happiness than our friend's robbery.

In addition, our emotions are often intensified by thinking about "bad" moments from the past and imagining "bad" moments happening in the future. For example, if our spouse leaves his dishes on the table, we might not just think, "That was lazy", we might think of all the previous times our spouse left his dishes on the table or all the other lazy things we think our spouse has done lately. If our kid gets a "bad" grade, we might not just think, "That was bad", we might imagine a future where our kid keeps getting "bad" grades and becomes a failure. In both of these situations, instead of just feeling a little anger or disappointment from thinking, "That was lazy" or "That was bad", our emotional reaction would be intensified by thinking about past "bad" moments and possible future "bad" moments. Each additional "bad" moment we think about multiplies the intensity of our emotion. In this way, we often react to our thoughts about the past and future, rather than just our thoughts about the actual event that just happened.

Throughout our lives we develop many concepts about what is "perfect" or "ideal", and, therefore, many beliefs about what is "bad" or "not good enough". Any time we make a decision as to whether something is "bad" or "good", this thought can be called a "judgment". Regardless of the subject of our judgments, or the words we use, believing that "something is bad" will create one of our unwanted emotions. Now let's take a look at some examples of what we judge to be "bad" in life, and how these judgments create our suffering and then lead us on our never-ending pursuit of happiness.

"The essentials for happiness"

As children, we are happy and content being single. At some point in our lives we then learn that marriage is essential to being happy. No matter what the source of this concept is—our parents, teachers, the movies—once we believe "marriage is needed for happiness", we automatically believe, "I don't have something I need to be happy". This makes us believe that "my life isn't good enough the way it is". This thought then creates a subtle sense of sadness or a feeling of being incomplete.

Unknowingly, we then blame these feelings on not having a spouse, as opposed to noticing that they were really caused by believing the *thought,* "marriage is needed for happiness". So, naturally, this belief makes us begin our long search for a spouse so that we can be happy. But since we believe marriage will make us happy, we inevitably believe that failure to find a spouse will leave us unhappy (a "bad" outcome). This causes us to experience fear that we will never find a spouse. And if we don't find a spouse by the time we think we should, we may then think, "I shouldn't still be single", which would cause us to feel sad or ashamed.

Depending on where and how we are raised, we learn different ideas about what we need to be happy. These ideas often show up as either our fantasies or our beliefs about what we should be doing with our life. The most common beliefs are that marriage, love, having children, success, wealth, major achievements, fulfilling potential, making history, fame, power, respect, or travelling the world will make us happy. As soon as we believe that something is the key to our happiness, and we don't have it, we have no choice but to think, "My circumstances aren't good enough right now to be happy", or "I need my circumstances to change for me to be happy". These thoughts make us feel as if something is missing from our lives, and as though we are somehow lacking or incomplete.

We then innocently blame our unhappiness on our seemingly insufficient circumstances instead of recognizing that it's only our *thoughts* about our circumstances that have created these feelings. Once this happens, we begin to pursue the circumstances we think we need to be happy. If we believe that certain circumstances are the key to happiness, then we must also believe, "If I don't achieve these circumstances, I will never be happy". Since this outcome is clearly seen as "bad", we start to feel anxious and worried that we might not ever get what we think we need to be happy.

Questions: *What do I believe is needed to be happy? What should my life be like? What key to happiness do I believe is missing from my life?*

Physical appearance

When we are babies and young children, we are completely fine with our bodies as they are, regardless of how much we weigh. Then, as we get older, we learn that skinny is "good" or "perfect" and fat is "bad". We learn this from TV, magazines, parents, or friends. Once we learn this, we start to believe, "I am not good enough the way I am", "I am too fat", or "I am not skinny enough". These thoughts then create the feeling of sadness. But since we attribute our sadness to our weight instead of our *thoughts* about our weight, we logically form a goal to become skinnier ("perfect") so that we can be happy again.

For every part of our bodies, we tend to have an idea of what is "beautiful" ("perfect") and what is "ugly" ("bad"). We compare each part of our bodies to our ideas of "beautiful" and then frequently decide it is "ugly" or "not good enough" in some way. These thoughts are then what create our emotional experience. If we judge our ankles to be too big, we may feel embarrassed when we have to wear a skirt. If we think our nose is "ugly", we may frequently worry about whether others are looking at it when we are in conversations.

We not only judge our body parts, but we also judge our clothes, posture, walking style, and anything else we see. Our judgments about our physical appearance create sadness, embarrassment, worries, and often even anger. But since we believe that our emotions are created by the facts and not by our *thoughts* about the facts, we often try to change our physical appearance (or hide it) in an attempt to make ourselves happy.

Just as we compare our own physical appearance to our ideas of "perfect", we also tend to compare every aspect of others' physical appearance to these ideas. These comparisons then create our judgments, and can often cause us to treat others without love.

Questions: What physical attributes about myself do I judge to be "bad"? Whose physical traits do I judge most often and what are they?

Actions

As children, we couldn't have cared less about whether people held doors open for us, burped, chewed with their mouths open, held forks in their palms, or talked on their cell phones at restaurants. But eventually we learned that these actions were "bad", "wrong", "inappropriate" or "shouldn't be done". Once we believe someone has done something "inappropriate", we begin to feel disappointed or angry at that person. Since we think our anger is created by others' actions, we conclude, "I need that person to change his or her actions for me to be happy". On top of that, when people don't change their actions after we conclude that they need to, we can experience additional anger towards them because we believe they are preventing our happiness. We don't realize that it is only our *thoughts* about their actions being "inappropriate" that create our emotions, not their actions themselves.

In almost every situation, we tend to have an idea of what people "should" do and say and how they should do and say it. This includes all of our concepts of "good manners", "respectful" or "appropriate" actions, as well as many of our own rules we have created about life (e.g., "no kissing in public"). There are also the widely accepted beliefs that it is "bad" or "mean" to yell, hit, verbally abuse, steal, cheat, or ignore people. There are also the beliefs that we are treating ourselves "badly" if we drink alcohol, smoke cigarettes, act lazy, overeat, eat unhealthy foods, or don't exercise.

Since we have so many ideas of the "right" way to act, and we habitually compare actions to these ideas, we often end up judging our actions and those of others to be "bad" in some way. Our judgments about others tend to create anger, while our judgments about ourselves usually spark disappointment, shame, guilt, or even anger. Whenever we believe we are the victim of any "bad" action, we become sad, and then often angry at whoever is seemingly to blame. These emotional reactions seem appropriate, instantaneous, and natural, but if we allow ourselves to look at any situation honestly—even if we feel doubtful or defensive about it at first—then it is possible to see that our emotional reactions are created by our thoughts about certain actions and not directly by the actions themselves.

The people whose actions we judge most are generally the people closest to us. These include our *partners, children, parents, friends, co-workers, and bosses.* With our partners, we tend to have beliefs about what is "perfect" for every aspect of their behavior – what is the "ideal" or "right" way for them to talk, act, walk, dress, eat, cook, clean, sit, watch TV, drive, caress, cuddle, make love, parent our children, and everything else. We continuously compare our partners' actions to our ideas of "the right ways to act", as if these ideas are true, and then we frequently judge our partners to be "insufficient" in some way when he or she does something that "he shouldn't have done" or that doesn't match up to our idea of "perfect". Even when our partner has no idea what our idea of "perfect" is. We feel disappointed and sad that our partners are "not good enough", and then on top of that we often get angry at them because we believe they are to blame for our unhappiness in the relationship. Since we don't realize that our emotions are the result of our own thoughts, not our partners' actions, we almost constantly try to "improve" our partners because we think that the "improvements" would make us happy again (or we fantasize about someone who is "perfect").

Questions: *Whose actions do I most commonly think aren't "good enough" or "should be different"? What actions do I most fre-*

quently judge to be "inappropriate", "disrespectful", "bad", or "mean"?

Situations

When we are young children, we are generally happy with the size of our house and type of car we ride in. However, once we are adults, many of us tend to believe that our house or car aren't "good enough", thereby making us sad or embarrassed about the house we live in or the car we drive. Because we believe our sadness or embarrassment is created directly by our situation, not by our thoughts, we often spend a great deal of time and money trying to get the "perfect" house or car in order to make ourselves happy. If we think the "perfect" house or car will make us happy, then we tend to think that it would be "bad" if we didn't get them. This concept then creates our fear and anxiety that we will never get the "perfect" house or car in the future.

By the time we are adults, we have an incredible number of ideas about how our lives "should be" or what the "ideal" situation would be. We tend to frequently compare our situation (and others') to our ideas of what are the "perfect" job, salary, marital status, and living situation. Inevitably, these comparisons cause us to frequently judge our situations to be "not good enough". For example, we might think it is "bad" to work as much as we do, to make the amount of money we do, to still be unmarried, to still not have children, or to still be living in a "small" apartment at our age. These situations themselves don't have the ability to create our sadness, anger, shame, or embarrassment. It is only our thoughts about our situations that create these emotions. But when we attribute our unhappiness to our situations, we begin to pursue the "perfect" situation and then start to fear not achieving it. Many of us then spend a lot of time worrying about whether we will ever achieve our idea of the "perfect" situation.

Questions: What situations in my life do I think aren't "good enough" or "shouldn't be the way they are"?

Thoughts

Not only do we have thoughts that certain external circumstances in our lives are "bad", we even have thoughts that decide that other *thoughts* are "bad". Throughout our childhood, no matter what thoughts we had about someone, we didn't have thoughts on top of them that said "the thought you just had was bad" or "you are bad because you just had that thought".

Now, as adults, most of us have many concepts about what are "good" thoughts and what are "bad" thoughts to have. For example, we may think that it is "bad" to think negatively about others, or we may consider it "bad" to think about the past or future. So instead of just having these thoughts, we add a layer of new thoughts on top of them, telling ourselves, "It is terrible that I am always judging people", "I am worthless for being so pessimistic about my relationship", or "I am stupid for always thinking about the future". This new layer of thoughts can make us feel disappointed, ashamed, or angry at ourselves just for giving attention to the thoughts that have entered our minds.

It is not as though our thoughts about others or the past and future create our shame and anger towards ourselves—it is only our negative thoughts *about* our thoughts that create this extra layer of suffering for us.

Questions: What thoughts in my mind do I often consider to be "bad"?

Emotions

When a toddler is sad, she certainly has no thoughts about how her emotion is "bad", and she won't think that she is somehow "worse" than others because she has this emotion. As adults, after our thoughts create emotions, we do often judge our emotions to be "bad". Most of us tend to think that it is "bad" to feel angry, sad, depressed, hopeless, frustrated, stressed, confused, jealous, guilty, fearful, or hurt. We also may think it is "wrong" or "inappropriate" to be happy in certain types of situations, such as when a loved one is sick. When we consider our emotions to be "bad", we feel sad, ashamed, or angry at ourselves on top of whatever emotion we are already experiencing.

If other people are experiencing any of these "bad" emotions, we often feel sad for them because we think it is "bad" that they have to experience them. But, it doesn't stop there. We also often judge others for their emotions because we think that these emotions signify something about the people who are experiencing them. Most commonly, we think that people who experience "too much" of these "bad" emotions are stupid, weak, emotional, fragile, immature, irresponsible, or "bad" in some other way. If we didn't believe the concept that some emotions are "bad", then we wouldn't get angry at ourselves or feel sad about the emotions we have. We could just experience them as a passing feeling in our body, like physical pain.

Questions: What emotions do I believe are "bad" or "negative"? What do I think these emotions mean about the people who have them?

Identity

As young children, before we learned our ideas of "perfect", we didn't think, "I am not good enough", no matter what our traits were. We didn't feel incomplete or unlovable. We also didn't worry about others' opinions of us. Once we become adults, this clearly changes.

To understand what changed, we first need to understand what our identity is. Our identity, or self-image, is our answer to the questions, "Who am I?", or "How would I describe myself?" Part of our answers to these questions includes the facts of our age, gender, physical measurements, job title, education, living situation, marital status, and so on. However, the facts themselves aren't what create our identity, emotions, or self-confidence. The basis for our self-image, and our ensuing happiness or unhappiness, is our opinion of ourselves (our thoughts about ourselves). For example, even if two people are the same age and have the same weight, education, and jobs, one person could be proud of himself, while the other person could be ashamed to have these very same characteristics. Basically, our self-image is predominantly made up of *our opinions* of all the facts, as well as our opinions of completely subjective topics such as our personality and whether we are attractive. Put simply, our identity is made up of thoughts (opinions).

When we compare any aspect of our self-image to our idea of "perfect" and decide that it is "bad" or "not ideal", we will feel sad, lacking, ashamed, incomplete, or even depressed. Naturally, we all tend to have many attributes that we consider to be "imperfect". For example, we may think, "I should be more successful", "I am not smart enough", "I am too boring", or "My body isn't attractive". As soon as we think any of these thoughts or make any other judgment about ourselves, we experience unwanted feelings of sadness and lack. *We blame these unwanted feelings on our perceived insufficiencies instead of recognizing that these emotions are only created by the thought, "Something about me isn't good enough".*

This misunderstanding causes us to try to "improve" our self-image to our idea of "perfect" in an attempt to make ourselves happy (otherwise known as "self-improvement"). Since we believe our happiness is dependent on whether we can achieve our goals (our ideas of what is "perfect"), our striving to "improve" our bodies, jobs, living situations, and everything else is often filled with the fear or anxiety that we won't be able to achieve these goals. This also causes us to worry about whether we will ever be able to make ourselves or our lives "perfect".

Questions: *How would I describe myself? What aspects of my self-image do I think aren't "good enough"? What do I do to try to improve my self-image?*

Now we will look at what life is like in any moment that we don't have these thoughts to create our suffering ... then we will examine the happiness we feel when we achieve our idea of "perfect".

A Guide to The Present Moment

Chapter Two

The Experience of
The Present Moment

Psychological thoughts create suffering

We are almost always thinking. Our thoughts broadly fall into two main categories: psychological thoughts and functional thoughts. All of the thoughts we discussed in the last chapter are psychological thoughts. Psychological thoughts are the ones that decide whether something is "good" or "bad", and these are the thoughts that create our suffering. For simplicity, our psychological thoughts are nearly all of our thoughts that have opposites. This is because if a thought has an opposite, then we will almost certainly consider one side to be "good" and its opposite to be "bad". For example, if we think it is "good" to be rich, funny, skinny, and intelligent, then we would consider it "bad" to be poor, boring, overweight, and unintelligent. Our minds tend to be filled with the same psychological thoughts repeating themselves over and over again.

Functional thoughts are mostly answers to the question "How do I do that?" Functional thoughts determine how to build something, how to get somewhere, or how to solve a particular problem at work. Purely functional thoughts don't create suffering, only psychological thoughts do. However, most of the time, our functional thoughts are tainted by psychological thoughts. For example, if we think about our tasks for the day (the to-do list), this would be a functional thought. However, these thoughts are often layered with thoughts like "it would be bad if I don't get everything done" or "it is bad that I haven't completed as many tasks as I wanted to". These thoughts would then create our unwanted emotions. In the rest of this book, when "thoughts" are mentioned, I am referring to psychological thoughts.

What is the experience of the present moment?

In any moment when we have no psychological thoughts, or we don't believe our psychological thoughts, what remains is the experience of the present moment. Whenever our psychological thoughts aren't creating our experience of life, we get to directly experience whatever is happening in a given moment. The direct experience of any moment is the experience of the present moment.

In general, we rarely get to directly experience whatever is happening in a given moment because our experience is constantly being created by our thoughts of what was "good" or "bad" in the past, what is "good" or "bad" right now, or what may be "good" or "bad" in the future. We don't just experience meeting a person, we experience our thoughts about how that person is "attractive" or "ugly", "respectful" or "disrespectful", "smart" or "stupid". We don't just experience our tasks at work, we experience our thoughts about how our work is "perfect" or "not good enough", how "boring" or "fun" the rest of the day will be, and whether our boss will be happy or unhappy with our work. These thoughts are what create our wide array of emotions.

When we don't have or believe the thoughts that create our unwanted emotions, none of these emotions are experienced, and we get to experience the present moment. This is one way to experience the present moment, and this is the way that will be addressed in this book. Regardless of how "bad" our circumstances may seem, when we experience the present moment (when we are present), we are free of all insecurities, anger, sadness, doubts, fears, anxieties, stress, depression, judgment, hatred, internal conflict, drama, arguments, jealousy, impatience, frustration, worries, and irritation. When we are present, what remains is an unconditional peace, freedom, contentment, and happiness combined (these terms will be used interchangeably). This peace is everything we have ever wanted. It is complete satisfaction.

Gratitude

Have you ever found yourself in a wonderful situation, but you still ended up thinking about what was missing or how the situation could be "better"? This is an incredibly common experience. We may have a great job, wealth, a lovely partner, and amazing children, but almost all of our attention is still given to thoughts about what we want to improve. We may be looking at a beautiful view and instead of just enjoying it, we often end up thinking, "This would be perfect if... my soul mate was here, it was sunnier, or I had my camera". We may have a wonderful partner, and instead of recognizing that, we focus on how she can improve. Our minds are too busy thinking about what isn't "good enough" in our lives or what "could be better" to be grateful and appreciative of what we have. This is typically the case even when we can admit our lives are *wonderful*.

But in any moment that we don't have or believe our thoughts that say, "Something isn't good enough", what remains is gratitude for what we have. Strangely enough, this is the experience we generally hope to achieve by trying to make life match our concept of "perfect".

Appreciation

Another common side effect of experiencing the present moment, is that we naturally appreciate and enjoy the simple things. We can be completely captured by the smell of a flower, the beauty of a tree, the sound of a child's laugh, the elegance of a landscape, the wonder of modern technology, the taste of a potato chip, or anything else. When our attention isn't on thoughts, this appreciation arises naturally.

Most of us can walk on a path every day and never notice the trees, the design of the houses, the texture of the path, the smell of the plants, or the sounds of the birds. The reason we rarely take notice of these sounds, sights, and smells in our daily lives is that our attention is almost continuously on our own thoughts of past and future. Even if we do look at a tree, our attention is on our judgments, labels, and commentary about the tree rather than on the tree itself. Our attention is on our thoughts about what we witness rather than just experiencing what we witness purely through our senses. When our attention is taken off thoughts, we naturally notice and appreciate so many simple things in our daily life that we never experienced before.

The ability to experience the awe of something simple arises in the moments when we have silence or space between our thoughts. It is like seeing something for the first time. This feeling is similar to the sense of wonder and innocent curiosity that young children have.

Peace, relaxation, and completion

Any feeling of insufficiency, unworthiness, or unlovability is created by thoughts. Therefore, we naturally don't experience these feelings when we don't have, or don't believe, the thoughts that create them. When we are present, we feel loved, approved of, completely worthy, and lovable, and we feel that nothing is missing from our lives. We feel complete. Not because we have thoughts that say, "Everyone loves me", or "I am great", but because we don't have, or don't believe, the thoughts that make us feel unlovable, unworthy, or incomplete.

Without our thoughts to create our unhappiness, we feel content right now. Since we are already happy, we no longer feel a constant need or pull to improve ourselves, others, and our situation just to try to make ourselves happy. This feeling is like "aaaaahh, I can rest now". We feel that our life is complete. We can still pursue any of our goals, but our pursuit will no longer contain the idea that we need to achieve our goal in order to make ourselves happy. This eliminates our anxiety because there is no downside to not achieving the goal—we are already happy.

We may not realize it, but thinking takes up a lot of our energy, tightens our muscles, and weighs us down. For example, you can see for yourself right now how thinking tightens your muscles by checking to see if your tongue is pressed against the roof of your mouth or if your teeth are clenched together. If so, let your tongue and teeth drop, and feel how your face softens. When we are present, our whole body softens and relaxes, it feels as if a huge weight that we never knew we had has been lifted off our shoulders, and we are left with an abundance of energy.

Lightness and laughter (like a child)

Normally, thoughts constantly create our unhappiness and then make everything in our life seem significant because we believe our happiness is on the line. In any moment that we are present, we don't need to take life so seriously because we are already happy. This naturally makes us take things much more lightly. When we are present, we can be filled with laughter and playfulness. We can enjoy ourselves and have fun right now without worrying about the future or what others might think.

We can still choose to act seriously, plan for the future, and give our complete energy and effort towards our current tasks. But when we act seriously, for example, in our job, we look at it as if we are playing a role rather than actually being worried about what "bad" outcome may happen. When our minds are silent, we can feel like a kid at playtime, yet still act however we feel is best for the situation at hand.

Love, acceptance, and connectivity

We tend to go through life spending an incredible amount of time looking for someone to love us because we believe (often unknowingly) that receiving love will make us feel happy and whole. *Basically, we create a vision of the "perfect" future where we are loved and happy, and then we look for someone to fill the open position of the one who will love us. Since we want to fill this position in order to make ourselves happy, once we find someone to love us, we expect that person to make us happy.*

The movies make this sound like a fairy tale, but as you may have discovered, reality is rather different. In reality, the pursuit of love makes us feel as though something is missing from our lives and often causes us to act and speak according to what we think others will love instead of allowing us to live with the freedom of being true to ourselves. If we do find someone to love, we start to fear that we won't receive that person's love in return, we need to frequently be reassured of their love, we worry about losing their love, we require our lover to fill our needs (after all, the lover did fill the position of the one who is supposed to make us happy), we compare them to how we think they should be, and we then feel disappointment or resentment towards our partner when they don't live up to our expectations or don't make us feel content.

This is how thoughts relate to love. But all of these thoughts actually *prevent* us from loving others. We think that we are loving someone, but these feelings are really created by the thoughts "I am excited because I believe you will make me happy", or "I love how you make me feel", or "I hate it when you don't make me feel how I want". In other words, we don't look for someone *to love*, we look for *someone to make us happy*. We love that person when we think they are making us happy, and we hate them when we think they aren't. As most of us have already discovered, this type of "love" doesn't fulfill us and often creates a lot of anxiety, anger, disappointment, and hurt.

If someone else loves you, but you don't care about that person, how much impact does that person's love have on your level of happiness? You may have noticed, it has very little impact. *The reason is because fulfillment doesn't come from receiving love; the feeling of happiness and completion we have always wanted comes from loving others.*

When we love someone without wanting or expecting anything in return, we feel free, open, and wonderful. This unconditional love isn't the same as positive thoughts about someone, and it isn't an affirmative thought that says, "I love you". Love is what we experience in any moment that we are with someone without having or believing any judgments about that person ("good" or "bad"). When we allow someone to be exactly as they are, without any belief that they would be "better" if they were different, this is love. True love doesn't want anything in return (such as another person's love), because there is nothing it needs. Love has no conditions. We just love for the sake of love.

When we believe our judgments about someone, we can feel anger, disappointment, or resentment, or we can just feel separate from that person. All of this blocks us from loving them. When we are present with others (not believing our judgments), we automatically feel a closer connection to, and more intimacy with, the people around us. Our feeling of separateness from people disappears. In the absence of judgment, love is what remains.

When we are present, we are already happy, so there is nothing we want from others. We don't have to worry about whether other people will love us, leave us, fill our needs, or make us happy, because we are already happy. None of that matters when we are already content. We can love others without anything to fear because we don't want anything in return. We are free to purely love others, and we completely forget about the idea of seeking love.

The beautiful thing about love is that we don't have to limit our loving to just our romantic partner or our family. We can love everyone we encounter. When we are with anyone without judging them in any way, we feel love for them. It doesn't matter if this person is our spouse or our waiter in a restaurant. Once you start to feel how wonderful it feels to love people, you want to just love everyone. When we are present, we have nothing to fear, so we don't have to create any boundaries about who can receive our love.

Peace in the midst of physical pain

It may seem that without our thoughts, we would still experience suffering when we have physical pain. However, pain is very different from suffering. Suffering is emotional while pain is a physical sensation. A physical sensation itself doesn't create our anger, sadness, self-pity, or depression. Only our thoughts about our physical sensations can create these unwanted emotions.

Have you ever been happy in the midst of a little pain? Most of us have managed to enjoy ourselves at some point while we were in pain from a bruise, a cut, a stomachache, or a headache. When our attention is taken off our thoughts about our pain or injury through a distraction like TV, sports, or sex, then we stop feeling angry, sad, self-pity, or depressed for those moments. If pain itself created these emotions (suffering), then we wouldn't be able to escape them purely by taking our attention off our thoughts.

Our pain only turns into emotional suffering when we think, "This pain is *bad*", "This pain may lead to something worse", "The cause of this pain might be something *bad*", "I shouldn't be in pain", "It is unfair that I am in pain", "I can't be happy because of this pain", "Something is wrong", "The pain is my fault", or "I don't get a break from pain". We tend to spend a lot of time and energy on these types of thoughts that just create and perpetuate our anger, sadness, and self-pity. Not only that, but focusing on these thoughts about our pain often has the effect of giving the pain more energy and increasing its intensity.

If we are waiting to be pain-free before we can finally be happy, we will likely be waiting for a long time. However, in any moment that we don't believe the thoughts about our pain, life can be lived just as peacefully with pain as without it. We will still have the physical discomfort, but no matter how strong our pain is, it does not have to lead to emotional suffering. But even though we won't suffer when we lose our thoughts about our pain, we can still put our full effort towards trying to prevent, alleviate, or mitigate the pain. When we are present, we are peaceful even in the midst of physical pain.

We follow our intuition

In any moment when we don't believe our thoughts, we are able to act from our intuition, our gut, or what can simply be referred to as acting from the present moment. Many traditions and cultures seem to emphasize following our intuition (sometimes called "heart"). Intuition appears as a subtle feeling of what to do, without providing any explanation or logic behind its decision. It often seems like a quick, succinct, and light suggestion of what to do.

On the other hand, thoughts provide endless explanations, analysis, and commentary when we are trying to make a decision. Intuition is not an emotion, is not created by thoughts, is not created by our genetics or life history, and is completely separate from thought. Our intuition is always here to guide us, but we aren't able to hear or feel it because our thoughts are too loud and take too much of our attention. Intuition is very subtle and can easily be overlooked when we are constantly listening to our thoughts and looking to our thoughts to help us make our decisions.

Normally, our decisions on what to say and do are based on thoughts. We decide what to do based on our ideas of what we "should" do, our beliefs about what will make us happy, and our beliefs about what will make us suffer (our fears). When we choose what we "should" do, we are choosing what society has decided is the "right" way instead of doing what feels true and natural to us. When we use our thoughts to make decisions, we often decide to stay in situations that we don't enjoy because our thoughts make us fear change. Since our thoughts are all inherently based on the past, if we listen to our thoughts on how to act, we are basing our decisions on the past instead of allowing ourselves to follow what feels true in this moment.

In addition, making decisions based on thoughts often leads to a lot of confusion and indecision because our thoughts often provide a variety of reasons for why different options could be both "bad" and "good". It is difficult to have confidence in our decisions when our minds provide us with reasons for why a certain option could be "better" and "worse" than another option. For example, if you receive a new job offer, you would think to yourself, "Should I take the new job or stay in the job I have?" Then you might think "my job isn't so bad and there is security in staying here". But, on the other side, you might think "the new job might be a better choice because it would pay more, but it also might be a worse choice because I won't have as much job security". Which option do you choose? Life is filled with unclear decisions when we are relying on our minds to make the decisions for us.

In any moment that we are present, we are better attuned to be able to feel what to say or do based on our intuition. Our intuition helps us to act and make decisions according to what feels right and natural to us. This keeps us in peace because it keeps us acting in ways that feel true for us, because it guides us into situations that are in alignment with our deepest or truest intentions, and because we don't have to deal with the normal difficulty of our decision-making process.

As we become more familiar with our intuition, we generally come to the realization that life is much more enjoyable when we follow our intuition, rather than when we base our words or actions on thoughts. Of course, we can still plan for the future when we think it would be helpful, but as we begin to trust intuition more, we tend to plan our future actions less and less. This tends to makes us more spontaneous. We choose to speak and act based on how we feel in the moment of choice rather than basing our decisions on what we think we should do, what we are afraid of, or what we thought was a "good" idea when we came up with our plan weeks, months, or years ago.

The concept of intuition is very difficult to grasp when we are not familiar with the experience of it. If it is not within our frame of reference, and we can't compare it to anything we have experienced, then we won't be able to understand intuition no matter how much it is explained. Therefore, let's see if you can remember a time when you acted from intuition or at least felt your intuition.

Can you remember a time when you had a big decision to make, and your mind gave you a number of reasons as to why one option would be "better" and how you should definitely pick that option, but yet a feeling somehow compelled you to choose a different option? If you had listened to your mind, you would have chosen to do what you thought you should do. But if you didn't make that choice, it was likely because your intuition guided you to the option that felt right.

Can you remember a time when you met a potential love-interest, and you felt, "This isn't a good idea", but your mind convinced you to go out with him or her anyway by telling you all the "good" things about him or her? In this moment, you likely felt your intuition, but yet you disregarded it and listened to your mind because it had so many "good" reasons (thoughts) for why you should go out with him or her.

Can you think of a time when you realized that your boyfriend or girlfriend was not right for you at all, and in that moment *you realized that you had known this all along*? Many times, in the moment that we acknowledge that a job, a lover, or a situation isn't right for us, we also notice that *we had always known that something wasn't right about it*. What happens in this moment is that we remember or become aware that our intuition had been trying to tell us what to do, but we just hadn't been listening.

When we pay more attention to our intuition and learn to trust it, we can make the decision that feels right to us from the start rather than waiting months or years to recognize what we had truly always known.

The happiness of the present moment is always here

The happiness we feel when we are present is not an emotion, and it is not even an experience. Emotions are temporary experiences that are created by believing thoughts. In other words, a specific action (believing thoughts) needs to take place for the emotion to be produced. On the other hand, if a thought doesn't arise, we are already present. In addition, if a thought arises, and we don't engage in the action of believing it, we are already present. This is why the present moment is our natural state and why we can't say that the present moment is a temporary experience.

Imagine a pair of glasses that have opaque black lenses, with only a circular transparent spot in the middle of each lens to see through. These glasses are your mind. The clear transparent spot in the middle of each lens is your attention. When you look through the lens, you are giving your attention to whatever is in front of the clear spot. Since this spot is empty, you see life clearly, without all of your thoughts about what you see. You are directly seeing the person, the tree, or anything else that is in front of you. This is the present moment, and this is complete peace, happiness, and freedom.

Now imagine that someone has stuck some small clear transparent plastic circles all over the lenses of your glasses. But these little plastic circles don't just stay in one spot. They constantly move around on their own, sliding all around your lenses. One plastic circle moves over the clear spot but just keeps on moving past it, and then another immediately takes its place. Each of these plastic circles is a thought, such as a concept about what is "good" or "bad". When one of the circles passes over the empty spot on your lenses, you are giving your attention to that thought. But since the plastic circles are transparent, the empty spot is still clear. You still see life as it is. If a thought just enters your attention, but you don't believe it, you are still present and happy.

However, normally, when a thought enters your attention, you don't just see it, you automatically believe that thought. Instead of just noticing the thought and allowing it to pass by, when you believe a thought, you are grabbing hold of it and giving it importance. Essentially, when you believe a thought, you are stopping the plastic circle as it covers the hole, and you are coloring in the transparent plastic circle. Therefore, as soon as a plastic circle passes over the clear spot on your glasses, that circle is stopped and colored in. Now, instead of seeing life clearly, whatever you are looking at takes on the color of the plastic circle. Your experience of life is now determined by what thought has entered your attention and been believed. If the thought is positive (a light color), then you experience a "positive" emotion. If the thought is negative (a dark color), then you experience a "negative" emotion. Instead of seeing a person or a tree in front of you, you now see a "mean" person or a "pretty" tree. In this way, your thoughts provide the prescription with which you view the world.

When you were a young child, there were practically no plastic circles on your glasses; you had an almost empty mind. You were happy and peaceful. Barely any psychological thoughts entered your attention because you had so few. A circle would slide over the empty spot and be colored in, but then it would quickly slide off, and it would take a while before another one would slide over the spot again. You experienced a lot of happiness, with only short-lived unwanted emotions, because there was much more silence and time in between the thoughts in your mind.

With each passing year, you learned more and more concepts of what is "good" and "bad", thereby adding and believing more and more psychological thoughts. With each new concept you learned, it was as if someone were throwing one more of these plastic circles onto your glasses. As you believed more concepts of "good" and "bad", the amount of time that your mind was silent between thoughts got smaller and smaller. Eventually, you get to the point where your mind becomes crowded with so many thoughts that you very rarely get a break from them. As one circle slides away from the hole on the glasses, another takes its place almost instantly. Your attention goes from one thought to another with almost no silence in between. Therefore, you have very little experience of the present moment.

Since we are used to the action of believing thoughts and we constantly do it automatically, it may seem as though the present moment is a temporary experience created by the action of *disbelieving* thoughts. However, if we don't commit the action of believing a thought (don't color in the circle), we are already present. When we disbelieve a thought, it is as if we are simply erasing the color of a circle that we just colored in, allowing us to see life as it is. We are essentially reversing our previous action. We wouldn't say that erasing the color of the circle is creating the uncolored transparency of the circle or the clearness of the spot on our lens. The circle has always been transparent, the spot has always been empty—it's just that we've rarely gotten to experience this because we automatically and unconsciously go from believing one thought to another with almost no break. The experience of the present moment is quite simply what remains when no thought arises in our mind or we don't engage in the action of believing a thought.

The experience of the present moment is what we have been searching for. Now we will take a look at why our pursuit of happiness has not been effective at providing us with the peace and happiness that we want ...

Chapter Three

Why Our Pursuit of Happiness Never Ends

The happiness of getting what we want

Since we believe that our circumstances create our unwanted emotions, the vast majority of our time, money and energy in life are spent trying to change our circumstances from "not good enough" to "perfect". If we manage to get anything in our life to match our definition of "perfect", when we get what we want, we often immediately experience happiness. *Despite how it seems, this immediate happiness is not created by the new circumstance itself. This happiness is actually the direct result of losing the thoughts that were creating our suffering.*

Once we believe our circumstances have become "perfect", there will be no more thoughts about how this particular circumstance is "bad", no more thoughts about who is to blame for the "bad" circumstance, and no more thoughts about the possible "bad" outcome of not getting what we want. These negative thoughts created our sadness, anger, and anxiety about this specific circumstance. Therefore, when these negative thoughts leave, we are left with happiness. Happiness is what remains when there are no thoughts to create our suffering. This is the experience of the present moment.

If you think, "I am fat", "I am a failure", or "My apartment is too small", then you will likely experience sadness, shame, or a feeling that something is lacking. If you blame someone else for any of these "bad" aspects of your life, then you are likely to feel anger or resentment towards that person. If you think that you will never be happy unless you "improve" these things, then you are likely to experience anxiety or feel worried about whether you will ever be able to make these things "perfect".

If you change your circumstances from "bad" to "perfect" and get to your ideal weight, achieve your definition of success, or buy a bigger home, then you will feel an immediate sense of happiness. It would certainly seem as though your accomplishment created your happiness, but if you look more closely, it's possible to see that your happiness is actually the result of losing some of your negative thoughts. As soon as you achieve your weight goal, get your success, or buy a bigger space to live in, you instantly lose the negative thoughts that were creating your shame, sadness, anger, and anxiety regarding your weight, success, or home. Each of these three circumstances now meets your definition of "perfect", so you would no longer have your negative thoughts about these particular circumstances. These thoughts created your suffering, not the circumstance themselves. Therefore, the absence of these thoughts leaves you with the inherent happiness of the present moment.

Contrary to what we have been taught to believe, neither a person's "ideal" weight, "ideal" level of success, nor "ideal" home can directly create happiness. If these circumstances themselves created happiness, then everyone who had them would be happy, and clearly some people who have these things aren't happy.

In addition, if a specific circumstance created happiness, then this circumstance would always create the same intensity of happiness when we achieve it. However, as you may have come to discover, achieving the same "perfect" circumstance can correspond with levels of happiness that are different for different people, and levels of happiness that are different for the same person at different times in that person's life.

Imagine you have been living in a small apartment for years, and you finally saved up enough money to buy a beautiful new three-story, five-bedroom house. How happy would this make you feel? It is likely to make you very happy, and it would certainly seem as though your happiness would be directly created by buying the house.

However, now imagine you had already been living in a beautiful and big house, but then you decided that you just wanted a bigger yard, so you decided to buy the three-story, five-bedroom house up the street. How happy would this make you feel? You would likely experience some immediate pleasure from buying the new house, but this pleasure likely wouldn't be very intense, wouldn't last very long, and wouldn't affect your overall happiness very much at all.

In both instances, you bought the exact same house, yet the intensity of your happiness in the first scenario would have been far greater than your happiness in the second scenario. The reason that achieving the same circumstance can correspond with different levels of happiness is simply because the happiness we experience from getting what we want is relative to how much suffering our thoughts were causing us. If you have suffered for years from thinking, "I shouldn't still be living in an apartment. It is pathetic that I can't afford to buy a house at my age", then buying a house will feel great because you will no longer have these thoughts to create your suffering. But if you only had the thought, "I would rather look at a different backyard", then buying a new house wouldn't make you much happier because losing this thought wouldn't affect your level of happiness very much.

The more intense our suffering is from our negative thoughts about a circumstance, and the longer these thoughts cause us to suffer, the happier we will seem to feel when we get what we want. Achieving our goals makes us happy because it eliminates our negative thoughts about a particular circumstance. Achieving our most difficult goals generally corresponds with a stronger, more intense experience of happiness or relief because we suffered for longer periods of time before achieving them.

Changing circumstances to "perfect" isn't enough to give us the happiness we want

Since getting what we want seems to make us happy, of course we are going to keep spending much of our life trying to make ourselves, our situation, and others "perfect". But, as we may have come to realize, this strategy doesn't really fulfill us. We tend to live life with a lot of suffering and discontent between our brief moments of happiness. When we get what we want, we only experience the present moment for a few minutes or days before our attention goes back to our other thoughts. The reason changing our circumstances to "perfect" isn't enough to give us the overall peace and happiness we are looking for is because it just doesn't address most of the thoughts that create our unhappiness.

Let's take a look at some of the thoughts that our pursuit of happiness through circumstances doesn't address:

• No matter how "perfect" our circumstances are, they don't change our thoughts about "bad" events from our past that create our sadness, guilt, and anger.

- We can't change many of the aspects about ourselves and others that we think are "bad" (e.g., height, weight, face, personality). This leaves us feeling ashamed and unworthy.

- We aren't always able to achieve our ideas of "perfect" (e.g., getting the "perfect" job, spouse, or house). When we don't get what we want, our thoughts create sadness, anger, guilt, or despair.

- When we manage to get the "perfect" circumstance we want, we often instantly begin to fear and worry about losing it. We may fear losing our "perfect" job or partner, or we may worry about losing our "great" appearance, our strength, or our athleticism as we get older.

- We can always lose any "great" circumstances that we have. When this happens, our thoughts clearly make us suffer.

- Changing circumstances can't help to alleviate most of our anxiety. No matter how "great" our circumstances are, we will still have almost all of our anxieties and worries about what others think about us, about losing what we love, about not getting what we want, about loved ones getting hurt, and about any other outcomes we think would be "bad".

- Regardless of how "perfect" we make ourselves and our situation on the outside, it often isn't enough to change our negative thoughts about ourselves, and stop us from feeling incomplete.

- It often takes a lot of time to change something from "bad" to "perfect". During this time, we are stuck experiencing sadness and anxiety from believing that "something isn't good enough" and "it would be bad if I don't get what I want".

- As long as we believe our idea of "perfect" circumstances, we will also believe our idea of "imperfect" circumstances. "Perfect" doesn't exist without "imperfect" because "perfect" isn't "perfect" unless we have something to compare it against. We can't think that someone is "pretty" without thinking someone else is "ugly". We can't think one comment is "nice" without thinking a different comment is "mean". In this way, as long as we are pursuing "perfect" circumstances to make ourselves happy, there will always be more situations, events, personality traits, appearances, actions, words, and events that we believe are "bad" or "not good enough". This means that there are always more negative thoughts to keep creating our sadness, anger, and anxiety.

For example, if you have a strong longing to get married, then you may have thoughts like "things aren't good enough because I haven't found the person I want to marry", "I shouldn't still be single", or "it will be terrible if I end up alone". These thoughts would create your sadness, shame, and anxiety. Then, in the moment that you get engaged or married, you would experience great happiness because these thoughts would have disappeared from your mind.

However, this initial happiness doesn't last forever, because it is only a matter of time before your attention goes back to all of your other thoughts. Achieving your goal for marriage doesn't eliminate your negative thoughts about how you are overweight, not attractive enough, or not caring enough; how your job isn't "good enough"; how you don't make enough money; how your living situation is less than ideal, and how you still don't have the children you want. In addition, you may have new thoughts about how your spouse isn't "good enough" at cooking, cleaning, loving, appreciating, and providing.

If you have already gotten a lot of what you wanted in life, you may feel a sense of relief to understand why you aren't fulfilled, and it may be nice to know that you are not the only one who is dissatisfied.

However, if you still have many goals, it can be tough to acknowledge that getting what you want doesn't have the ability to fulfill you. But it is important to understand that this doesn't mean that you shouldn't pursue your goals, and it doesn't mean that you won't be happy. It just means that if you really want peace, you need to directly address the thoughts that are keeping you from it. And the beauty of this is that you can do it right now. You don't have to wait until you get everything you want and make life "perfect" for you to be happy (as you may have thought was the case). You can be happy now. Then, once you are happy, you can pursue any goal you want and really enjoy your pursuit because you know your happiness isn't dependent on the outcome.

Positive thoughts aren't enough to fulfill us

The experience of the present moment doesn't last very long when it comes from achieving something that meets our idea of "perfect". However, some happiness does remain after the initial few minutes or days. This type of happiness can be created by positive thoughts about any of the circumstances in our life right now, as well as by positive memories. The happiness created by positive thoughts is definitely enjoyable and makes us happy. However, positive-thought happiness isn't very strong or very fulfilling. To see this for yourself:

1)   Please take a moment to think back to a time when you achieved something you had really wanted for a long time. This could be the moment when you got a job offer, learned that you had passed an important exam, won a championship title, found a spouse, or anything else. Try to remember how happy you were in the first moment when you got what you wanted. Remember how that felt.

2)   See how happy you feel right now when you tell yourself, "I am in my dream job", "I am a licensed lawyer", "I am a champion", "I am married", or whatever else it was that you achieved.

3)   See how you feel right now by thinking about the moment when you achieved your goal. How does the memory make you feel?

Was the quality of your happiness the same in each of these three scenarios? For the vast majority of us, the first few moments after we achieve a goal, we are fulfilled and overtaken with happiness. On the other hand, later, our positive thoughts about those new circumstances we now have, and our memories about when we achieved those circumstances, only provide us with a pleasant feeling. This pleasant feeling is completely incomparable to the happiness we experienced in the initial few moments when we got what we wanted. The reason that our experiences of happiness are so different is simply because they are created by two very different causes. *The first few moments of happiness when we get what want are created by the absence of thoughts, while our happiness later on is created by positive thoughts about the present or the past.*

There are a few reasons why our positive thoughts aren't very fulfilling and don't create the all-pervasive happiness that we experience when we get what we want.

By nature, when we think some aspect of our lives is "great", we also still believe that other aspects are "bad". Therefore, when we think a positive thought, our happiness is generally being held back by the attention, whether conscious or not, that we're giving to some negative thoughts in the background.

When we have a positive thought about something, it is usually easy (or at least possible) for that thought to change so that it becomes "worse". Therefore, when we rely on positive thoughts to make us happy, there is almost always a constant subtle anxiety that our positive thought might change and we might lose our happiness.

For example, if you think about yourself, "I am attractive", this would give you a little pleasure. Since you like this pleasure, of course you would not want this thought to change to "I am unattractive". But once you decide that it would be "bad" to think "I am unattractive", you start to feel a subtle anxiety about the possibility of becoming unattractive as a result of gaining weight, skin problems, ageing, or anything else. In addition, to maintain your thought "I am attractive", you may frequently worry about whether your face, clothes, and body meet your definition of "attractive". If others were to tell you that you are unattractive, it would be harder to continue to believe, "I am attractive", so you would naturally begin to worry about what others think.

Since we usually go to our memories when we aren't content in a given moment, if our attention isn't completely on our story (the memory), a small portion of our attention is still given to our negative thoughts. These negative thoughts in the background prevent us from fully experiencing the happiness of our memory (a positive thought). In addition, memories are also often tinged with the anxiety of knowing that we have to come back to this "worse" moment or from thinking that we may never have such a "good" moment again.

For example, if you think about your wonderful vacation on the beach last month, this will give you some pleasure, and maybe put a smile on your face. However, telling yourself this great story will also at least create subtle thoughts about how where you are right now isn't as "good" as where you were, which creates the feeling that you are lacking something. We usually aren't aware that the anxiety or negative thoughts are present when we are giving attention to our positive memory, but this is part of the reason why positive-memory happiness is a much less peaceful and satisfying experience than present-moment happiness.

Distractions provide us with some relief from thoughts

Since getting what we want doesn't fulfill us, we have developed a different way to make ourselves happy. We try to have fun and enjoy ourselves. We do this by distracting ourselves from the thoughts that cause our suffering, discontent, and restlessness.

We have learned from watching our parents and friends, as well as from our own experiences in life, that distractions are an easy way to make ourselves happy and to escape from our unwanted emotions. We may be unaware of it, but we look to TV, movies, music, food, work, relationships, internet, phones, friends, shopping, drugs, and alcohol to distract us from the thoughts that create our suffering. These are the tools we have been given to make ourselves happy, so of course we are going to use them.

Since our thoughts make us suffer, we naturally do everything we can to avoid them. This is why most of us don't want to be with ourselves with no distractions and always need to be with friends, on the phone, listening to music, watching TV, keeping ourselves busy, or engaging in some other form of distraction. Even when we are with others, our thoughts make us nervous or worried about what people think, so many of us choose to drink alcohol in order to take our attention away from the thoughts that prevent us from feeling free and happy. The more intense our suffering is, the stronger our urge will be to escape from our unwanted emotion and to engage in our favored distractions. This is why it is often very difficult to stop engaging in our "bad" habits.

Questions: What do I do when I feel sad, lonely, stressed, worried, or anxious? What types of distractions do I use to take my attention away from the thoughts that create my unwanted emotions?

Distractions like those mentioned above take our attention away from the thoughts that are creating our unwanted emotions, and they make us happy by directing our attention to other more positive thoughts. If we decide to do work, then our thoughts will shift to thinking about how to get our work done. If we decide to spend time with a friend or partner, then we could have entertaining or engaging conversations about whatever topic we want. If we go on the internet, then we will be giving attention to our thoughts about whatever content we are looking at. These activities give us relief by shifting our attention from negative thoughts to more positive thoughts. Therefore, these distractions make us happier during the time that we engage in them.

There's also another kind of distraction. When we engage in an activity (distraction) that we love, sometimes we give our complete attention to the present moment, with no attention given to any thoughts. When thoughts aren't given any attention, they stop. This is an experience of the present moment. This may happen when we are playing sports, dancing, creating art, playing with our children, listening to music, meditating, or doing yoga. No matter what the activity is, the experience is the same: peace and happiness. There are no thoughts about the past or future, ourselves or others, or what is "good" and "bad", because the activity we are engaged in is engrossing enough or enjoyable enough to somehow give all of our attention to it.

But we can recognize that the happiness doesn't come from the activity itself because we could easily be unhappy while doing any of these activities. For example, sometimes we may have a lot of fun dancing or playing with our children, while at other times those activities may be no fun at all. This may happen because we are thinking that something about the activity isn't "good enough", we aren't "good enough" at it, or because we are preoccupied worrying about something else, such as our job or what others think. This would create the experience of frustration, anger, sadness, or anxiety instead of peace.

Questions: What types of activities have made me happy in the past? Have I ever been doing the same activity but not been happy while doing it? If the same activity sometimes makes me happy and sometimes doesn't, can I admit that the activity itself must not be what is directly creating my happiness?

Distractions aren't enough to keep us in peace

Distractions are wonderful for us. They are the source of much of our happiness in life, and they provide us with much-needed relief from our suffering or discontent. But, as helpful as they are, they aren't enough to make our lives really happy, bring us peace, make us feel whole, or make us content with our level of happiness. No matter how happy we are when we are being entertained, we can't always be distracted from our thoughts. No matter where we go, no matter who we are with, no matter what situation we are in, we have to be with our thoughts. All of our thoughts that judge, analyze, and compare, as well as all of our thoughts that create annoyance, anger, sadness, shame, and guilt – they all come with us. In any moment that we aren't being distracted, we will come right back to the thoughts that were creating our suffering and discontent before we distracted ourselves.

In our jobs, in our interactions with friends, when pursuing love interests, in the times with our family, and any time by ourselves, our thoughts will continue to create our experience of life. It may seem as though our attention is on others when we are with them, but we are almost always unconsciously judging them, thinking about how to get their approval, and thinking about whether we are getting their approval. For example, we might be unaware that we are thinking, "He shouldn't have said that", "Should I tell him about my past?", and "Did I make a good impression?" *Our relationship with our own thoughts dictates how enjoyable all of our relationships in life will be.*

It can really be tough to admit that we have certain unwanted thoughts, but the longer we avoid our thoughts and the emotions they create, the more these emotions grow and control our lives, making it harder and harder to really be happy. If we don't allow ourselves to acknowledge the thoughts that create our emotions, then we can't address them. However, if we address the thoughts that create our unwanted emotions, then we can be happy in any situation without any distractions.

It's time to end our pursuit of happiness

Since we have been trained to believe that circumstances should be able to make us happy, when we get what we want but don't feel content, we wind up assuming, "I am not happy because I just don't have *enough* of what I want". We think, "If I had enough, then I would be happy". For example, many of us have been taught that success, wealth, respect, or love will make us happy. But when we get these things, we still don't feel fulfilled. These achievements don't have the ability to fulfill us because they don't eliminate the vast majority of our negative thoughts. Instead of recognizing this, we unknowingly decide, "I am not happy because ... I don't have *enough* success, power, love, appreciation, respect, wealth" or "I am not happy because ... my house isn't big enough, my car isn't fancy enough, my body isn't attractive enough, I'm not smart enough".

When we think we aren't happy because we don't have *enough* of what we want, we keep seeking more and more of what we already have. We think that we will stop pursuing more once we are happy. But since the things we try to achieve, acquire, or change to make us happy don't actually have the ability to make us happy (other than temporarily), we never stop pursuing more of what we want.

It may seem as though others have achieved happiness through circumstances because we see them smiling or laughing, but this phenomenon of being dissatisfied isn't unique to any one individual. Our lack of peace is not a personal issue. We were all taught to believe our concepts of "perfect" and "bad", and we were all taught that circumstances create happiness and suffering. Since none of us have been taught to directly address the thoughts that make us unhappy, we are all in the same boat of being dissatisfied.

The result of our pursuit of happiness through "perfect" circumstances and distractions is moments of happiness, but also a real lack of overall, lasting peace and contentment, and often a lot of suffering. We almost always seem to be waiting to be happy. We are either waiting for the next fun moment to distract ourselves from our discontent, or we are waiting to achieve the "perfect" circumstances. We might be waiting for work to be over, waiting for the weekend, waiting for our next vacation, waiting to find our soul mate, waiting for our children to get through their teen years, waiting for our children to go to college, waiting for success, waiting for retirement, or waiting for our partner to change.

The promise of happiness almost always seems to be in the future. And it always will be in the future unless we start to address the thoughts are preventing us from feeling happy. It's time to go to the source of our unwanted emotions and directly address the thoughts that are making us unhappy.

Let's now take a look at how to do it ...

Chapter Four

The 5 Steps to
The Present Moment

If you want to stop holding on to your sadness about a past event, stop worrying about what someone thinks about you, stop feeling anger towards someone, stop feeling ashamed about your life, or stop experiencing anxiety about the future, then all that's necessary is to stop believing the thoughts that create these emotions. That's it. You don't need to fix yourself, change others, or improve your situation. All these emotions are created purely by thoughts in your mind and not by anything about you, your circumstances, or the people in your life.

As I mentioned in the introduction, the people who come to me are able to disbelieve these thoughts and experience the present moment when they are with me but tend to have a hard time identifying and disbelieving the thoughts that create their unwanted emotions on their own. In order to address this issue, I designed a 5-step process that will help guide you to experience the peace of the present moment, and make you happier in your daily life.

This chapter will outline the whole process in brief and will provide you with several examples, while the chapters ahead will break down the steps in more detail, taking you through the process as you read. Once you get familiar with this process, you can use it anytime, anywhere, with any thought and any emotion. No matter how intense your emotion is, no matter how long you've had it, and no matter what circumstances you think created it, if you stop believing the thought that causes your emotion, you will come right back to the peace of the present moment.

1) Pick an unwanted emotion

The first step is to pick an emotion you are experiencing that you want to stop experiencing. For example, you may want to stop feeling resentment towards your partner, you may want to stop feeling guilty about something you did, you may want to stop feeling anxiety at work, or you may want to stop worrying about what your friends think about you.

If you have any of these emotions but you want to experience them, then that's fine. There's certainly nothing "wrong" or "bad" about feeling any of our emotions. This is not about getting rid of all of our emotions. This is just about giving us the option to choose happiness instead of suffering in any moment that we want to be happy. Sometimes, after "bad" events, we may want to experience our grief, sadness, or guilt for a few weeks or months before we decide that we really want to be happy again. Sometimes we may feel sad or angry, but yet we are completely fine about it. If this is the case, then there is certainly no need for us to engage in the 5-step process for these emotions.

2) Identify the thoughts behind your unwanted emotion

Before you can stop believing the thoughts that creates your unwanted emotion, you first need to pinpoint the thoughts behind your emotion. These thoughts generally appear as whatever we think caused our emotion ("my husband shouldn't have shown up late"), whatever we think needs to change in our life for us to be happy ("I need a promotion for me to be happy"), or whatever story is running through our minds as we experience the unwanted emotion ("what if she doesn't like me?"). Since it can often be difficult to find the thoughts for yourself, you'll be provided with a variety of questions in the next chapter to aid you in the process of identifying the specific thoughts behind your emotion.

3) Recognize that your emotion has been created by your thoughts and not your circumstances

In order to have any interest in questioning your thoughts, you first need to recognize that your thoughts, not your circumstances, have created your unwanted emotion. As a result of this recognition, your attention can be taken away from who you think is to blame, how you are the victim, what should be different, or how to change things, and directed to questioning the validity of the thoughts that are actually causing your suffering. Chapter 6 contains five questions to help you directly discover that your thoughts have actually created your unwanted emotion.

4) Discover that you don't know whether your thought is true

For each thought that creates one of your unwanted emotions, it is possible to discover that you don't know whether it is true. Once you no longer believe a thought to be true, the corresponding emotion dissolves. If a friend told you that your house just burned down, *and you believed them*, how would you feel? You would likely feel upset. But if your friend told you this, *and you didn't believe your friend at all* (maybe because they are always talking nonsense), then how would you feel? If you didn't believe what your friend said, then you would have no reason to feel upset, and you therefore wouldn't be emotionally affected by the comment. In the same way, if you don't believe a thought (word) in your mind to be true, it won't create an emotion.

When we are believing a thought, we are essentially believing "my thought *is* true". But, when we recognize "my thought is not true" or "I don't know whether my thought is true", we have stopped believing "my thought *is* true". When we stop believing that our thought *is* true, this can also be referred to as "disbelieving a thought". Once we disbelieve a thought, our emotion dissolves. Chapters 8 through 15 contain 34 different questions to help you directly discover that the thoughts that create your suffering might not actually be true. Each question will show you a different reason why a specific type of thought might not be true.

Here is an exercise to help you to directly experience the difference between believing a thought to be true and admitting that you don't know whether the thought is true. For each of the following ten examples, tell yourself the first thought given and imagine how you would feel (or have felt) if you were in a situation where you had this thought. Make sure to strongly emphasize the words that are italicized. Then tell yourself the alternative second thought in the example, pretending that you just became aware of some new piece of information, and now you really don't know whether your original assertion was true. Imagine that you completely recognize the second thought to be true, and see how this thought makes you feel. Notice the difference in feeling and how your emotion loses most or all of its power.

1)   "She *was* disrespectful to me" — "I don't know if she was being disrespectful"
2)   "It *is* bad that I didn't get the job offer" — "I really don't know whether it will be good or bad for my life that I didn't get the job offer"
3)   "I *am* not worthy of love" — "It is definitely possible that I am worthy of love"

4)   "My boyfriend *doesn't* care about me" — "My boyfriend might care about me"

5)   "It *was* terrible that my parents didn't give me attention when I was young" — "I really don't know if the way my parents treated me was good or bad for my life overall"

6)   "Now that my wife left me, I *will* never find someone to love me again" — "I may find someone new to love me who is even more wonderful than my wife"

7)   "She *is* to blame for what happened" — "I don't know if she is to blame"

8)   "I *need* to have a child for me to be happy" — "I actually don't know that I won't be just as happy without a child"

9)   "It *would* be bad if my daughter doesn't get accepted into her top choice college" — "The truth is that I don't know if it would be bad for my daughter's life for her to get rejected from her top choice college"

10)   "I'm 30 and I *should* be married by now" — "I honestly don't know that there's anything wrong with not being married by 30"

Did you feel how the emotion dissolves or loses most of its power when you acknowledge that you don't know whether the thought is true? Once we realize, "I don't know whether my thought is true", we have already stopped believing, "My thought *is* true". When we no longer believe our thought is true, our thought stops creating its emotion. In its place, we experience the peace of the present moment (until our attention goes to other thoughts). This feeling often seems like a big relief at first.

However, since this exercise involves hypothetical examples, it is unlikely that you felt the full suffering from believing the first thought, and so you wouldn't experience as much relief from disbelieving the thought. Also, this exercise doesn't fully enable you to experience the relief of disbelieving a thought because you are just pretending to believe "I don't know whether my thought is true" instead of actually discovering it.

5) Question the validity of any reason to continue suffering (if relevant)

Even though you may want to be happy, your mind may still try to convince you that you are "better" off keeping your unwanted emotion by creating a reason for why it might be "bad" if you lost it. For example, if you start to see that your worries about a sick family member are caused by a thought that you don't know is true, then your mind may try to keep you worries by saying, "If I don't worry, that means I don't care about him". If you start to see that the thoughts that create your stress might not be true, your mind might react by thinking, "My stress helps me to get my work done". If you begin to realize that your thoughts, not the person you were blaming, have created your anger, then the thought, "I need to hold him accountable for what he did" may show up.

Just as you can question the truth of the thoughts that create your suffering, you can also question the validity of any thoughts that try to convince you to continue suffering. Common forms of resisting happiness, and questions to help you disbelieve these thoughts (if they arise), are addressed in chapters 16 and 17. However, if you find yourself believing a reason to keep your unwanted thoughts or emotions at any step along the way, feel free to just jump ahead to Step 5 in order to challenge your reasons to continue suffering. You don't need to wait until you go through all of the first four steps.

The 5 Steps to The Present Moment in real life

To see how The 5 Steps work with real thoughts and real circumstances, we will now look at examples of how two different people used this process in their lives.

Ben has a job interview coming up with a small advertising firm that he really wants to work for. His stomach is in knots because he is worried that he won't get the job offer. He is filled with anxiety, constantly thinking, "What if I don't get the job? How will I come across in the interview? What if they aren't impressed?" A few nights before the interview, he is so stressed that he can't sleep. This is when he decides that it is time to go through The 5 Steps that I had given him a few weeks prior (for a different issue). The following script represents his process of using The 5 Steps to go from feeling anxiety to peace. The questions are all part of The 5 Steps, and Ben's answers are in italics.

Step 1: Pick an unwanted emotion

I am stressed about my upcoming job interview and I don't want to feel this way anymore.

Step 2: Identify the thoughts behind your unwanted emotion

What outcome would be "bad"?

It would be bad if I don't get the job offer.

Step 3: Recognize that your emotion has been created by your thoughts and by not your circumstances

How do I feel when I think this thought or tell myself this story?

I feel anxious, tense, nervous.

If no "bad" circumstance is actually happening right now but yet I can create an emotion (stress) right now just by thinking, then can I admit that thoughts have created my emotion rather than circumstances?

Yes, I can admit that my situation isn't causing my anxiety, my thoughts are. Nothing bad has happened—I haven't even had the interview yet.

Step 4: Discover that you don't know whether your thought is true

Can I think of a few possible "bad" effects of getting the outcome I want?

While I think that I will like the job a lot, I can't know for sure that I will like it since I never actually worked there. So I might not like the job. I might not be good at it. It is possible that I won't like the people that work there. This job might give me more stress or require more hours of work than other jobs that I'm looking at.

Do I know with absolute certainty that this outcome would be "bad" for my life? Can I think of a few possible "good" effects from getting the outcome I don't want?

If I don't get this job offer, I might find a different job that makes me happier, I am better at, pays more, or requires fewer hours. In my extra free time without a job, I might meet someone great, or have some experiences that teach me something important that ultimately makes me happier.

While I do really want to get this job offer, the truth is that I don't know that this job would be best for me or make me happiest.

Just saying that to myself gives me such relief. I can breathe again. I don't have to worry about not getting the job offer because I

really don't know whether that would be better or worse for my life.

Step 5: Question the validity of any reason to continue suffering (if relevant)

But if I don't stress about the interview then I won't work hard to prepare for it, which will hurt my chances of getting the job offer.

Can I think of any reasons why not having anxiety might help me get what I want?

Without anxiety, I suppose that I would enjoy my studying for interviews more, which might help me to spend more time preparing for the interview. I would definitely be able to be more focused while preparing for interviews if I wasn't stressed. That might make me understand the information I'm learning more easily, and help me to prepare better answers to the questions they might ask. If I am not nervous and anxious while I'm at the interview, then I am highly likely to answer the questions better. The interviewer will probably like me more, and enjoy being around me more if I am relaxed and not filled with worry.

I guess not having anxiety might actually help me to get the job offer. Considering that, I definitely don't see any reason why I would want to keep my anxiety.

Here's another example. Amanda comes to me complaining about how she feels that her connection with her husband doesn't have the energy and joy it once did. He doesn't bring her flowers anymore, and he doesn't seem to appreciate all she does around the house (let alone pitch in himself). She feels resentful, let down, and doubtful that things can get better. This is how she changed that. Once again, the questions given are all part of The 5 Steps, and Amanda's answers are in italics.

Step 1: Pick an unwanted emotion

I want to stop feeling sad about my marriage.

Step 2: Identify the thoughts behind your unwanted emotion

What "bad" outcome happened?

It is bad that my husband doesn't appreciate me.

Step 3: Recognize that your emotion has been created by your thoughts and by not your circumstances

How do I feel when I think this thought or tell myself this story?

I feel sadness, disappointment, and resentment towards my husband.

If no "bad" circumstance is actually happening right now but yet I can create an emotion (sadness) right now just by thinking, then can I admit that thoughts have created my emotion rather than circumstances?

It still seems like my husband is causing my anger and disappointment.

Am I able to be happy (have fun) when I am being entertained and distracted from my thoughts? If I can be happy when I am distracted from my thoughts, even though the "bad" circumstance still exists, then can I admit that my "bad" circumstance is not causing my unhappiness?

When I am out with my friends, at the movies, or doing yoga, I can definitely still enjoy myself. Even though my problems with my marriage still exist, I can still be happy when I'm not thinking about it. This does make it pretty clear that it must be my thoughts that are creating my unhappiness about the marriage, not the marriage itself.

Just admitting that my husband isn't to blame for my sadness already seems to alleviate some of my resentment towards him.

Step 4: Discover that you don't know whether your thought is true

What are the facts and what is my interpretation of the facts? Am I absolutely sure that my guess about their thoughts, feelings, or intentions is true?

Well, the facts are that he rarely says "thank you" or "I appreciate that", never brings me flowers anymore, and doesn't help with cleaning the house. I guess my interpretation is that "these actions mean he doesn't appreciate me". It definitely seems like my interpretation is true and that he must not appreciate me.

Have I interpreted the facts based on what I would be thinking if I acted that way? Am I sure that they express their feelings or choose their actions in the same way as I do? Is it possible that he doesn't express his love, approval, or appreciation in the way I am looking for it because he doesn't feel the need to receive love, approval, or appreciation in that way?

When I appreciate someone, I try to let them know. If I don't show gratitude and love, it usually means it's because I don't appreciate them. It is possible that it just doesn't occur to him to show his appreciation through flowers and saying "thank you". He definitely doesn't seem to need or want appreciation in these ways, so maybe that's why he doesn't put much effort into showing me appreciation in these ways.

Can I think of a few reasons or examples as to why the opposite thought (interpretation) might be true?

It might be signs of appreciation that he pays for our mortgage, and that he pays for my food and yoga classes, amongst other things. He has bought me a few presents in the last year. He

compliments me sometimes. Sometimes I can see he appreciates me by the way he looks at me.

Maybe he does appreciate me and just doesn't show it in the ways I was looking for it. Just saying that makes me feel as if a huge weight has been lifted off my shoulders. Maybe my marriage is just fine the way it is. It was just my thoughts about my husband that made me feel that it wasn't good enough, and in-turn made me feel sad and resentful. I really feel much better about it now. It's nice not to have to worry about that anymore.

There is no fifth step because her mind did not come up with any reason to keep her sadness.

How The 5 Steps immediately brings us present and makes us happier

When we are suffering, we are often giving a large portion of our attention to a few specific thoughts or stories. When we disbelieve these thoughts, our attention is free for a moment. Our attention is then left completely on this moment, and all of a sudden, we are fully present. What remains is the experience of the present moment. We feel free, whole, and happy.

But, as you can imagine, this experience of the present moment often doesn't last very long. This experience ends when our attention returns to other thoughts. We may be present for a few seconds, a few minutes, or a few days before this happens. How long we stay present is hard to predict because it depends on a wide variety of factors. In general, the more attention we gave to a thought (e.g., 10% of our day), and the longer we gave it attention (e.g., two months), the longer our present moment experience will be when we disbelieve the thought.

This may seem like a short time to be present. However, even when our attention does return to other thoughts, we are now happier than we were because we no longer have the specific unwanted emotion that our thought was creating. If our thought was creating a large amount of sadness, then we won't have that sadness anymore, regardless of whether our attention is transferred to the present moment or just other thoughts.

Imagine that you are an aspiring singer and you just performed a new song on stage for the first time. Then, when you get off the stage and ask your friend how you did, he says to you, "That was terrible!" This would likely make you feel hurt or embarrassed. If you believed your friend, you would likely feel hurt or embarrassed. But if your friend then smiles, and you recognize that he was joking, how would this affect your emotional state? You would likely feel an instant sense of relief. Your hurt or embarrassment would have dissolved in an instant. Why would this happen? It would happen solely because you stopped believing your friend's words to be true. As soon as you stop believing someone's words, the emotion they created instantly dissolves. This is the same type of emotional impact that we experience when we disbelieve a thought that was creating suffering for us.

When we disbelieve a thought, the change to our emotional state will be relative to how much suffering the thought has been causing us. If a specific thought has created a large portion of our suffering (for the last hour or 10 years), then we will be much happier without it. However, if a specific thought hasn't been creating any noticeable suffering, and it hasn't been taking up much of our time or energy, then disbelieving this thought will have very little emotional impact on us and our attention will just go directly back to all of our other thoughts.

How disbelieving thoughts makes us happier in life and helps us to live in the moment

Imagine you go to a magic show and you watch the magician cut his assistant in half. The first time you see this, you might feel scared or shocked by it, because you believe that what is happening is real and true. But if the magician then shows the audience how the trick works, the next time you see someone get cut in half, you won't be emotionally affected because you won't believe that what you're seeing is true.

In the same way, when you experience an emotion, you are believing a thought to be true. When you discover that you don't know whether your thought is true, you have essentially exposed how the trick works. If the same thought arises again in your mind, you are much less likely to be fooled by it (believe it) because you have already seen why the thought isn't known to be true. As with the magic trick, if you don't believe the thought to be true, it won't create an emotion. For this reason, once you disbelieve a thought, that thought is much less likely to arise or be believed again in the future.

Therefore, when we disbelieve the thoughts that create our suffering in any specific situation, we often wind up being happy in that situation in the future. Even if we are thinking in those situations, and our minds aren't silent, we still won't be believing the negative thoughts we previously had. This means we won't experience the emotions these thoughts created. Let's look at a few examples of how this could look in a typical day:

• In the morning, we may experience anxiety about trying to get our children to school on time with everything they need. If we can recognize that we don't really know whether "it would be bad if my children were late" or "I need to get my children to school on time", then we can be at peace as we prepare our children in the morning. We can start our days with enthusiasm and energy instead of feeling overwhelmed.

• We may feel anxiety at work when our boss doesn't show us appreciation. If we stop believing our guess that "he doesn't think I am good at my job" or "I am going to get fired", then we can stop feeling anxiety at work. We can be happy at work and even improve the quality of our work because we can give it our full attention.

• We may get angry when our co-worker doesn't offer to help us. If we can acknowledge that we aren't sure whether our co-worker is being selfish, and therefore stop believing the thought "he shouldn't be so selfish", then we can more easily enjoy our interactions with our co-worker. We can have fun with our co-worker, treat him with genuine kindness, and still offer to help him when he needs it.

• We may not say what we want to say or do what we want to do when we are with our friends because we are afraid of what they will think. If we realize that we don't know whether our thought "it would be bad if they had a negative opinion about me" is actually true, then we can finally feel free to just do and say whatever feels right and natural to us. We can stop worrying all the time about what others think about us.

• When we get home at night, we might feel disappointment or resentment towards our spouse for not picking up the groceries we needed. If we can see that our interpretation "she doesn't care about my time" might not be true, then we can feel love towards our spouse instead of animosity.

Situations themselves don't create our emotional experience; it is only our thoughts about them that make us suffer. If we disbelieve these thoughts about our situations and the people in our lives, then we can remain loving, happy, and peaceful when we are in these situations in the future. We can go about our day without anxiety, anger, sadness, and worry.

If the unwanted thought arises again, we often see this thought as funny, useless, irrelevant, delusional, or just interesting, rather than believing it. However, it is important to note that we often believe thoughts that we previously disbelieved. This is most likely to happen when we had believed a thought for a long time, we closely identified with a thought, or we didn't fully disbelieve it.

But even if we do believe one of our thoughts again: 1) The intensity of the emotion it creates is usually substantially weaker, because we don't believe the thought as strongly; 2) We more quickly realize that our emotion has been created by the thought (as opposed to circumstances) because the emotion often triggers our memory of disbelieving the thought when we last experienced it; 3) It is much easier to disbelieve the thought because we already know that the thought creates our emotion, what questions to ask ourselves, and why the thought isn't known to be true. After a few times, we often don't even need to ask ourselves any questions to disbelieve the thought because we almost instantly recognize we don't know whether the thought is true.

As we disbelieve more of our thoughts, we can be happy in more and more situations. In addition, if we disbelieve the negative thoughts we have about ourselves, our lives, and past events, then we can be peaceful and content even when we are alone with no distractions.

There is no such thing as "lasting happiness"; there is only a series of single moments. So becoming happier simply means there are more frequent moments of happiness (although there are varying degrees) and fewer moments of suffering. We become happier for a larger percentage of our time. As we believe fewer thoughts, we experience more freedom and peace in our life.

Put differently, as we disbelieve more thoughts, there is more silence (or space) between thoughts. The fewer thoughts we believe, the more we are living in the present moment. This means that there is more experience of the present moment between thoughts that create suffering. As this space between thoughts grows, we experience more peace, love, laughter, and gratitude in our life.

How to engage with The 5 Steps

The most helpful and effective way to read the rest of this book is to engage with The 5 Steps to The Present Moment as they are described in the following chapters. If you just think about the concepts on a theoretical level, it might be interesting, but it won't provide you with much value. By engaging with the process while reading, you can actually experience the peace that results from disbelieving thoughts as you read.

However, this book isn't just meant to guide you to the present moment while reading. The real value comes from applying this process to life in any moment that you experience an unwanted emotion. This process is meant to be used when your spouse or child does something "wrong" and you're about to yell at them and start a fight. It can be used when you have just gotten rejected, and you're feeling hurt. It is there for you when you're feeling unlovable. It will help bring you peace when you can't stop worrying about an upcoming event. If you're about to go to food, drugs, or alcohol to escape the way you're feeling, this process can relieve the underlying cause of your urge. Or whenever your thoughts are causing dissatisfaction, you can question your thoughts to become present again.

Reading this book will get you familiar with each of the steps and all of the questions. To help you engage with this process on your own after reading the book, you can access all of the questions and explanations on my website www.liveinthemoment.org through the free interactive web app "The 5 Steps to The Present Moment". This way, when an unwanted emotion starts to impinge on your life at a later date, you will have the tools you need to bring yourself back to the peace of the present moment.

Chapter Five

Steps 1 & 2: Pick an Unwanted Emotion and Identify the Thoughts Behind It

Pick an unwanted emotion

Please take a moment right now to pick an emotion you don't want to have anymore. You should pick an emotion that is specific to a certain time, situation, or circumstance. You may want to lose your anger towards someone who seemed to have hurt you. You may not want to feel shame about some aspect of your life. You may want to stop experiencing anxiety at work. You may want to stop judging your partner because it causes tension in the relationship. You may want to stop worrying about what others think when you're in a particular situation.

Alternatively, if you are already aware of a specific thought that you know is making you unhappy (or taking a lot of your attention), then you can just write this thought down and go straight to Step 3. For example, if you have a specific judgment about yourself and you don't like the way it makes you feel, then you wouldn't need to engage with Step 2 to help you find that thought.

This process is most helpful when you make it personal and choose one of your own emotions, not someone else's emotion or a hypothetical example. If you are really open to engaging with this process, then you can feel free to start out with any emotion, no matter how intense it is or how long you've had it. However, if you are hesitant about this process or are engaging with it just to test it out, then it would likely be more helpful for you to start off picking an emotion that is less intense. If you try to question intense emotions or really deeply held beliefs just as a test, you often aren't really ready and willing to discover that your thoughts might not be true. Once you experience the benefits of questioning your thoughts and become familiar with how the process of questioning works, then you can much more easily question the thoughts causing intense emotions, or long-held emotions, or "really bad" circumstances.

At first, just pick one specific emotion. After you go through all 5 steps for this emotion, you may want to come right back to Step 1 and pick another emotion to dissolve.

How to identify the thoughts behind your unwanted emotion

Our most common unwanted emotions generally fall into four main categories: 1) anger or judgments about others; 2) worry about what others think or feeling hurt by others' opinions; 3) anxiety, stress, worry, or fear about the future; 4) sadness, sense of incompleteness, unworthiness, shame, guilt, or judgments about ourselves. In order to help you find the thoughts behind your unwanted emotion, this chapter contains a list of the most common thoughts (beliefs) that create each of these types of emotions. Then, for each emotion, there is a list of questions that will help you to identify the specific thoughts that are most likely behind your unwanted emotion. Please take a moment to decide which category your unwanted emotion falls into.

When you ask yourself the questions in the next section, your answer to each of the questions is potentially one of the thoughts behind your emotion. The most important thoughts (answers), the ones behind your emotion, will be referred to as the "core" thoughts. Your core thoughts will be the answers that resonate with you, provoke a feeling response as you think them, hit you with a feeling like "yeah, that's it", or at least seem to accurately describe what you are believing. Before you get to the questions, here are a few guidelines to help ensure that you will be able to identify the thoughts behind your emotion.

• It is very important to write down the answers (thoughts) that feel important (regardless of whether there are one or 10). This allows you to see your thoughts more clearly and helps you to look at them more objectively, which makes it much easier to investigate whether the thoughts are true. When our thoughts are just in our head, it is easier for them to take on incredible importance, be over-dramatized, and seem very true.

• Answering the questions honestly is really important. It is very common for us to instantly judge our thoughts as mean, selfish, or "bad" in some way and then choose not to write them down. However, this process is only helpful if we write down and question the thoughts that we actually have. Any form of "editing" the thoughts or only picking the thoughts that "aren't so bad" decreases the effectiveness of the process substantially. If you don't want to have a specific thought or emotion, you first need to admit you have it. If we keep hiding them, they will continue to run our lives and create our suffering. It can take real courage and honesty to be open with ourselves, but try to remember that everyone has these so-called "bad" thoughts, not just you.

• It can sometimes feel difficult for us to answer the questions that help us to identify the thoughts behind our suffering. This is usually because we are unknowingly afraid of seeing a negative thought we have about ourselves. We unconsciously think some version of "if I look at the negative thoughts I have, or even admit I have them, I will feel worse". We may not realize it, but we tend to have this idea that as long as we don't admit we have certain negative thoughts, they won't affect us. But the truth is, all of our anxiety, worries, sadness, sense of insufficiency, and problems with our relationships come from thoughts that we don't want to look at. The bottom line is that we can't address these thoughts, and the issues they cause, until we identify them.

• Most of the questions are formatted as "fill-in-the-blank". This may make your answer (your thought) sound differently than it does when you are just thinking it to yourself. There are two major reasons why the questions are formatted in this way. 1) When we experience an emotion, we often have long stories about what we think caused our emotion. However, we want to try to make this thought or story as succinct as possible in order to really get at the heart of the issue. 2) We want to frame our answers to the questions (our thoughts) in a way that makes our thoughts easiest to disbelieve. The "fill-in-the-blank" format helps to ensure that this happens. In addition, the examples under each question are meant to serve as a guideline for how to answer the question.

• Lastly, it is also helpful to take a couple of deep breaths or focus on your breathing for a few moments before attempting to identify the thoughts.

Identify the thoughts that create your unwanted emotion

Please jump to whatever emotion is relevant to you, and skip all of the questions for the other emotions. Also, just answer the questions that are relevant to your situation.

Anger

If you are angry at someone (or judging them), this anger is almost always created by believing one or more of the following thoughts:

- "Someone did something bad."
- "Someone is to blame for the bad action they committed."
- "Someone is bad or something about them is bad because of what they did or how they are."
- "A bad outcome has happened." (The "bad" outcome could be that you are unhappy in some way, or you believe some event turned out "badly".)
- "Someone is to blame for the bad outcome." (If the "bad" outcome is your unhappiness, then that person is the cause of your unhappiness or is somehow preventing or blocking your happiness.)
- "If someone acted differently (better), then the outcome would be better (e.g., I would be happier)."
- "The future will be worse because of what someone did."

Questions for anger

In the moment that I am angry at this person or judging them, what thoughts or stories are usually running through my mind?

1) What did they say or do that was "bad"? What "bad" outcome are they to blame for?

It is/was bad that _____

Sample answers: "It was bad that Ashley insulted me", "It is bad that my husband doesn't show me appreciation" "It was bad that my parents got divorced", "It is bad that she got injured", "It is bad that I am not happy", "It was bad that we didn't make it to the show on time", "It is bad that she yelled at her child"

2) What are they doing that isn't "good enough"?

_____

Sample answers: "Ashley doesn't respect me enough", "My boss isn't nice enough", He isn't appreciative enough", "He isn't helpful enough around the house", "My child doesn't talk to me enough"

3) What do I think about the person who did something "bad", is to blame for the "bad" outcome, or is doing something that isn't "good enough"?

_____ *is* _____ *because* _____
(who)   *(something "bad")*

Sample answers: "Ashley is disrespectful because she insulted me", "John is inconsiderate because he doesn't show me enough appreciation", "He is selfish because he divorced my mom", "He is lazy because he allowed her to get injured", "He is stupid because he made us arrive late at the show", "She is a bad mother because she yelled at her daughter"

4) What should be different about the way they are, or should have been different about the way they acted?

_____ *should/shouldn't* _____
(who)

Sample answers: "Ashley should respect me", "John should appreciate me more", "She shouldn't have been so selfish", "He shouldn't have been so lazy", "He should have been ready earlier", "She shouldn't have yelled at her daughter"

5) What do I need to change about them, or the way they act, for me to be happy?

I need _____ to _____ for me to be happy
       (who)

Sample answers: "I need Ashley to respect me more for me to be happy", "I need my boss to be nicer for me to be happy", "I need John to be more appreciative for me to be happy", "I need him to clean up more around the house for me to be happy", "I need my child to talk to me more for me to be happy"

6) How would I feel if they were to change the way they act or if the "bad" outcome had never happened?

I would feel happy if _____

Sample answers: "I would feel happy if Ashley respected me", "I would feel happy if John showed me enough appreciation", "I would feel happy if my father hadn't divorced my mom", "I would feel happy if she hadn't got injured", "I would feel happy if we made it to the show on time", "I would feel happy if she was nicer to her daughter"

7) If I believe that something needs to be different for me to be happy, or that changing something would make me happier, then what must that mean I believe is the cause of my unhappiness?

My feeling of _____ is caused by _____
       (unwanted feeling)

Sample answers: "My feeling of unhappiness is caused by Ashley's insults", "My feeling of resentment is caused by John's lack of appreciation", "My feeling of bitterness is caused by my parents' divorce", "My feeling of anger is caused by him allowing her to get injured", "My feeling of anger is caused by not making it to the show on time", "My feeling of anger is caused by seeing her yell at her daughter"

8) What impact will this "bad" outcome have on how I feel in the future? What will they be doing in the future?

_____ *will* _____

  (who)

Sample answers: "Ashley will keep disrespecting me", "I will never feel happy with my marriage because John doesn't appreciate me", "I will stay bitter", "I will stay angry at him", "My husband will continue to ignore me and make us late for events", "She will continue to unnecessarily yell at her daughter"

Anxiety

If you have anxiety, stress, worry, or fear about the future, then you are almost certainly believing one or more of the following thoughts:

- "A specific outcome would be best and make me (or others) happiest."

- "Any outcome other than the best one would be worse and make me (or others) less happy."

- "A specific outcome would be bad."

Questions for anxiety

In the moment that I am feeling anxiety, stress, worry, or fear about the future, what thoughts or stories are usually running through my mind?

— If your thoughts or stories are about how a specific outcome would be "bad" for someone else, it is important to be honest with yourself and check whether you actually have anxiety because you think the outcome would be "bad" for you.

1) What do I (or others) need to get, change, or keep to be happy?

_____ *need(s) to* _____ *for* _____ *to be happy*
   (who)   *(who)*

Sample answers: "I need to get success for me to be happy", "I need to keep my boyfriend for me to be happy", "My son needs to leave his girlfriend for him to be happy", "I need to stay healthy for my children to be happy", "My daughter needs to have a better job for me to be happy", "I need to get married for me to be happy"

2) If I need to get or change something for me to be happy, then what must that mean I believe is causing my unhappiness?

My feeling of _____ *is caused by* _____
               (unwanted feeling)

Sample answers: "My feeling of shame is caused by not having success", "My feeling of sadness is caused by my daughter having a bad job", "My feeling of incompleteness is caused by being single"

3) What outcome would be "best" or make me (or others) happiest?

_____ *would be happiest if* _____
   (who)

Sample answers: "I would be happiest if I became successful", "I would be happiest if I kept my boyfriend", "My son would be happiest if he broke up with his girlfriend", "My children would be happiest if I stayed healthy", "I would be happiest if my daughter got a better job", "I would be happiest if I got married"

4) If I believe this "perfect" circumstance would be "best" or make me (or others) happiest, then what do I think about the possibility of not achieving this outcome?

_____ *won't be as happy if* _____
  (who)

Sample answers: "I won't be as happy if I don't get success", "I won't be as happy if I lose my boyfriend", "My son won't be as happy if he stays with his girlfriend", "My children won't be as happy if I get injured or sick", "I won't be as happy if my daughter doesn't get a better job", "I won't be as happy if I don't get married"

5) What outcome would be "bad"?

It would be bad for _____ *if* _____
                (who)

Sample answers: "It would be bad for me if I don't get success", "It would be bad for me if I lost my boyfriend", "It would be bad for my son if he stayed with his girlfriend", "It would be bad for my kids if I get injured or sick", "It would be bad for me if my daughter doesn't get a better job", "It would be bad for me if I never get married"

Worrying about what others think

If you find yourself worried about what others think, worried that you won't get others' love and approval, or if you feel hurt because you lost or didn't get love and approval, then you are almost certainly believing one or more of the following thoughts:

- "Someone has a negative opinion about me or doesn't love, approve, or appreciate me." (Regardless of whether they explicitly told you or you're just guessing.)
- "The opinion someone has about me is true."

- "It would be good to get love and approval from someone because it would make me happy, secure, worthy, or whole, or it would cure me in other ways."

- "It would be bad to not get someone's love and approval or to lose someone's love and approval because it would either prevent me from being happy or it would make me suffer (e.g., confirm that I am unworthy, unlovable, or not good enough)."

- "Someone won't love and approve of me if they knew the real me"

Questions for worrying about what others think

In the moment that I am worried about what others think, or feeling hurt by what someone else thinks, what thoughts or stories are usually running through my mind?

1) What do they think of me?

_____

Sample answers: "Adam doesn't appreciate me", "Tara doesn't really love me", "He thinks I am not good enough for him", "My boss thinks I'm stupid", "He thinks I'm unattractive", "My father thinks I'm a failure"

2) What do I think their opinion signifies about me?

If _____ _____, *then that must mean I am*
   (who)   *(unwanted opinion)*

_____
(something "bad")

Sample answers: "If Adam doesn't appreciate me, then that must mean I am not worthy of appreciation", "If Tara doesn't love me, then that must mean I am unlovable", "If she thinks I am not good enough, then that must mean I am not good enough", "If my boss thinks I'm stupid, then that must mean I am stupid", "If he thinks I am unattractive, then that must mean I am unattractive", "If my father thinks I am a failure, then that must mean I am a failure"

3) What do I want them to think about me?

I want _____ *to think I am* _____
　　　　　(who)　　　　　　　　　　　*(something "good")*

Sample answers: "I want Adam to think I am worthy of appreciation", "I want Tara to think I am lovable", "I want him to think I'm good enough", "I want my boss to think I'm smart", "I want him to think I'm pretty", "I want my dad to think I am worthy of approval"

4) How would their love, approval, or appreciation make me feel?

If _____ _____, *that would make me feel*
　　(who)　　　*(wanted opinion)*

_____
　　　　　　　　(wanted feeling)

Sample answers: "If Adam appreciated me, that would make me feel whole", "If Tara loved me, that would make me feel secure", "If he thought I was good enough, that would make me feel good enough", "If my boss thought I was smart, that would make me feel like I could relax", "If he thought I was pretty, that would make me feel lovable", "If my father approved of me, that would make me feel content with myself"

5) If I think that their love, approval, or appreciation would make me feel happy, then what must that mean I believe is the cause of my unhappiness?

My feeling of _____ *is caused by* _____
　　　　　(unwanted feeling)

Sample answers: "My feeling of incompleteness is caused by not receiving appreciation", "My feeling of insecurity is caused by not having someone to love me", "My feeling of insufficiency is caused by him thinking I'm not good enough", "My feeling of being overwhelmed is caused by my boss thinking I'm not smart",

"My feeling of sadness is caused by him thinking that I'm not attractive", "My feeling of unhappiness is caused by not having my father's approval"

6) What am I scared they will think of me?

I am scared that _____ will think I am _____
             (who)   *(something "bad")*

Sample answers: "I am scared that Adam will think I am not worthy of appreciation", "I am scared that Tara will think I am not lovable", "I am scared that he will think I'm not good enough", "I am scared that my boss will think I'm stupid", "I am scared that he will think I'm unattractive", "I am scared that my dad will think I am not worthy of approval"

7) Why can't I be myself when I'm with them? Why can't I speak or act honestly in these moments? What am I scared will happen?

_____ *will* _____
  (who)

Sample answers: "Adam won't appreciate me if I only do what I feel like doing", "Tara will not love me if he knew the real me", "She will think I'm stupid if I act like myself", "He will not want to spend time with me if I don't act happy", "She will be hurt if I'm honest", "She will reject me if I don't pretend to be interested in the same things as she is", "He will think I'm boring if I don't keep talking"

8) How would I feel if people had these negative opinions about me, I didn't get their love and approval, or I lost their love and approval?

I would _____ if _____
       (unwanted feeling)

Sample answers: "I would stay unhappy if they don't approve of me", "I would never feel whole if I don't find someone to love me", "I wouldn't be able to relax if I don't win her love", "I would feel worthless if he stops loving me", "I would feel hurt if he thought I wasn't good enough"

Sadness

If you feel sadness, self-pity, guilt, shame, embarrassment, un-worthiness, or a sense of something missing (incompleteness), then you almost certainly have at least one of the following thoughts:

- "The perfect circumstances would make me happy (or would otherwise satisfy me)."
- "Something about me or my life is bad, not good enough, or isn't the way it should be."
- "I did something bad."
- "I am to blame for my bad action or for whatever is bad about me or my life."
- "A bad outcome has happened to me or someone else."
- "I am to blame for a bad outcome."
- "I am bad because of the bad characteristic, action, circum-stance, or outcome in my life"
- "The bad characteristic, action, circumstance, or outcome happened or is the way it is because I am bad"
- "The future will be bad."

Questions for sadness

In the moment that I am feeling sad, guilty, ashamed, embarrassed, unworthy, or incomplete, what thoughts or stories are typically running through my mind?

1) What are the "perfect" circumstances that I want? What do I need to get or change about myself or my life for me to be happy?

I need to _____ *for me to be happy*

Sample answers: "I need to be thinner for me to be happy", "I need to be successful for me to be happy", "I need to find someone to love me for me to be happy", "I need to fulfill my potential for me to be happy", "I need to give my children a better neighborhood to grow up in for me to be happy"

2) How would getting the "perfect" circumstances make me feel?

I would feel happy if _____

Sample answers: "I would feel happy if I was thin", "I would feel happy if I was successful", "I would feel happy if I found someone to love me", "I would feel happy if I fulfilled my potential", "I would feel happy if we could move to a nicer neighborhood"

3) If I believe that I need these "perfect" circumstances to be happy, or that getting these "perfect" circumstances would make me happy, then what must that mean I believe is the cause of my unhappiness?

My feeling of _____ *is caused by* _____
　　　　　　　(unwanted feeling)

Sample answers: "My feeling of shame is caused by my weight", "My feeling of insufficiency is caused by my lack of success", "My feeling of incompleteness is caused by being single", "My feeling of unhappiness is caused by not having fulfilled my potential", "My feeling of unhappiness is caused by living where we do"

4) What aspect about myself, my life, or my previous actions am I ashamed about? What "bad" outcome happened?

It is/was bad that _____

Sample answers: "It is bad that I am overweight", "It is bad that I am shy", "It was bad that I didn't get the promotion", "It is bad that I am still single", "It is bad that my son got into trouble at school", "It is bad that I am sad", "It was bad that I yelled at my wife", "It was bad that she got injured"

5) What isn't "good enough" about me or my life?

_____

Sample answers: "I am not thin enough", "I am not outgoing enough", "I am not successful enough", "My son doesn't behave well enough", "I have not achieved enough", "My neighborhood isn't nice enough"

6) What should be different about my life or the way I am? What should I have done differently?

I should/shouldn't _____

Sample answers: "I shouldn't be overweight", "I should be more outgoing", "I shouldn't still be in this low position at work", "I shouldn't still be single at my age", "I should have raised my kid better", "I shouldn't be sad", "I shouldn't have yelled at my wife", "I shouldn't have let her get injured", "I should be able to afford living in a better area"

7) What do I think this "bad" characteristic, action, circumstance, or outcome in my life signifies about me?

I am _____ *because* _____
    (something "bad")   *("bad" circumstance etc.)*

Sample answers: "I am ugly because I am overweight", "I am a coward because I am shy", "I am worthless because I work in a low-paying job", "I am worse than others because I am still single", "I am a bad mom because I raised a trouble-maker", "I am weak for being sad" "I am a bad husband because I yelled at my wife", "I am selfish because I let my friend get injured", "I am an embarrassment because I can't afford to live in a nicer neighborhood"

8) Why is this "bad" characteristic or circumstance the way it is? Why did the "bad" outcome or action happen?

_____ *because I am/have* _____
("bad" circumstance etc.)   *(something "bad")*

Sample answers: "I can't keep up my diet because I am worthless", "I can't speak up for myself because I am a coward", "I haven't got a promotion because I am not good enough", "I can't find someone to love me because I have something wrong with me", "My child is a trouble maker because I am a bad mom", "They got injured because I am stupid"

9) What impact will this "bad" characteristic, action, circumstance, or outcome have on the future?

_____ will _____
   (who)

Sample answers: "I will never find someone to love me", "I will always be a failure", "My child will keep getting into more and more trouble", "I will never get a job that uses my potential", "I will never be happy", "He will hate me forever because I injured him"

All of these questions are meant to serve as a guide to help you find the th ughts behind your emotions, but feel free to ask yourself any other questions that may help you get closer to the heart of what you are believing. Once you have several core thoughts written down, please review your thoughts, and pick the most important one to take through the rest of The 5 Steps. You will then apply different questions to this thought in order to discover that *it* is the cause of your emotion and that you don't know whether it is true. Once you have gone through The 5 Steps with this one thought, you can do it again with any other thought that you want to disbelieve. If any new thoughts or judgments come up for you as you go through the other steps, be sure to write them down so that you can question them just as you will do with the thoughts you just found.

Chapter Six

Step 3: Recognize that Your Emotion has been Created by Your Thoughts and Not by Your Circumstances

Even though you have now identified a few thoughts behind your unwanted emotions, you probably still believe that your emotions are directly created by your circumstances. It can certainly seem as though someone else's actions have caused our anger, an unwanted event has made us sad, or a specific situation is making us unhappy.

This chapter contains five different questions that aim to help you directly discover that the thoughts and stories behind your emotions are actually the cause of your emotions, rather than the circumstances themselves. You can ask yourself the following questions based on the thoughts you found in the last step. You can choose to answer these questions mentally or you may find it more helpful to write down your answers. Normally, when you engage with this process on your own, you would stop asking yourself the questions once you recognize that your emotion was created by a thought. However, for now, it would be helpful to read through all of the questions in order to get familiar with them.

1.   How do I feel when I think this thought or tell myself this story?

Please take a moment to close your eyes and give some attention to the thought you have found. Tell yourself the story in detail and give it your complete attention. Picture the situation in your mind. Envision the scenario with all the relevant details. Look at everyone's facial expression, look at the background details, and give it all your attention. Take a few seconds to stop reading and imagine this now.

How do you feel when you think this thought? Does thinking about this story create an emotion? A moment ago you likely weren't feeling any emotion. Then, just by thinking, you began to experience an emotional reaction.

It may seem as if a "bad" circumstance or event is responsible for creating your unwanted emotion, but there is no "bad" circumstance or event happening in this moment to create your emotion. You are just reading a book, but yet you experienced an emotional reaction nonetheless. If a specific event created a specific emotional experience, it would only be able to create that emotional experience while the event was actually happening. A specific event or circumstance might have happened in the past, but it is not happening now. Therefore, the event can't be creating your emotional reaction right now. If you experience an emotional reaction right now, it must have been created by something that's going on right now. Since you were giving attention to thoughts, your emotion must be a direct reaction to the thoughts you just had, not any circumstance or event. You might not have been able to have thoughts about the event if the event had never happened, but it is still your thoughts that are creating the emotion and not the event.

In comparison, if you took a shower last week that made your hair wet, could you make your hair wet again right now just by thinking about the shower you took? No. This is because the water created your wet hair, not your thoughts. If you could create wet hair right now just by thinking, then you would know that thoughts alone create wet hair. In the same way, since thoughts can create an emotion right now just from thinking about a past event, we know that thoughts alone are creating our emotion.

If your thought is about the future, since no "bad" event has actually happened, the emotion can't be created by an event. The emotion can only be created by a thought. If you think about taking a shower next week, could this make your hair wet right now? No. This is because water creates wet hair, not thoughts. If thinking about taking a shower next week made your hair wet right now, you would know without any doubt that thoughts caused your hair to be wet, and not water. In the same way, since thinking about a future event can create anxiety, worry, or anger right now, we know that thoughts alone are creating these emotions.

Even if you didn't get to feel the emotions from these exercises, you can probably admit that we often seem to experience emotions as a result of circumstances that happened in the past or may happen in the future. We may grieve for years after the death of a loved one. We may be angry at our parents twenty years after we have left home for things they did in our childhood. Similarly, we could experience fear and anxiety over the prospect of having a meeting or a job interview go badly well before the meeting or interview even happens. If we are experiencing the emotion now when no event is happening now, or no event ever happened, then an event can't be creating the emotion. The only action happening right now is our thinking. Therefore, it can only be our thinking that is creating our emotion.

The Questions: What emotions or physical sensations do I experience when I think this thought? If an event itself created my emotion, then wouldn't the event only be able to create the emotion while it was actually happening? If no "bad" circumstance is actually happening right now but yet I can create an emotion right now just by thinking, then can I admit that thoughts have created my emotion rather than circumstances?

2.   Could I or someone else be happy despite having the same factual circumstances?

Certain circumstances seem to create specific emotional responses. It seems obvious that some circumstances are responsible for creating sadness or anger, and other circumstances create happiness.

However, in order to claim that a specific circumstance *creates* a specific experience, it must always create that same experience, for every person, every time. For example, a turned on light bulb creates light. Everyone who sees a turned on light bulb will experience light, every time, for as long as they are around the light bulb. A flame creates heat. When anyone comes into contact with a flame, they will experience heat every time, for as long as they are near the flame. Beating a drum creates sound. If any person moves near a beating drum, they will experience sound, every time, for as long as they are near the beating drum.

If specific circumstances created specific emotional reactions, each circumstance would always create the same emotional reaction, for everyone, every time. For example, if a specific living situation directly created shame, then everyone who had that same living situation would always have no choice but to feel ashamed. If a performance review at work created anxiety, then everyone would always experience anxiety before their reviews. If a specific insult created anger, then everyone would always react with anger to that insult.

Clearly, this isn't the way life works. The same circumstance often corresponds with vastly different emotions for different people, and different emotions for the same person at different points in time.

If two people each live in the same sized one-bedroom apartment, one person could be proud about their living situation and the other could be ashamed about it. If two people are called "ugly", one person could get very upset, while the other could laugh it off. If two people have a performance review coming up at work, one person could feel anxiety about it, while the other might feel confident and excited about it. In addition, the same person might sometimes feel happy about their living situation and sometimes ashamed. The same person might sometimes be angered by an insult and sometimes completely unaffected by it. The same person might sometimes feel anxiety before a performance review and sometimes confident.

If two people are mugged at gunpoint, one person could be outraged at the violation, and the other could just be relieved he wasn't hurt. A "bad" hair day may make us upset some days and not at all on other days. Sometimes it may drive us crazy when our roommates leave their dishes in the sink, and other times it may not bother us at all. If the same circumstance can correspond with vastly different emotions at different points in time, then our emotions must not be created by the circumstances we encounter.

To take it even further, people can be happy in the midst of seemingly tragic events, and they can suffer amid seemingly great circumstances. If a family member dies, we can still be happy if we are excited to get the inheritance or are glad to see their suffering end. If we get fired from our job, we can be happy about it if we were looking for an excuse to leave or if we are excited about the possibility of finding a job that we love more. If our husband files for divorce, we can still be happy if we had stopped loving him but were scared to file for divorce ourselves or if we're looking forward to being single again.

Similarly, we can worry about our financial security no matter how wealthy we are. We can feel unloved and sad even when our spouse and family truly love us. We can feel depressed about being overweight even if everyone else thinks we are thin. We can get angry at someone even if they treat us with love and kindness. We can feel ungrateful and incomplete even if we have almost everything we ever wanted.

We often tend to think that our shame or embarrassment is the result of our insufficient physical appearance, personality traits, marital status, job, car, or living situation. But when we were young children, almost all of us were happy (with no shame) regardless of how "bad" these circumstances were. If we used to be happy with a given circumstance, and now we are ashamed about the same circumstance, it can't be the circumstance itself that is creating our shame.

If the "worst" of circumstances can leave us happy, and the "best" of circumstances can result in suffering, then it is clear that circumstances don't create our emotions. Circumstances themselves are neutral. The same circumstance often corresponds with different emotions for different people because we can all have different thoughts about the circumstance. Even if our emotional reaction happens immediately after an event and seems completely logical and connected to that event, it is still our thoughts that create our emotional reactions. There are always thoughts that arise between a circumstance and our emotional reaction to it. We rarely notice these thoughts only because we haven't been directed to pay attention to them.

Regardless of what the circumstance is, and regardless of whether the circumstance is happening now or in the past, it can only be our thoughts about the circumstance that create our emotions.

The Questions: Could someone else be happy despite having the same circumstance? Have I ever been happy, or experienced a different emotion, under the same conditions? If the circumstance itself created a specific emotional response, wouldn't it always produce the same emotional response for me and everyone else? Could I be happy in this situation if I had different thoughts about it? If someone else could be happy despite having the same seemingly "bad" circumstance, if I could be happy if I had different thoughts about the circumstance, or if I have been happy at one point with the same circumstance, can I admit that the circumstance itself is not creating my emotion?

3.   If I didn't know that the event had happened, would I still be suffering?

Imagine that you have to go to the doctor for a routine medical test, and when you get back the results, you find out that you have a harmful disease. How do you think you would feel in that moment? You might feel anger, sadness, despair, or anxiety. What would have created your emotions in that moment? It would certainly seem as though the disease itself created the emotions. But, if the disease itself created sadness, then you would have felt sad as soon as you developed the disease. If you didn't know that you had the harmful disease, would you still experience sadness, anger, despair, anxiety about it? No. If you already have the disease, but yet don't experience an emotional reaction to it, this must mean that the disease itself (the circumstance) isn't what creates your emotions.

While it seems that circumstances directly create our emotions, we actually can't experience an emotion unless our minds know about the circumstance. In other words, we can't have an emotional reaction to a circumstance until we have thoughts about it. If an event itself directly created an unwanted emotion, the event would create the unwanted emotion as soon as it happened.

If a loved one is injured in a car accident while you are asleep, when would you experience an emotional reaction to this event? You would only start to feel sad once you found out what happened and could have thoughts about it. If your loved one's injury (the circumstance) directly created your sadness, then you would immediately experience sadness as soon as the event happened. If you wouldn't experience sadness until you started to think about what happened, then it has to be your thoughts that are creating your sadness.

In comparison, if you were asleep and someone poured water on your head without waking you up, your hair would still get wet. Your hair would get wet because water directly causes wet hair. If your hair didn't get wet until you woke up and thought, "Someone poured water on my hair", you would know that your thoughts were necessary in creating your wet hair. Clearly, a circumstance cannot create an emotional reaction without thoughts.

The Questions: Would I be suffering if I didn't know the event happened? If the circumstance wouldn't have created an emotion without my mind knowing what happened (thoughts), then can I admit that the circumstance itself doesn't have the power to create my emotion? If my thoughts can create my emotion with no event happening now (e.g., thinking about past or future), but an event can't create an emotion without my thoughts (mind knowing what happened), then can I admit that my thoughts have created my suffering, and not a circumstance?

4. Am I able to be happy (have fun) when I am being entertained and distracted from my thoughts?

If a "bad" circumstance itself creates a specific unwanted emotion, then as long as we have that same "bad" circumstance, we would not be able to escape the specific unwanted emotion that the circumstance creates. If our unattractiveness directly creates our sadness, then we wouldn't be able to escape this sadness as long as we are unattractive. If our "bad" relationship creates our unhappiness, then we wouldn't be able to feel happy while still being in the relationship. If our "bad" job causes our feeling of shame, then we wouldn't be able to have a break from this shame as long as we are in our "bad" job.

However, in life, regardless of how "bad" our circumstances are, often all it takes to stop feeling one of our unwanted emotions is to simply engage in our favorite hobbies or some form of entertainment. It may seem that our unattractiveness directly creates our sadness, but all we need to do to stop feeling sad is turn on one of our favorite TV shows. It may seem that our "bad" relationship creates our unhappiness, but all we need to do to stop feeling unhappy is to go dancing. It may seem as if our "bad" job is creating our shame, but all we need to stop to feeling ashamed is to go play with our children.

No matter how "bad" our circumstances are, and no matter what unwanted emotion we are experiencing, we generally stop feeling the unwanted emotion when we are playing with our children, watching TV, dancing, playing music, doing yoga, eating delicious food, or playing sports. So why are we able to stop experiencing our unwanted emotions and have fun (be happy) just by entertaining ourselves? This happens simply because entertainment distracts us from the negative thoughts that are actually creating our suffering. If a "bad" circumstance created our unwanted emotion, then we wouldn't be able to escape the unwanted emotion simply by distracting ourselves from our thoughts.

If our "bad" circumstance still exists, but yet we can make ourselves happy purely by distracting ourselves from our negative thoughts, then it must be our thoughts that are creating our unhappiness.

The Questions: What do I like to do to entertain myself and have fun? When I am feeling my unwanted emotion, do these activities enable me to enjoy myself and stop feeling the unwanted emotion? If my "bad" circumstance still exists, yet I can make myself happy from engaging in activities I enjoy, then can I admit that my "bad" circumstance is not causing my unwanted emotion? If I can go from experiencing an unwanted emotion to being happy simply by entertaining myself (distracting myself from my thoughts), then can I admit that my thoughts must be creating my unwanted emotion?

5.   What are the facts and what are my thoughts about the facts?

We generally don't realize it, but we constantly form thoughts about circumstances and then unknowingly consider these thoughts to actually be part of the facts. For example, we may think, "I *am* ugly", "He *is* mean", "This situation *is* terrible", "Her actions *were* inappropriate", or "He *doesn't* appreciate me". We generally consider these thoughts to be no different from facts such as "her name *is* Amanda", "that *is* an apple", "my house *is* red", or "I *am* six feet tall". We innocently and often unknowingly think these thoughts as if they are facts and then conclude that our emotions were created by these "facts". However, the thoughts mentioned above are not facts. They are thoughts about facts.

Imagine you are waiting in line for a cup of coffee, then a man says to you, "Get out of my way!", as he tries to cut through the line to get to the seating area. Now imagine that this incident leaves you a little angry at the man. What would have caused your anger in this situation? Most of us would naturally think, "His disrespectful words caused my anger". In other words, it seems as though the facts themselves created our anger. But the key question to ask ourselves in this scenario is, "What were the facts and what was my thoughts about the facts?" The only facts were the words "get out of my way". It is not as though his words were factually disrespectful; his words were just his words, completely neutral. Therefore, he didn't speak "disrespectful words"; we just had a *thought* about his words that says, "That is disrespectful".

Our thoughts have nothing to do with his words (the facts). They are two separate things. *They exist in two completely separate places. His words were spoken in front of us and detected through our senses, whereas our thought "that is disrespectful" only exists as a concept in our mind.* Our emotion is created by the concept (thought), not by the facts. Our emotion is caused by what is going on in our minds, not by what is going on in front of us. Our anger is caused by the thought "that is disrespectful", not by the words "get out of my way". If we didn't have this thought about his words, we would experience no emotional reaction to them.

We consistently label people, actions, words, situations, and events as "bad", "not good enough", or "wrong". We say, "She *is* annoying", "She *is* boring", and "She *is* ugly" as if they were facts. Then we experience an emotional reaction to these labels, and we treat ourselves and others according to them. But what are the facts and what are our thoughts about the facts? A girl can't *be* "annoying", "boring", or "ugly". These concepts are not part of the facts. Someone can only perform actions or speak words, which our thoughts then label as "boring" or "annoying". "Boring" and "annoying" can't be seen and can't be touched. Any concept that certain words or actions are "boring" or "annoying" only exists as thoughts in our own minds.

It may seem as if "ugly" can be seen and touched. Think about it, though: a face, eyes, a nose, and hair can be seen and touched. These are not "ugly", these are only body parts. After we witness a body part through our senses, we then have the thought "her nose *is* ugly". Her nose can't *be* "ugly", her nose can only be her nose. "Ugly" is just a thought about her nose. Our thought is completely separate from the facts.

Similarly, we tend to believe thoughts like "my life shouldn't be like this", "he shouldn't have done that", or "I should be different". We believe these thoughts as if they are true, so they tend to run our lives and create a lot of shame and anger. But where does "should" exist? Can you see it or touch it? Is it really a rule written in stone somewhere that must be followed? The whole idea of "should" is just a concept that only exists in our minds. It is not a fact that we really should act a certain way, our life should be a certain way, or they should act a certain way. Our actions and our lives are just what they are. Any idea that they should be different doesn't exist anywhere but as a thought in our own mind.

Facts are what we know to be true. What we directly experience through our senses are the facts. The facts are reality. Then we superimpose our ideas of "good" and "bad", "right" and "wrong", "should" and "shouldn't" onto reality and claim those ideas are facts. Facts are completely neutral. Reality just is. Reality doesn't have a perspective. Nothing can be factually "bad" or "not good enough", and nothing "should" be a certain way, because facts don't contain perspectives within them.

Once we can see that part of what we considered to be facts is actually just our thoughts about the facts, then we can begin to recognize that our emotions are created by our thoughts and not by facts. Only then does it become possible to start questioning whether these thoughts are really true. Reality itself is freedom. It's only our thoughts about reality that create all of our suffering and discontent.

The Questions: What are the facts and what are my thoughts about the facts? Does "bad" exist as part of the facts, or is it just part of my thoughts about the facts? Can I see, hear, or touch the "bad" of something or someone, or is the "bad" of something or someone just thoughts about what I see, hear, and touch? Is "bad" physically located outside or only in my own mind? Does the idea of how things "should" be exist anywhere other than as a thought in my own mind? Is my emotion being created directly by the facts or is it created by my thoughts about the facts?

Recognizing that a thought created our emotion eliminates some of our suffering

Recognizing that your emotion has actually been created by a thought, and not your circumstances, is a big step towards freedom. Seeing this often weakens our belief in our thought and can substantially weaken its ensuing emotion.

If you can see that your thought has created your suffering, then you can stop blaming whatever person, action, event, or circumstance you thought was the cause of your suffering. This recognition alone can free us from a large amount of anger and resentment in our lives. It may also stop us from acting hurtfully towards whoever we believed was to blame.

Since we don't have control over many of the circumstances or events in our lives, it often seems as though we don't have control over our emotions and that they have been inflicted upon us without our permission. This can often make us feel as though we are powerless. We feel as if we are a victim. But if you are able to acknowledge that your thoughts are causing your suffering, then all of a sudden you are no longer powerless. You are no longer a victim. You now have some control. This means that no circumstance, no event, and no person has the power to make you suffer. You no longer have to believe that your emotions are inflicted upon you without your permission. And you don't have to believe the thoughts that would make you unhappy. This is a truly liberating discovery.

Even though it is thoroughly unenjoyable to live life feeling like a victim or holding onto anger towards others, it can often be hard for us to admit that thoughts are causing our suffering. If you find yourself strongly resisting this recognition, you can jump ahead right now to the first section in Chapter 17 called "I want to keep blaming others for my suffering".

Chapter Seven

Step 4: Discover that You Don't Know Whether Your Thought is True

We can't force our thoughts to stop or leave

Now that you have recognized that your thought has created your unwanted emotion, you most likely want to get rid of that thought. But trying to silence your mind, control your thoughts, stop your thoughts, let go of your thoughts, or push your thoughts away doesn't work. Our minds are too clever to allow thoughts to stop other thoughts. Our thoughts don't go away when we think, "I don't want to think these thoughts", "Go away thought!", "I am going to let this thought go", or "I am going to stop thinking now".

For example, if you are worrying about whether your child will get a "good" grade on his school exam, then telling yourself, "I don't want to worry", isn't going to stop you from worrying, because it doesn't address the cause of why you are giving attention to your worrisome thoughts.

Thoughts survive through the energy they get from our attention. We have no choice but to give our attention to whatever is most important to us. So if we are giving attention to a thought, it is because we unconsciously believe that thought is more important than whatever is going on in front of us. Generally, we give the most attention to thoughts that seem important to either our happiness or our survival. For example, our judgments about others help to improve our opinion of ourselves. We worry about the future because we believe our happiness is dependent on getting the future outcome we want. We tell ourselves sad stories from the past because doing so helps us to maintain some aspect of our identity (our survival).

It may seem as though we know that our thought only creates suffering, but if the thought held no importance to us, we quite simply wouldn't give it any attention. Since we automatically believe our thoughts, they almost always seem more important than the present moment, more important than what's actually happening in front of us.

The more we try to stop or control thoughts, the more attention we are giving to them. And in addition to our original thoughts remaining, we also end up adding a layer of new thoughts about how to get rid of our original thoughts—as well as a layer of internal conflict, because we think, "Why won't you thoughts go away!", "I don't want to think these thoughts!", or "It must be my fault that I can't stop my thoughts!"

Exercise: To illustrate this point, try to silence your mind right now. Close your eyes and try whatever strategy you want and see what happens. If you don't have a preferred strategy, try to count your breaths and see how high you can count while focusing on each breath. For most of us, we can only do this for a few seconds, maybe a few minutes at most. How high did you count before your mind interrupted you and took your attention? That is almost certainly not long enough to make you much happier. Now imagine how difficult it would be to silence your mind when you are in the midst of feeling sad, angry, stressed, or worried. To take it one step further, try to imagine how difficult it would be to silence your mind while you are engaging in your daily activities (especially the ones that seem to "cause" anger or stress).

Thoughts that aren't believed don't create emotions

Luckily, we don't need to get rid of our thoughts in order to stop experiencing the emotions they create. If you watch a movie in which the main character is cheated on by her husband, you would likely feel sad or angry if you believe the acting. But if you don't believe the actors, then even the saddest or most dramatic scenes will not provoke an emotional reaction. If a friend tells you that your child was injured in a car accident yesterday, and you believe them, you would likely feel upset. But, if you don't believe your friend at all, you would have no reason to feel upset.

Just as watching a movie or listening to others' words only creates emotions when we believe them, listening to our own thoughts only creates emotions when we believe them. No matter what thought arises in our mind, we won't experience an emotional reaction to it if we don't believe it.

There is no need to worry about getting rid of your thoughts, stopping them, dropping them, or letting go of them. Regardless of what someone is saying to you, if you don't believe what they are saying, you can keep listening to their words without them creating unwanted emotions. The same is true of our thoughts. *Regardless of what a thought is saying, if we don't believe that thought, it can remain in our minds without creating any emotions. Therefore, our thoughts themselves were never the problem. It is only our belief in thoughts that creates all of our suffering.*

Once we stop believing a specific thought to be true, that thought no longer provides us with any value. For example, if we stop believing our judgment about someone, then this judgment won't make us feel better about ourselves anymore. If a thought doesn't provide us with value, then it has no importance to us, and we have no reason to give it attention. Since attention provides a thought with the energy it needs to survive, the loss of attention usually causes the thought to disappear on its own. Our thoughts almost always drop away entirely on their own when we don't believe them to be true.

Our emotions are created by unknowingly believing our thoughts to be true

Please take a moment to locate the thoughts you found in Step 2. Is there any uncertainty about what you think *is* "bad", *was* "bad", or *would* be "bad"? Is there any doubt about what you think you need to get, change, or keep to be happy? Or do you believe that each of your thoughts is true? If we are experiencing an emotion, it must be because we are believing the thoughts behind it, because if we didn't, they wouldn't create the emotion. Our emotions can only be created by believing a thought to be true.

We tend to go through life unknowingly believing our thoughts about circumstances to be completely true. We don't think, "I am not sure whether this situation is terrible", we think, "This situation *is* terrible". We don't think, "I am not sure whether I am ugly", we think, "I *am* ugly". We don't think, "I don't know if he is mean", we think, "He *is* mean". We don't think, "It might make me happier if I get the promotion", we think, "I *need* this promotion to be happy". We don't think, "Failing the test might be bad for my life", we think, "Failing the test *would* be bad". Even though there seems to be uncertainty in a thought like "something bad could happen", the uncertainty is only about whether it will happen, whereas our anxiety is created from being certain that the outcome we fear "*would* be bad" if it did happen. As soon as we believe any of these thoughts, we experience our seemingly "negative" emotions.

Since we believe our thoughts to be true, our emotions almost always seem completely justified and logical, and seem as though they are the only appropriate reaction. We think it makes sense to be sad when we fail at getting something we wanted. But it only seems this way because we fully believe, "It *is* bad that I didn't get what I want" or "It *would* have been better if I had gotten what I wanted". It seems logical for us to get angry at our husband when he forgets about our dinner date. But this reaction only seems logical because we believe, "It *is* bad that he forgot" or "He *must* not care about me". However, the fact of the matter is, all of these types of thoughts are just assumptions. These thoughts aren't facts, and they aren't known to be true. They are simply uninvestigated theories and interpretations of events in our life.

We ask ourselves questions to help us disbelieve our thoughts

The point of Step 4 is to help you realize that you don't know whether your thoughts are true. The way we do this is by asking ourselves questions. Let's look at a couple of quick examples of how questions can help us to disbelieve a thought:

• If we think, "She *was* disrespectful to me", then we could ask ourselves "Could someone else have a different perspective on the situation? If someone else could have a different perspective, can I know for sure that my thought is true?" This might help us to realize, "I don't really know for sure that she was being disrespectful".

- If we think, "It *is* bad that I didn't get the job offer", then we could ask ourselves, "Do I know for sure that this circumstance is bad for my life and won't have some good effects?" This could help us to recognize, "I don't know whether it was good or bad to not the get the job offer".

- If we believe, "I *am* not worthy of love", then we could ask ourselves, "Can I think of a few reasons or examples as to why the opposite might be true?" This just might help us to discover, "It is definitely possible that I am worthy of love".

Sometimes the questions may show us that we don't know whether our thought is true, and sometimes we will see that our thought actually isn't true at all. Either way, when we have stopped believing our thought to be true – when we disbelieve the thought – we stop experiencing the emotion that our thought created. The peace that remains is the experience of the present moment.

How to use the questions to disbelieve your thoughts

In the following eight chapters, there are 34 different major questions to help you disbelieve your thoughts. Each of these questions is a separate solution and has its own section dedicated to explaining its use. All of the questions are meant to hit at your thoughts from different angles, exposing different reasons why your thoughts might not be true, trying to find a way for you to realize that you don't know whether your thought is true. Some questions may show you that your concept of "bad" doesn't really exist, while other questions are meant to show you that a specific circumstance may not even meet your own definition of "bad".

There are 34 different questions to provide you with different options (solutions) to help you disbelieve your thoughts, and because certain questions are only meant to be applied to certain thoughts. You may only need to ask yourself one of the major questions (and its sub-questions) in order to disbelieve your thought, or it may take several questions to disbelieve the thought.

Rather than just reading right through the next eight chapters, you will find that this process is more likely to dissolve your unwanted emotion and bring you present if you jump to the chapters and questions that are relevant to the specific thoughts you found in Step 2. In order to help you figure out which questions to ask yourself, the 34 questions are broken down into chapters by type of thought. Below is a list of the chapters and quick explanations of when to use the questions inside them.

Chapter 8 – Questions to Disbelieve Any of Your Thoughts. No matter what thought you are believing, you always start with these questions.

Chapter 9 – Questions to Disbelieve Your Thoughts about Current or Past Circumstances. This chapter is for when your thought is about a "bad" event from the past, or you think anything about your life is "bad" or "not good enough". Feelings of something lacking in your life are addressed here.

Chapter 10 – Questions to Disbelieve Your Thoughts about Future Outcomes. Your thoughts about the future (including all anxiety thoughts) are addressed in this chapter.

Chapter 11 – Questions to Disbelieve Your Thoughts about Others' Opinions. This is meant to help you disbelieve all of the thoughts that make you emotionally react to what people think and make you worry about what people think.

Chapter 12 – Questions to Disbelieve Your Judgments about Others.

Chapter 13 – Questions to Disbelieve Your Judgments about Yourself.

Chapter 14 – Questions to Disbelieve Your Concept of Blame. The questions in this chapter are to help you stop believing the thoughts that cause your anger, resentment, shame, and guilt. If you think anything about yourself or others is "bad", these questions are meant to help you realize that no one is to blame for whatever action or outcome we think is "bad".

Chapter 15 – Questions to Disbelieve Your Idea of How Things Should Be. These questions are for any of your thoughts that contain a "should".

When one of the questions has helped you to disbelieve your core thought, there is usually a corresponding feeling like "aaahh, I see", peace, relief, or some clear feeling that the emotion has lost its power. If you ask a question but it does not help you to disbelieve your thought, don't worry about it, just move on to another question. Each question is helpful at different times, for different thoughts. Not every question will work every time.

If the feeling of relief or peace from disbelieving a thought doesn't seem to correspond to how much suffering the thought seemed to be causing, then it is likely that the thought was not completely disbelieved or you were not investigating the core thought. When this happens, it is worth questioning the thought more, questioning a different thought you found, or going back to Step 2 to see if you can identify other thoughts that are at play.

Once your emotion has dissolved, there is no need to ask yourself any more questions regarding the thought that created it. You can either pick another emotion and go through the process again, or you can choose to read through all of the questions in this book to help you become familiar with them. Then, when you apply this process to one of your thoughts at a later date, you can go directly to the questions that will best help you to disbelieve your thought.

Uncertainty about the future doesn't create anxiety

It may seem that the uncertainty as to whether a thought is true or not—the very uncertainty we're trying to create here—might lead to anxiety. We tend to have this idea that anxiety is created by not knowing the future. However, uncertainty about the future doesn't create anxiety. Anxiety is created by the belief that a "bad" outcome is possible. Would you experience any anxiety if your friend told you, "I will give you $100 tomorrow for your birthday, but I am not going to tell if it will be $20 bills, $10 bills, or $1 bills"? There is uncertainty, but each outcome is equally "good", so the uncertainty is irrelevant and won't lead to anxiety.

However, after we disbelieve a thought, our minds may form a new thought that creates anxiety. For example, if we believe the thought, "My boyfriend doesn't care about me anymore", then we may experience sadness. If we disbelieve our thought, recognizing "I don't know if it's true that my boyfriend doesn't care about me anymore", then we would no longer feel sad. But, we may then form the new thought, "It would be bad if my boyfriend stopped caring about me", which would create anxiety.

Therefore, if you ever find that disbelieving a thought has created anxiety for you, all you need to do is ask yourself the question "What outcome do I think would be bad?" Once you have identified what future outcome you think "would be bad" (what outcome you fear), then you can go to Chapter 10 to question whether you actually know this future outcome "would be bad".

How to answer the questions

When we ask ourselves one of the questions given, the immediate answer often seems to confirm what we have been thinking all along. If the question is, "Are you sure?", the immediate answer may be, "YES I'm sure!" This type of answer is what comes when our mind thinks it already knows the answer and we don't actually stop to discover the answer for ourselves right now. Answering a question based on the first thought that pops into our mind will not allow us to discover the answer that is true for us.

Rather than answering a question in this way, stop and take a breath after you ask yourself one of the questions. Be patient, wait a few seconds, and allow the answer to come. Don't refer to your knowledge, what you think the right answer is, or what you think the answer should be. The answers you are looking for, by nature, will often conflict with what you know, what you have been taught, and what you have believed. This is why we start from scratch. Answer the question honestly and innocently. Treat this as a completely new discovery, as uncharted territory. If necessary, look at your own experience in life to discover what is true for you.

Since our minds partially don't want to disbelieve thoughts, our thoughts may try to trick us in a few ways.

• Thoughts can try to answer questions with a story or justification that only provides evidence that seems to prove our thought is true.
• Thoughts can prevent us from seeing the truth by overcomplicating the answers so much that it is hard to find the truth.
• Thoughts can go on tangents in order to avoid directly answering the question.
• Thoughts can try to answer the questions, *"Do you know for sure?"* or *"Is it true?"*, with answers such as "I am almost sure", "I am almost positive", or "I am 99% sure". However, if we

aren't 100% sure that our thought is true, if there is a possibility that it isn't, then the fact is, we don't actually know whether our thought is true. Our own truth becomes, "I don't know if this thought is true". The only two possibilities are that either we are sure that our thought is true or we aren't sure. Regardless of whether we are ninety-nine percent sure or one percent sure, we are not sure. Either the thought is a fact ("this *is* an apple") or it is not known to be true. There is nothing in between. If we are not sure, then our answer must be, "I don't know if this thought is true".

When we answer, "Is it true?", with "I am almost positive", or "there is a small possibility that I am wrong", then we have not yet disbelieved our thought, and we are going to continue to experience our unwanted emotion. But if we can take it one step further and just acknowledge that our answer "I am almost positive my thought is true", actually means, "I really don't know whether my thought is true at all", then the emotion dissolves. If our answer is, "I am almost 100% sure that my thought is true", then we would have to admit that since we are not positive our thought is true, it must mean that, "I really don't know whether my thought is true".

For example, we may experience anxiety from thinking, "It would be bad if my girlfriend broke up with me". But after asking ourselves a few questions, we may be able to recognize that there is a small possibility that this outcome could be "good" for our life. If we answer, *"Am I sure this thought is true?"*, with "I am almost positive it would be bad if my girlfriend broke up with me", then our anxiety will remain. However, since we don't actually know with certainty that "It would be bad if this happened", the truth is, "I really don't know whether losing my girlfriend would be good or bad for my life". If we can admit this, then we are no longer believing the thought that created our emotion, and we would have no reason to feel anxiety anymore.

Because of these tricks, the most effective way to answer questions such as, "Do you know for sure?" or "Is it true?", is with either "yes", "no", or "I don't know". For other types of questions, you can choose to mentally answer the questions or you may find it more helpful to write down your answers.

Chapter Eight

Questions to Disbelieve Any of Your Thoughts

From an early age, we are conditioned to judge things—actions, words, situations, events, experiences, feelings, people—as "good" or "bad". Regardless of what you're thinking, or what emotion you are experiencing, the questions in this chapter can help you to disbelieve your thoughts.

1.   Is it true?

As soon as we find a thought that creates our suffering, the first question we must always ask ourselves is the very simple question, "Is it true?" If we stop for a few moments and allow ourselves to really look, this question is often enough to help us discover that we don't know for sure whether our thought is true. On the other hand, if the answer is an immediate "yes my thought is true!"—as it often is—it's worth asking yourself, "Am I absolutely sure my thought is true?"

Many times, when we experience intense emotions, it is because we are believing thoughts with extreme words such as "everyone", "no one", "always", "never", "everything", or "nothing". These extreme words intensify our emotions because they leave no room for positivity at all. For example, we may think, "Everyone hates me", "No one likes me", "He is always mean to me", "I am never going to find a wife", "Everything hurts on my body", or "Nothing ever goes my way". But if we just ask ourselves, "Am I sure this thought is true?", then it is usually possible to recognize that we can't be certain such extreme statements are true.

Similarly, we also tend to unknowingly have thoughts that exaggerate the "bad" effect of unwanted events. For example, we might think, "My father will kill me if I get fired from my job", "My life is over if my boyfriend leaves me", "I need this job", or "I have to get everything done". When we believe these thoughts, we can experience a lot of fear. But if we allow ourselves to question the truth of these thoughts, it is often clear that these thoughts aren't really true.

When we recognize that our extreme statement or exaggerated "bad" effect either isn't true or isn't known to be true, we lose our reason to feel whatever intense unwanted emotion we had been experiencing.

The Questions: Is it true? Am I absolutely certain that my thought is true? Can I be absolutely sure that such an extreme statement is accurate? Am I certain that I am not exaggerating the effects of a "bad" outcome?

2.   Can I think of a few reasons or examples as to why the opposite might be true?

Any time we are experiencing an emotion, it is because we are believing a thought to be true. Since we don't want to think of ourselves as "wrong", we unconsciously want to keep believing that we were "right" to believe our thought is true. Because of this dynamic, once we believe a thought, our minds generally only look for evidence that will support our thought. Doing this, of course, perpetuates our unwanted emotions.

For example, once we think, "My husband doesn't appreciate me", we may immediately see a bunch of images of past events projected in our mind that all help to prove our thought is true. We would only think of the times when we didn't get any praise from our husband, and we would not think of the times when he did give us praise. We might leave out key details of a story, like the fact that our husband didn't even know that we did something worthy of praise. If our minds think back to any time when he said "thank you", then we generally interpret that "thank you" to be said in an unthoughtful and uncaring way.

The evidence we use to prove our thoughts to be true is almost always biased, almost always includes only memories that back up our claim, and is almost always based on whatever perspective or interpretation we think proves our point. This process of finding nothing but supportive evidence for our thoughts winds up strengthening our beliefs and intensifying our emotions.

Now that we know how our minds keep us believing thoughts, we can flip this process upside down in order to help us disbelieve our unwanted thoughts. Once we are aware of a thought we want to disbelieve, instead of looking for supportive evidence, all we have to do is look for a few possible reasons or examples as to why the opposite of our thought might be true. In other words, if we think a situation is "bad", we can look for reasons or examples as to why it might be "good". If we can find some genuine reasons or examples why the positive thought might be true, then this often makes us realize that we can't be sure whether our negative thought is true.

If we think, "My boss is mean", then we might be able to remember a few times when he was nice to us or others. If we think, "My job sucks", we can try to remember all the aspects of our job that we like. If we think, "I am unworthy of anyone's love", then we can try to find a few reasons why we think someone would want to love us. If we have decided, "I don't make enough money", then we can look for a few reasons as to why we do actually have enough money. If we think, "My girlfriend said 'thank you' in an unappreciative way", then we can try to find reasons why it is possible that we misread her intentions and that she was appreciative when she said it. If we think it is "bad" that our husband always leaves his dirty clothes on the floor, then we can try to find reasons why his habit might be "good" for us or our relationship (e.g., it gives us consistent opportunities to do things for the person we love).

When we only look for evidence to prove that our negative thought is true, or only remember and think about the negatives of any situation, we will always be proved right and will inevitably suffer as a consequence. But it is almost always possible to come up with genuine reasons or examples why any situation, person, or event is positive. *When we are used to thinking of a circumstance as "bad", it may take some effort, creativity, or even brutal honesty to find some reasons why the opposite thought might be true, but it is always possible.* It may even require a few minutes (or more) of thinking in order to find genuine reasons or examples as to why the opposite might be true.

If we are able to recognize that the opposite of our thought could be true, this usually makes us realize that we can't really be sure that our thought is true. Once we are able to recognize that we don't know whether our thought is true, then the emotion our thought was creating naturally dissolves, or at least loses much of its power.

This question can be applied to any thought and is often the only question we need to ask ourselves in order to disbelieve a thought.

The Questions: Can I think of a few reasons or examples as to why the opposite might be true? If there are a few reasons or examples (memories) as to why the opposite thought might be true, can I be absolutely certain that my thought is true?

3.   Am I sure my thought is true, or is it just a perspective?

Imagine you went to see a movie with a few friends. When you come out of the theatre, you say to your friends, "I didn't think that movie was very good". You say this with a certain softness or lightness; you know that you are just giving your opinion, your perspective. Then imagine your friends respond by telling you how they thought the movie was really great. Since you understand that your statement was just an opinion, you acknowledge their opinions, and you may find them curious, but you don't argue about it.

Now imagine a different scenario in which you leave the movie telling your friends, "That movie *was* so boring and terrible!" This time, your statement is still just an opinion, but yet you don't see it as an opinion. You think your statement is true. There is a sort of hardness or certainty about your statement. So when your friends tell you that the movie was really great, you either argue with them, try to convince them to see it your way, think they are stupid, or think they don't know what they're talking about or are just wrong.

In both of these scenarios, you had a thought about a movie. However, in one of these scenarios you saw your thought as an opinion, whereas in the other one, you believed your thought was true, or a fact, and didn't recognize that it was just an opinion. When you saw your thought as just an opinion, it didn't have any power to create emotions when your friends disagreed. However, when you believed your thought to be true, you experienced anger and judged your friends when they disagreed. No matter how sure you are that a movie is "bad", it is still just a thought you have about a movie, and not a fact. If you can acknowledge that others could disagree with your thought, then you can admit that you really don't know whether your thought is true, and you can acknowledge that your thought is really just a perspective.

In the same way, all of the thoughts in our minds are just perspectives. *The only time our thoughts create emotions is when we confuse our perspective to be what's true.*

Throughout our life, we have absorbed the belief that certain types of words, actions, situations, and appearances *are* "bad". Over time, we each have created our own definitions of what words and actions *are* "disrespectful", "mean", or "annoying" and what physical attributes *are* "ugly". When we hear certain words, witness certain actions, or see certain physical attributes, we unconsciously ask ourselves, "Does this meet my definition of disrespectful or respectful, annoying or pleasant, funny or boring, pretty or ugly?" Then we answer this question by making the judgment (decision) that what we witnessed *is* "disrespectful", "annoying", "boring", or "ugly". We have no uncertainty about whether our thought is true. We don't view our thought as a perspective, we unknowingly view it as a fact, as true. Once we make this judgment, we react with the corresponding emotion.

What's important to understand here is that the facts themselves are neutral. It's our individual minds that label the facts as "good" or "bad", "right" or "wrong", "pretty" or "ugly". But since we all have different genetics and life histories, it is always possible for other people to label the same facts differently. We can all have different definitions of what types of actions, words, appearances, situations, or events qualify as "bad", "inappropriate", "unattractive", "disrespectful", and so on. We may believe a circumstance *is* "bad", but someone else could disagree with us if the circumstance doesn't meet their definition of "bad". If someone else can disagree with us, this may help us to realize that we don't know whether our thought is true and that it is really just a perspective.

As we have now seen, our emotions are created by innocently believing our thoughts to be true and factual. However, if we believe our thoughts are true, we are unknowingly claiming that every other perspective on the subject is wrong. If we experience anger from believing, "His actions *were* inconsiderate", we are unknowingly believing that anyone who thinks, "His actions *were* considerate", is wrong. If we experience anxiety from thinking, "It *was* bad that she left me", we are unknowingly believing that anyone who thinks, "It *was* good that she left you", is wrong. Any time we believe, "This *is* bad", we are inherently believing, "Anyone who thinks this isn't bad *is* wrong". But what we are not seeing here is that if others could disagree with us, then our thought must just be a perspective. Can we really know with absolute certainty that our thought is true when others could disagree with us?

Our thoughts often seem true because the people around us tend to reinforce our beliefs by frequently agreeing with our perspectives about what *is* "good" and "bad". They often have similar perspectives because they live in the same area or were raised in the same culture, because the same type of job often draws similar people, or just because we often choose to spend time with people who have beliefs that are similar to ours. In this way, when we think something *is* "bad" and we get sad, angry, or worried, our friends usually agree with our judgments instead of offering us a different perspective.

For example, if you tell your friend that you are angry because "my husband shouldn't have said that to me", your friend will most often say, "You're right, he shouldn't have said that". If you tell your friends, "I am worried that my son will fail his exam", your friends usually tell you, "He will do fine". This may seem as if it is helpful, but by making this statement, your friends are agreeing with your decision that "failing the exam would be bad", while at the same time they are trying to calm you by saying, "He probably won't fail". If you are sick, the people around you usually tell you, "That's such a shame, I hate it when I'm sick, I'm sorry you have to be sick". These comments are telling us, "Being sick is bad", which strengthens our belief "sick is bad" and perpetuates our sadness and self-pity. We often unknowingly choose not to be around people who would disagree with us, because it can be confronting. We want people to tell us we're right, and we want their sympathy. But by being offered sympathy, we are effectively being told by others, "Your thought is true", and therefore, "Your reason for suffering is completely valid and true". This causes us to continuously have our concepts of "bad" reaffirmed as true and perpetuates our suffering.

We may think, "My boss *is* too demanding", "It *is* bad that I still don't have a husband", "I *am* not attractive", "He *is* selfish", "It *would* be bad if I don't land the new client", or "My boyfriend *doesn't* appreciate me". But is it possible that someone else could have the opposite thought on any of these issues? Could someone think that your boss is reasonable, that it is more enjoyable to still be single, that you're good-looking, that he is considerate, that not getting the client would be "good" for your business, and that your boyfriend really does appreciate you? If it is possible, then can you really be completely sure that your thought is true?

This simple question might help us realize that our thought is just a perspective. We might recognize, "I think my boss is demanding, but maybe he is reasonable", "It seems bad that I'm still single, but maybe this gives me more freedom to enjoy myself", "I think I'm not attractive, but it's possible that I am attractive to others", "He often seems selfish, but it is a possibility that he is a considerate person overall", "There would be some bad effects if I didn't land the new client, but it could wind up being good for my business", "My boyfriend doesn't show me appreciation, but that might not actually mean he doesn't appreciate me".

If we acknowledge that others can have a different thought about the same circumstance, then we may be able to recognize that our thought is just a perspective, and that it is not a fact, nor is it what's true. We can come to understand that our opinion is just an opinion. Once we acknowledge that our thought is just a perspective, we may be able to recognize, "I don't really know whether my thought is *true*". If we truly see that our thought is just a perspective that we don't know to be true, then even our seemingly "bad" circumstances won't cause us to suffer anymore because we won't believe our thought that says, "This *is* bad".

The Questions: Am I sure my thought is true, or is it just a perspective? Is the agreement from others enough evidence to prove that my thought is true? Could someone else from a different culture, gender, age group, geographic region, religion, or economic status have a different perspective? If someone else could have a different perspective, can I know with absolute certainty that my thought is true? Am I sure that my thought is true, considering that the belief, "My thought (perspective) is true", inherently means that I must also believe, "Every other thought (perspective) about this circumstance is wrong"? If someone else could react with a different emotion, can I be sure that the thoughts which create my emotion are true?

4. Am I sure that my feeling proves that my thought is true, considering that feelings are created by believing thoughts to be true?

It sometimes seems as if we aren't just believing a thought to be true, but rather, our thought feels true for us. If someone says to us, "Get out of my way", we might think, "That is disrespectful". Even if we were to admit that other people could have a different perspective and believe, "That was not disrespectful", we might think,

"It doesn't matter what anyone else thinks, because this is what is true for me, this is valid for me".

But what does it really mean when we think, "This thought is true for me"? Think about this for a second. Doesn't it just mean, "I believe this thought is true"? It certainly seems as if it is more than that. It seems this way because the thought corresponds with a physical feeling in our bodies. *What happens is that once we believe a thought to be true, that thought creates an emotion. Once we have this emotion or feeling in our body, this feeling seems to help prove to us that our thought is true. It makes the thought feel true.*

To give an example, when we think, "That was disrespectful", we may immediately get tense or angry. These feelings in our body seem to prove to us that our thought is true. It feels true. However, these feelings are only present because we believe the thought to be true. An emotion, or feeling in the body, can't help prove that a thought is true, because it is only created by *believing* a thought to be true. No matter how strong our emotions are, they are never a sign that our thought is true. Thoughts create feelings; feelings don't create thoughts.

We have been raised to believe that sadness, anger, fear, and happiness are the direct result of specific circumstances. Since emotions seem to be directly caused by circumstances, it seems that our thoughts about any circumstance come after we experience the emotion. Therefore, it seems that the feeling proves our thought is true.

If our husband is travelling on business and hasn't called us, we may think, "He doesn't care about me anymore", and experience sadness. When we believe that our sadness is a direct result of circumstances, we think that our sadness proves that he doesn't care about us. But really, we have no idea whether he still cares

about us. This is just a guess; he might car[e]
as he always has. Our sadness is not a resu[lt]
band's love and care, it is created from believi[ng]
doesn't care about me anymore".

If we think, "My relationship shouldn't be like this", th[en]
likely feel sadness about our relationship. If we believe the
is directly caused by circumstances, then we will think our sa[d]
proves that there is something "wrong" with our relationship a[nd]
that it shouldn't be the way it is. In reality, our sadness was only
caused by believing our thoughts about the relationship, and therefore our sadness can't help to prove our thought is true.

If we feel fear or anxiety that we are going to get fired from our
job, we may believe that this feeling is created because we are
actually going to get fired. We think that our thought "I am going
to get fired" must be true because we feel the fear and anxiety that
we would expect to feel if we were actually going to get fired.
However, we can't know the future. Our fear and anxiety are only
felt because we believe the thought "I am going to get fired", not
because we are actually going to get fired.

For many of us, one of the major reasons why we believe our
thoughts to be true is because we believe that our feelings serve to
prove that our thoughts are true. Therefore, when we stop believing
our feelings to be evidence that proves our thought is true, we have
lost a major reason to believe our thought is true. Without this
belief, it becomes much easier to see that any thought might not be
true.

The Questions: Is it true that emotions (feelings) are directly
caused by circumstances? Is it true that emotions come before
thoughts? Can my emotions genuinely act as proof that my thought
is true, considering that my emotion is only created because I believe my thought to be true? If my thought *feels* true, does that

t this feeling is only created
?

ave   created   my
at I need to change
:, or others in order

tly create emotions, we
... of "imperfect" circumstanc-
..., I need something to change for me to be
...ppy and wind up almost constantly trying to "improve" ourselves, our situation, and others. This pursuit of change tends to
take on incredible importance, and seem very serious, because our
happiness seems to be on the line. We have anxiety that we will
never achieve the desired change, we feel sad or angry at ourselves
when we don't achieve the desired change, and we get angry at
others when they don't change for us.

However, we have now discovered that our unhappiness, or our
unwanted emotion, has actually been created by believing thoughts.
If our circumstances aren't causing our unhappiness, then this
means we don't need to change our circumstances in order to be
happy. We can admit it's not true that "my circumstances aren't
good enough to be happy", "I need my circumstances to change for
me to be happy", or "I can't be happy unless my circumstances
change". When we recognize that these thoughts aren't true, all of
a sudden we can relax. We don't have to change or improve everything we thought we had to in order to finally be happy. We can be
happy right here, right now, without changing anything about ourselves, our situation, or others. All we need to do is disbelieve a
few thoughts.

The Questions: Can I admit that thoughts have created my unhappiness or unwanted emotions, rather than circumstances? If my unwanted emotion isn't created by circumstances, then is it true that I need to change something about myself, my situation, or others in order to be happy? If my thoughts have created my unwanted emotion, then am I absolutely certain that I can't be happy with my circumstances exactly as they are right now?

Chapter Nine

Questions to Disbelieve Your Thoughts about Current or Past Circumstances

The questions in this chapter are meant to help you disbelieve the thoughts that claim, "The outcome was bad", "This circumstance is bad", and "Things aren't good enough right now". When you stop believing these thoughts, you no longer have your reason to keep feeling whatever sadness, anger, or guilt you have had. In addition, without the belief that something in your life isn't "good enough", there is no longer a sense that something is missing.

6.   Do I know for sure that this circumstance is "bad" for my life and won't have some "good" effects?

Let's say you break your leg. You would consider that to be "bad", right? Now imagine that while you are sitting in the doctor's waiting room with your broken leg, you meet the man who eventually becomes your loving husband and the father of your children. Considering this, would you now consider it to have been "good" or "bad" for your life that you broke your leg? You would almost certainly consider the broken leg to have been "good" for your life. In isolation, you decided that the broken leg was "bad", but after experiencing its "good" overall effect on your life, you would now consider it to be "good" that you broke your leg.

In the same way, as we go through life, events that seem "bad" can always wind up having many "good" effects and end up being "good" for our life overall. Since we don't know all of the effects of any circumstance, we don't really know whether any circumstance is "good" or "bad" for our life.

Whenever we consider a circumstance or outcome in our life to be "bad", we are only judging it based on the immediate effect that we are aware of (e.g., the pain or inconvenience of a broken leg). But one cause does not have only one effect. We may think that a specific circumstance or outcome is "bad" and will make us suffer, but there are countless effects that could arise from any one outcome or circumstance in our lives. Then there are countless effects of each one of those effects. We have no idea what all of the effects of any event will be for ourselves and others (long-term or short-term).

If we just acknowledge that a specific "bad" outcome in our life could have "good" effects, then we can recognize that we really don't know whether the "bad" circumstance will make us happier overall in the long run. In other words, we can recognize that we don't really know whether the "bad" circumstance is "bad" for our life. Now let's look at some examples of how this dynamic can play itself out.

We may think that having our partner cheat on us, getting injured, being overweight, getting a low grade, discovering that our child is using drugs, or missing our train to work is "bad". But could the cheating provide us with the incentive to change something about ourselves, force a conversation that improves the relationship, or give us the courage to leave? Could getting injured result in our having the time to read a book that changes our lives, taking a test that detects cancer early, or helping us realize how much the people in our lives love us? Could being overweight lead to finding a wonderful lover, protect us from severe injury in a car accident, or help us find nice friends who aren't superficial? Could a low exam score teach us that we need to study differently, show us that this topic isn't right for us, or spur us to change a lifestyle that's not conducive to learning? Could our child's drug use lead him to realize that drug use can't make him happy, scare him into changing his life, or help to teach others how not to live? Could missing our train to work result in avoiding a fatal accident, give us time to read a news article that helps our work, or allow us to meet someone great?

These possible effects may seem realistic or they may seem highly unlikely, but the fact is that they are all possible. *When we label a circumstance "bad", we are making an uninvestigated assumption that the circumstance or event will make us unhappy or less happy.* But the bottom line is, for every seemingly "bad" circumstance, there can be many "good" effects that wind up making us happier. When we decide that a circumstance is "bad" just because we are aware of a few seemingly "bad" effects, we are ignoring all of the possible "good" effects that could come from it.

Haven't you been through an event in the past that you thought was "bad" at the time but ended up working out "great"? This happens all the time. But we don't have to wait until long after an event in order to realize that we don't know whether it is "good" or "bad". As soon as an event occurs, we can see that we don't know whether it is "good" or "bad" if we just allow ourselves to admit that we can't possibly know what all of the effects will be. If we can just admit that our "bad" circumstance could wind up having "good" effects or could help to make us happier in the long run, then we can stop believing our circumstance *is* "bad".

If we believe, "It is bad that I got cheated on, got injured, am overweight, got a low exam score, or missed my train", then we will likely experience sadness, shame, or anger. But if we can admit that we don't know with absolute certainty whether an event is "bad" for our life, then we can acknowledge, "I don't know for sure that it is bad". When we don't know whether an event is "good" or "bad" for our life, then we don't know whether it was "good" or "bad" that it happened. Once we see this, we have stopped believing our thought "this is bad" to be true, thereby freeing us from whatever suffering this thought had been creating.

The Questions: Am I upset because I think that this circumstance is "bad" for me or for others? Do I know all of the effects of this circumstance, and all of the effects of those effects? Can I think of a few possible "good" effects that could come from this "bad" circumstance? (be creative). Is it possible that this "bad" circumstance could lead to "positive" effects in the future that wind up making me (or others) happier? Is it possible that this circumstance is exactly what I (or others) need in order to learn a lesson that will make me (or them) happier in the future? If I can remember a time in the past when I thought a circumstance was "bad" but it ended up working out really well, then can't it happen again? If I don't know whether this "bad" circumstance will make me (or them) happier or not in the long run, then isn't it true that I don't know whether this circumstance is "good" or "bad" for my (or their) life?

7.   Do I know for sure that life would be "better" if I could change what was "bad" in the past?

Almost all of us have things in our past that we believe *were* "bad", whether it's something seemingly small or something more substantial like a lost job, hurtful words, physical abuse, cheating, a partner leaving, a child getting in trouble, an injury, or the death of a loved one. When we go through one of these events, we often suffer for a long time afterwards because we keep telling ourselves the story about how "bad" the event was. These thoughts or stories just keep recreating our sadness, anger, and guilt. But if we can recognize that we don't know whether the event was actually "bad" for our life, then we will naturally stop giving attention to these thoughts.

Normally, when we are giving attention to a thought about how a past event was "bad", it is because we believe that life would be "better" and we would be happier if the event hadn't happened. This seems like a logical conclusion. However, this relies on an overly simplistic view of cause and effect. We consider the "bad" event or action to have one effect—suffering—so we assume that if the "bad" action or event were eliminated, the suffering would be eliminated. But one cause does not have just one effect. This isn't the way life works.

For example, if one of your parents died when you were young, that would obviously seem like a "bad" thing to have happened. Almost all of us would naturally assume that it would have been "better" for our life if our parent hadn't died. But let's say you're now grown up, you're happy, you have a great marriage, and you're a wonderful mother. Isn't it possible that these seemingly "positive" aspects of your life are effects of having lost your parent at a young age? We don't know what all of the effects are of losing our parents, as there are many immediate effects from that event and then countless effects from all of those effects.

It's always possible that anything "good" in our life could have been the result of an event from our past that we labeled "bad". Regardless of whether we can draw a connection, if we like certain aspects of our life now, the "bad" event from our past could easily have helped to make these aspects of our life come to fruition. If we can acknowledge that the "bad" event may have helped lead to some of the "good" in our life, this may help us realize that the "bad" event might not have been "bad" for our life overall.

To think that life would be "better" if the "bad" event hadn't happened would be to ignore all of the "good" that may have come from it. If the "bad" event hadn't happened, it is possible that we might not have a lot of the "good" in our life right now. If we knew that the "bad" event helped to create much of the "good" in our life, then we probably wouldn't want to remove the "bad" event from our past. If we wouldn't want to remove the "bad" event from our past, then this means we consider it to have been a more "positive" than "negative" contributor to our life overall. Since we actually don't know whether the "bad" event created some of the "good" in our life, we really don't know whether the event was "bad" or "good" for our life.

It's even possible that if the "bad" event hadn't happened, some seemingly "worse" event could have happened. If our reckless driving hadn't caused that "bad" car accident, we might have caused an even more serious accident instead. If our child hadn't gone to jail for drug possession, then maybe he would have kept using drugs until he overdosed. If our husband hadn't cheated on us, we might still be suffering in our marriage instead of being in our much more fulfilling new relationship. In other words, "It could have been worse". To assume that life would be "better" if the "bad" event hadn't happened is to ignore the fact that life could be "worse".

If we believe, "It was bad that my husband made us move when he changed jobs", this will create anger and resentment. If we are able to find some "good" in our life or our children's lives, then this may help us to realize that we can't really be sure whether this event was "bad" for our life. If we aren't certain whether the event was "bad" or "good" for our life, then we can finally stop believing, "The event was bad". Once this happens, we stop experiencing the suffering these thoughts created, and we no longer have any reason to give attention to these thoughts.

The Questions:

a) Do I like any aspects of my life right now? Is it possible that the "bad" event from the past actually led to this "good" in my life? Just because I can't draw the connection between the "bad" event and the "good" aspects of my life, does that mean there isn't a connection? If the "bad" event could have helped to create "good" parts of my life, then am I completely sure that the event was "bad" for my life?

b) Is it possible that I wouldn't have some of the "good" in my life if the "bad" event hadn't happened? Would I be willing to give up the "good" in my life just to remove the "bad" event from my past? If not, then doesn't this mean I consider the "bad" event to have had more of a "positive" than a "negative" effect on my life, and therefore I consider it to be "good" for my life overall?

c) Is it possible that I (or others) would have suffered more if the "bad" event hadn't happened? Is it possible that a seemingly "worse" event could have happened if the "bad" event hadn't happened? If so, then am I certain that it was "bad" that the "bad" event happened? Do I know for sure that my (or their) life would be "better" if I could change what was "bad" in the past?

8. Would I consider this event to be "bad" on my universal scale, or is it only "bad" relative to my normal experience?

The "worse" we consider an event to be, the lower the score we would give it on a scale of "1 to 10", and the stronger our unwanted emotion will be. For example, you would experience more intense anger when witnessing someone getting robbed than watching someone getting yelled at because you would consider the robbery to be "worse" (a lower score). We generally don't realize it, but we have actually created two different scales with which we judge circumstances and events. The first scale is our "personal scale", which is based on the types of experiences we have had in our own life. The second scale is our "universal scale", which is based on all of the possible "good" and "bad" circumstances in the world.

When an event occurs in our life that is "worse" than what we normally experience, we often consider it to be "really bad" and react accordingly. This is because we automatically rate circumstances according to our personal scale. This often causes us to experience strong unwanted emotions to events that would actually be considered "pretty good" on our universal scale.

For example, if you are on your way to a Broadway show, and then all of a sudden you get stuck in traffic, you might think, "This is terrible" and get really frustrated about it. If you are generally healthy, and then you catch a cold that prevents you from going out over the weekend, you might think, "This really sucks" and get upset or feel self-pity about it. If your daughter, the "straight A" student, gets a B grade on a test, she may think, "This is horrible" and become sad or depressed about it.

But what is "bad" or "terrible" on your universal scale? You might think that death, disease, and poverty are a "1", or "terrible". You might think that sustaining a severe injury or having your house burned down would be a "2", or "really bad". Now, how does the "bad" event or circumstance in your life compare to these "bad" circumstances? For most of us, the vast majority of events that make us angry, frustrated, or sad would actually be considered "okay" or "pretty good" on our universal scale. If we see that what we thought was "bad" isn't really "bad" at all, then we don't have a reason to feel upset.

We all may know that the "bad" circumstances in our lives pale in comparison to those of many, but yet it is very easy to lose sight of this in our daily lives because we automatically judge the circumstances in our lives according to our personal scale. But if we want to recognize that a circumstance in our life isn't "bad", then often all we need to do is take a step back and ask ourselves how we would rate the circumstance according to our universal scale. This can often give us just enough perspective to see that our situation is not really "bad" at all.

This doesn't mean some events are "bad", or that some events are "worse" than others. Essentially, what this means is that many of the events in our lives that we decide are "bad" often don't actually meet our own definition of "bad". Whenever we notice that a circumstance we thought was "bad" isn't actually "bad" (according to our own definition), the unwanted emotion this thought had been creating is likely to weaken substantially.

The Questions: What types of events or circumstances in the world do I believe are actually "really bad"? Would I consider this event to be "bad" on my universal scale, or is it only "bad" relative to my normal experience? If my circumstance is only "bad" for a short time, wouldn't it be considered much "better" than a long-term "problem"? Where does my circumstance or event fit into my universal scale of what is "great" and "terrible"?

9. Am I sure that making my circumstances "perfect" or "good enough" would make me happy? If "not good enough" circumstances are causing my unhappiness, then wouldn't "good enough" circumstances make me happy?

When we believe, "Something isn't good enough", we almost always unknowingly mean, "Something isn't good enough *for me to be happy*". In other words, the belief doesn't come from a particular circumstance matching our concept of "bad"; it comes from comparing some aspect of our life to our idea of what would make us happy. There are two major ways this plays out.

a)   When we believe that a specific circumstance is needed to be happy, and we don't have it, this makes us believe, "Something isn't good enough right now for me to be happy". If we believe marriage is essential to happiness, and we aren't married, then we think, "My life isn't good enough because I'm not married".

b)   If we believe that a specific circumstance will make us happy, yet we still aren't happy when we get it, then we may decide, "I'm not happy because I don't have enough of it". Say you thought that being rich would make you happy, and you made a lot of money but still weren't happy, then you might assume, "I am not rich enough". If you think love and appreciation would make you happy, yet you have these in a relationship and still aren't happy, you may decide, "He doesn't love and appreciate me enough".

Since our thought "something isn't good enough" is based on the underlying idea that "getting what I want would make me happy", this is actually the thought whose truth we need to question. For example, if we believe, "My husband doesn't appreciate me enough", then we can question whether it is true that "I would be happy if he appreciated me enough". If we believe, "I'm not successful enough", then we can question the truth of the thought "I would be happy if I became successful".

At first glance, it may seem sad, scary, or depressing to question whether it is true that getting what you want can make you happy. On the surface, it seems as though our fantasies give us an escape from the insufficient circumstances of our reality and provide us with the hope of achieving happiness in the future. But this is actually one of our mind's most clever tricks.

Believing in the idea that our fantasy will make us happy makes us compare reality to our fantasy, which causes us to feel as though this moment isn't "good enough" the way it is—as if something is missing from our life. It's not true that our circumstances aren't "good enough", and it's not true that something is missing from our life; it only seems this way because we are constantly comparing reality to our fantasy.

As long as you believe that your fantasy will make you happy, you will almost certainly believe your life isn't "good enough" the way it is, and it will seem as though something is missing from your life. If you believe that love from a spouse can make you happy, then you will probably believe that your husband doesn't love you enough. If you believe success can make you happy, then you will probably believe that you aren't successful enough. If you believe that physical attractiveness can make you happy, then you will probably believe that you are not attractive enough.

And as long as you believe that your fantasy will make you happy in the future, you'll see the present moment merely as a means to get to your fantasy, and you'll be willing to sacrifice your happiness in this moment in order to achieve your goal. What's more, your attention will be on the future rather than this moment, because our attention naturally gravitates to whatever we believe is most important. When our attention is on the future, we automatically feel dissatisfaction because we are not able to experience the fullness of this moment.

Achieving your fantasy isn't your only hope of being happy. Believing in your fantasy is what's preventing you from feeling happy. If we realize that getting what we want can't make us happy, then we can stop comparing our circumstances to our fantasy. This stops us from believing that our circumstances aren't "good enough", and allows us to be at peace with our situation. We no longer feel this sense of incompleteness and lack.

When we stop believing that our fantasy will make us completely happy and fulfilled, our attention comes off our future fantasies of how life will be when we achieve our goal, and brings us back to the present moment. When our attention is on the present moment, on the task at hand, we enjoy ourselves. We find what we are doing to be fulfilling. This simple change eliminates a lot of our dissatisfaction in life.

So we need to ask: *Can getting what I want make me happy?* Let's look at what happens when we get something we want. Whenever we get what we want, we only experience happiness because we lose our negative thoughts about that particular circumstance. If we move from our small apartment to a big house, then we may no longer have our thoughts about how our apartment isn't big enough, how we are a failure because our apartment is small, or how we are "worse" than our friends because we live in such a small apartment. If we get married, then we may no longer have our shame about being single or worries about never finding someone to love us. Even if we become really wealthy, all our wealth can do is help us to improve our opinion of ourselves, make a few of our circumstances "perfect", and help us to afford more distractions from our thoughts. *But no matter what circumstance we are able to make "good enough", and no matter what type of distractions we engage in, we will not lose all of our insecurities, anxieties, worries, anger, sadness, shame, sense of something missing, judgments about others, and ideas about what is "bad" in our life.* This is why no matter what we get, and no matter how much of it we get, it can never be *enough* to fulfill us.

If "not good enough" circumstances were the cause of our unhappiness, then "good enough" circumstances would make us happy. But if "good enough" circumstances wouldn't make us happy, then that means it's not true that our "not good enough" circumstances are the cause of our unhappiness. If getting what we want won't

A Guide to The Present Moment

make us happy, then that means our lack of peace and contentment is not the result of not having what we want, and not the result of something in our life not being "good enough".

If we admit that respect doesn't have the ability to make us happy, then we can stop thinking, "I don't have enough respect to be happy". If we admit that love and affection from our partner can't make us fulfilled, then we can stop believing, "They don't show me enough love and affection to make me happy". If we stop believing that physical beauty can make us happy, then we can stop believing, "I am not attractive enough to be happy".

If you admit that getting what you want won't fulfill you, then you can finally stop comparing reality to your fantasy (your idea of "perfect"). This simple recognition allows us to stop believing that our circumstances aren't "good enough" to be happy, it stops us from blaming the apparent insufficiencies in our life for our unhappiness, and it makes us stop sacrificing our happiness in this moment just so we can try to achieve our fantasy.

Our pursuit of happiness has been based on the premise that our circumstances are "not good enough" right now to be happy. Whereas the reality of it is that we aren't happy because we believe a thought that says "something isn't good enough right now". We have been spending all of our time and energy trying to make everything in our life meet our definition "perfect" just so that we could eliminate the thought "something isn't good enough". Therefore, if we can just stop believing "something isn't good enough", then regardless of how our current circumstances seem, we can be completely fulfilled right now with our circumstances exactly as they are.

The Questions: If "not good enough" circumstances are causing my unhappiness or blocking my happiness, then wouldn't "good enough" circumstances make me happy? Would making my circumstances "good enough" eliminate all of my insecurities, anxieties, anger, sadness, shame, sense of incompleteness, and judgments about myself and others? Has my fantasy of getting what I want left out all of the negatives? If "good enough" circumstances wouldn't make me happy, then is it true that "not good enough" circumstances are causing my unhappiness? If getting "enough" of the circumstance I want (love, appreciation, success) wouldn't give me the happiness I want, then is it true that my "not good enough" circumstance is blocking my happiness? Is it true that something is "not good enough" for me to be happy?

Chapter Ten

Questions to Disbelieve Your Thoughts about Future Outcomes

Thoughts about the future can create anxiety and fear, intensify your existing emotions, and make you feel dissatisfied just by taking your attention off the present moment. Regardless of the subject of your thoughts, if you are giving attention and energy to thoughts about the future, the questions in this chapter can help you disbelieve them. When you disbelieve these thoughts, the emotions they create subside, and you lose your incentive to give attention to them.

10. Do I know with absolute certainty that these future "bad" moments, events, or situations will happen?

If you get fired from your job, you don't just feel sad from thinking, "It is bad that I got fired". Much of your suffering comes from thinking about all of the future consequences you believe having gotten fired will bring: "I *won't* be able to afford going on my vacation", "I *will* have to stop going out to my favorite restaurants", "I *won't* be able to find another job", "I *will* be sad for months". If someone you love leaves you—say, through divorce or death—then you don't just feel sad because you think, "I would be happier right now if they were here" or "It is bad that they aren't here with me now". Your suffering is compounded by your mind projecting images of a future where you "*will* be all alone", "*will* not find another genuine connection", or "*will* be sad all the time".

In other words, instead of just reacting to a thought that says, "One moment is bad", we react to a thought that says, "Many future moments *will* be bad". In this way, the intensity of our suffering is multiplied by however many future moments we decide "*will* be bad".

These types of thoughts show up quite frequently for parents about their children. If our child fails a test, we might think, "If I don't set him straight, he *will* be a failure". If we find out our child is using drugs or alcohol, we might think, "She *is* going to ruin her life". Then we react to our thoughts about the future, and not to the situation. We can easily get very angry or disappointed with our children over seemingly small events because we're reacting to what we think *will* happen as opposed to what has happened.

In order to stop suffering from future "bad" moments, we can take a step back and question whether we actually know that the future "bad" event or situation *will* happen. Is it a foregone conclusion that our son will be a failure? Can we know for sure that our daughter will ruin her life? Is it possible that we'll find another job quickly? If we can see that the future "bad" event or situation might not happen—or at least that we can't know for sure it will—then we can stop believing, "These bad events *will* happen" or "This *will* lead to something really bad". When we stop believing that these thoughts are true, they quite simply stop creating our suffering.

The Questions: Is it true that I know the future? Do I know with absolute certainty that these future "bad" moments, events, or situations *will* happen?

11. Can I handle my situation in this moment, right now?

Imagine experiencing a strong pain for one second. Now imagine doing a task you hate for only one second. Lastly, imagine experiencing anxiety or sadness for just one second. Would it be a big deal if you had to experience this pain, do this task, or experience this emotion for one second? Would it be hard for you, or would it be easy to handle it for only one second? Most of us would likely think that we could easily handle one second of any of these types of experiences, and it wouldn't be a big deal at all.

The truth is that regardless of whether our "bad" pain, task, emotion, or situation lasts one moment or 1,000 moments, we can only ever experience one moment at a time in life. If we can easily handle one moment of any experience, and we only ever experience one moment at a time, then why do our experiences in life often seem overwhelming?

Generally, instead of just experiencing this seemingly "bad" moment, we are busy thinking about all of our future (and past) "bad" moments. When we think of all the future moments when we believe we are going to be suffering, in pain, or doing something we don't like, we escalate our current suffering substantially. Bringing the future into the equation thoroughly exacerbates our emotions. We can always handle any type of "bad" task, situation, physical sensation, or emotion in this moment. It's thinking about all the future "bad" moments that makes us feel self-pity, angry, intimidated, fearful, anxious, and overwhelmed.

We tend to get really upset about our "bad" situations in life largely because we have a habit of trying to manage all of our future suffering or "bad" moments *right now*. If we are absolutely sure that our "bad" situation will continue, or if we aren't able to disbelieve the thought that "future bad events *will* happen", then instead we can question whether we need to be able to handle all of our future "bad" moments right now.

Imagine a specific pain you have experienced or are currently experiencing. If you think, "I will be in pain for only the next one second", how is this likely to make you feel? You almost certainly wouldn't suffer very much, if at all. Now, if you think, "I will be in pain for the next month", how is this likely to make you feel? You would probably feel moderately strong self-pity, anger, anxiousness, or fear. In both of these situations, your pain is exactly the same in this moment. *In both of these situations, the only pain you have to experience is the pain in this moment, right now.* If this is the case, then why is your emotion likely to be much stronger in the second instance? The second thought would create a much stronger emotion because you are reacting to the idea that you will experience a month of pain instead of to the idea that you will experience one moment of pain. But the idea that you will experience a month of pain is simply not true. *No matter how long your pain may last, you can only ever experience one moment of pain. It is impossible to experience more than one moment of pain at a time.*

Since we can only live one moment at a time, we can only experience any "bad" feeling, task, situation, or emotion for one moment at a time. *We don't need to be able to handle all of our future "bad" moments. We only have to be able to manage this moment right now.* This is always much easier.

If you get fired, and then start thinking about all your future hardships, you can stop and ask yourself, "Can I handle my situation in this moment, right now? Is this single moment right now too much to manage?" If you lose your partner, and then start thinking about all the future moments when you will be sad or lonely, you can stop and ask yourself, "Is my sadness in this very moment manageable right now? Is it true that I need to be able to handle all my future loneliness right now?" If you are doing a task at work that you don't like, and then start thinking about how "bad" it is that you will have to continue doing this task for the next week, you can ask yourself "Can I handle doing this task right now? Is it that terrible in this moment?" If you break your ankle, and are in a lot of pain, and then you start thinking about all the future moments when life will be hard and painful, you can ask yourself, "Can I handle the pain right now? Is it bearable in this moment? Is it true that I need to be able to manage more than one moment of pain at a time?"

No matter how "bad" our situation seems, we can always handle one moment. Since you can only experience one moment at a time, you only need to be strong enough to manage one moment. You don't have to be strong enough to manage a week, a month, or a year of your "bad" pain, emotion, task, or situation. You just have to be able to handle this moment, right now. And when you realize that *you can* handle this moment, you are free.

The Questions: Can I handle what's happening in this moment, right now? Is it true that I need to be able to handle any moment other than this moment?

12. Do I know with absolute certainty what outcome would make myself or others happiest? Can I think of a few possible "bad" effects of getting the outcome I want?

Since we believe our "insufficient" circumstances are the cause of our unhappiness, we try to make our circumstances "perfect" in order to make ourselves happy. We almost always seem to operate under the assumption "I know what's best for me", "I know what's best for them", "I know what would make me happiest", "I know what would make them happiest". We might think, "It would be best if"… "I arrive on time", "My boss is impressed by my work", "The guy is interested in me", "My child gets a good grade", or "My wife lands the new client".

When we treat what we want as what is "best" for us or as what would make us happiest, then we naturally believe that not getting the circumstance (outcome) we want will leave us unhappy or at least less happy. As soon as we decide that what we want will make us happiest, we simultaneously and unconsciously decide that every other outcome would be "bad" or "worse". Our fear, stress, anxiety, pressure, and worries all arise from this one simple idea that "some bad outcome could happen".

Not only that, but if we don't get the outcome we want, we then experience anger, sadness, hopelessness, and frustration because we think that the outcome we've gotten is "worse" and that we can't be as happy with it. The same applies to our ever-present idea that we know what is "best" for our friends, partners, and children. We have anxiety about whether they will get "what's best" for them, and we get sad or angry when they don't get (or do) "what's best".

But if we can discover that we don't really know what outcome would be "best", this stops us from deciding that all other outcomes are "worse", and thus eliminates our fear of not getting what we want for ourselves or others. So, do we actually know what outcome would make ourselves or others happiest? It may seem as if we do, but there are actually a number of reasons why we can't really know what outcome would be "best". Let's take a look at few:

a)   If some people who have what you want aren't happy, then can you know for sure that getting what you want would make you happy? For example, are all people with wealth, success, fame, respect, or love happy?

b)   If you never experienced getting the particular outcome that you want, then can you know for sure that you will like it? For example, is it possible that you won't like the responsibilities of the job you want? Is it possible that your daughter won't enjoy the college you think would be "best" for her?

c)   Since you don't know all of the effects of any outcome, can you know for sure that a specific outcome would be "best" for you or for others? For example, is it possible that success, a promotion, or power would lead to longer hours, a demanding boss, more anxiety, more pressure, less job security, or make you less available to spend time with your family, thereby making your wife unhappy and your kids disappointed?

d)   If others can believe that the outcome you want wouldn't be "best" for you, then can you really be sure that this outcome would make you happiest? For example, could someone else think that you wouldn't be as happy if you got success, fame, or marriage?

When we recognize that we don't know what outcome would be "best" for ourselves or others, we can realize that we don't know whether it would be "bad" not to get the outcome we want. This allows us to recognize that our happiness does not depend on getting the outcome we want. This takes the pressure off everything we do. We can pursue what we want without stress or worry. Then our pursuit of what we want takes on a certain feeling of lightness, and we can be happy while pursuing any goal we want.

In addition, when we stop believing that failure to achieve "what's best" will make others less happy, we can stop worrying about whether the people we love will achieve what we think is "best". We can still give advice to others and tell people what we think, but just without the idea that we actually know what outcome will make them happiest.

The Questions: Is everyone who has what I want happy? If some people who have what I want aren't happy, can I know for sure that getting what I want would make me happy? If I never experienced the particular outcome that I want, can I know for sure I will like it? Can I think of any possible new problems or "bad" effects of getting the outcome I want (for me or for others)? If so, then can I know for sure that this outcome would be "best" and make me happiest? Could someone else think that getting what I want wouldn't make me happiest? If others could have a different perspective, can I be absolutely certain that I know what outcome would be "best"?

13. If circumstances themselves don't create happiness, then is it true that I can't be as happy if I don't get the circumstances I want?

Where does the happiness come from when we get what we want? We know the happiness can't be created by the thing itself because:
a) Many people who have the circumstances we want aren't happy;
b) Achieving the same goal results in different degrees of happi-

ness depending on how difficult it is to achieve; c) If circumstances themselves made us happy, we would remain happy as long as we had them. But in reality, we only end up truly happy for a short period before we start to oscillate between discontent and happiness, either from worrying about losing the circumstance or from believing all of our other negative thoughts.

The happiness we experience when we get what we want is purely the result of losing our negative thoughts about that particular circumstance. If we think, "It is bad that I am single" and "It will be bad if I never find someone to love me", then finding a lover will make us happy by eliminating these thoughts along with the sadness and anxiety they created. But this happiness is short-lived, because there will always be other circumstances we believe aren't "good enough", which will continue to create all of our unwanted emotions. *If we believe that getting what we want will make us happy, we are actually believing that getting what we want will eliminate all (or most) of our negative thoughts.* In reality, getting what we want can only eliminate a few of our thoughts, a small percentage of the thoughts that create our unhappiness.

If we feel fearful, anxious, worried, or stressed because we believe, "It will be bad if I don't get what I want", we are really believing, "I can't be as happy without getting what I want". *If we believe, "I can't be as happy without getting what I want", we are really believing, "I can't get rid of any of my negative thoughts unless I get what I want".* Since we have now learned how to question our thoughts, this statement is no longer true. We now know of another way to eliminate our negative thoughts other than changing our circumstances from "bad" to "perfect". The recognition, "I can be just as happy without getting what I want", eliminates our anxiety because we no longer have any reason to fear not getting what we want.

The Questions: What do I want? Is everyone who gets what I want happy? Does achieving this goal give everyone the same amount of happiness every time? Does everyone who achieves this goal remain happy as long as they have it? If not, then can I admit that the happiness I would experience by getting what I want would not be created by the circumstance itself, but only by losing a few negative thoughts about the circumstance? Will getting what I want eliminate all of the negative thoughts that cause my insecurities, anxieties, sadness, shame, and anger, or will it just eliminate my negative thoughts about that one particular circumstance? If I don't get what I want, isn't it still possible to eliminate my negative thoughts through disbelieving them? If so, then am I absolutely sure I will be less happy if I don't get what I want?

14. Do I know with absolute certainty that this outcome would be "bad" for my life? Can I think of a few possible "good" effects from getting the outcome I don't want?

Imagine that you are offered a new job that is "better" than your current job and pays twice the salary. But in order to start the job, you first need to get fired from your current job (you can't quit). If your boss fires you, would you consider it to be "bad"? In isolation, getting fired seems "bad", but overall you'd almost certainly consider it to be "good" because it helped you to get the new job. You would be happy that you'd gotten fired because you couldn't have gotten the new job without it.

If we think, "Getting fired from my job would be bad", we will experience anxiety when we think about the possibility of getting fired in the future. But if we know that getting fired will have "good" overall effects on our life (i.e., in this example, we could start a "better" job), then we would consider getting fired to be "good", and we would have no anxiety about it.

In real life, it may seem obvious that getting fired would be "bad", but the fact is, one cause has innumerable effects. Could getting fired lead us to find a new job that we like more, give us invaluable time with our family before we find a new job, make us realize we were in the wrong career, or enable us to meet our future spouse during normal work hours? If we can just acknowledge that it is possible for "good" effects to come from getting fired, then we can no longer be certain that getting fired would be "bad". We can recognize that we don't know whether getting fired would make us happier or unhappier in the long run. Once we realize this, our anxiety is gone because we have stopped believing, "Getting fired would be bad". Since this thought created our anxiety, when we stop believing it, we are left in peace.

This is the same logic we've used to question past events or current circumstances that seem "bad". No matter what outcome we think would be "bad", we can't possibly know what all the effects of it are. Even if it seems as though the immediate effect of an event would be "terrible", it is always possible that the event will lead to many "good" effects that outweigh the immediate "bad" effect. With some "really bad" outcomes, at first glance, it can seem as if there couldn't possibly be any "good" effects. It may even seem ludicrous to suggest such a thing. But if we allow ourselves to be truly open and honest with ourselves, and if we actually take a few minutes to use our imagination, then we can almost always come up with some plausible "positive" scenarios.

If we are just willing to admit that a specific "bad" outcome could have "good" effects, then we are acknowledging that this "bad" outcome could make us happier overall. *If we aren't completely sure whether an outcome will lead to more suffering or happiness in the long run, then we can't be sure whether the outcome would be "bad" or "good".* Believing that a specific outcome "would be bad" creates our anxiety, but when we acknowledge, "I don't know whether this specific outcome would be good or bad", then all of a sudden we have nothing to fear.

The Questions: Do I know all of the effects of this "bad" outcome, and all of the effects of those effects? Can I think of a few possible "good" effects that could come from this "bad" outcome? (be creative). Is it possible that this "bad" outcome could lead to "positive" effects in the future that wind up making me (or others) happier? Is it possible that this outcome is exactly what I (or others) need in order to learn a lesson that will make me (or them) happier in the future? If I can remember a time in the past when I thought an outcome would be "bad", but it ended up working out really well, then can't that happen again? If I don't know whether this "bad" outcome would make me happier or not in the long run, then isn't it true that I don't know whether this outcome would be "bad" or "good" for my life?

15. Do I know for sure that I need to keep my "great" circumstances in order to be happy?

When we are happy, we often believe that our "perfect" circumstances have created our happiness. We think that we are happy because "I am thin", "I am successful", "I have a wonderful girlfriend", "I have my dream house", "I have the job I wanted", or "Everyone thinks I am great". However, our happiness can't be created by a job, a girlfriend, physical appearance, or any other circumstance. We are happy because we have either lost some of our negative thoughts, we are distracting ourselves from some negative thoughts, or we have some positive thoughts about our circumstance. Take romantic partners: some of the main reasons we are happy when in a relationship are because our partner's positive opinion of us (e.g., their love and appreciation) helps us to have a more positive opinion of ourselves, we create excitement for ourselves through fantasies about a wonderful future with them, and they distract us from some of our negative thoughts about other aspects of our life.

This misconception about the source of our happiness wouldn't be a problem if it didn't create suffering. However, as soon as we decide, "My happiness is the result of a circumstance", we begin to fear losing the circumstance that we believe makes us happy. Naturally, if we believe, "My job makes me happy", we will likely think, "I can't be as happy if I lose my job", and this will make us fear losing our job. If we think, "I am happy because I have such a wonderful girlfriend" then we will likely think, "I can't be as happy without her", which creates the fear of losing her. The funny thing about this scenario is that by believing, "My girlfriend makes me happy", we actually make ourselves less happy, because now we're spending some of our time worrying about losing her, monitoring whether she still loves as much as she used to, and worrying about whether she is faithful instead of just enjoying her company.

But the truth is that our "great" circumstances don't create our happiness, it is only our positive thoughts and loss of negative thoughts that have made us happy. We don't need to keep our "great" circumstances to be happy, because we can also eliminate our negative thoughts by disbelieving them, we can find other circumstances to have positive thoughts about, and we can engage in other distractions to make us happy. No specific circumstance is needed to eliminate our negative thoughts, to have positive thoughts, or to distract ourselves from our negative thoughts.

If we want to truly enjoy whatever circumstances we have and not be preoccupied with our worries about losing our "great" circumstances, all we need to do is question whether our happiness is actually a direct result of our circumstances. If we are able to recognize that our happiness has not been created by our "great" circumstance, then we might realize that our thought "I can't be as happy without this great circumstance" or "I need to keep this great circumstance to be happy" is not actually true. As soon as this happens, our fear of losing our "great" circumstance naturally leaves because there is no longer any reason to fear losing it.

The Questions: Is everyone who has the "great" circumstance I have happy? Have I been happy in every moment while I have had this "great" circumstance? If this "great" circumstance directly created happiness, then wouldn't everyone who has it be happy for every moment that they have it? Can I admit that my happiness is not directly created by my "great" circumstances, but is actually created by either losing some of my negative thoughts, having some positive thoughts, or distracting myself from some negative thoughts? If my circumstance hasn't created my happiness, then am I absolutely sure that I couldn't be just as happy after losing this "great" circumstance, considering that I could disbelieve my negative thoughts, find something else to have positive thoughts about, or find a different distraction?

Chapter Eleven

Questions to Disbelieve Your Thoughts about Others' Opinions

As we previously discussed, our identity is made up of all the thoughts we believe about ourselves. We may think, "I am attractive", "I am uninteresting", "I am funny", "I am a failure", "I am caring", "I am a good mother", and so on. When we believe positive thoughts about ourselves (positive identity), we experience some happiness or confidence. When we believe many negative thoughts about ourselves (negative identity, low self-worth), we experience sadness, loneliness, lack of confidence, sense of incompleteness, and feelings of unworthiness. We naturally want to think of ourselves as "great" or "worthy", because we believe that would make us happy.

So how do we try to create positive thoughts about ourselves? It's not as easy as just changing the thought "I am unlovable" to "I am lovable", "I am boring" to "I am fun", or "I am ugly" to "I am attractive". One of the main ways we look to improve our self-image is by trying to find other people to convince us to think more positively about ourselves. We look for positive comments from others in order to change specific thoughts about ourselves from negative to positive, and to reaffirm the positive thoughts we already have about ourselves. If we think, "I am not attractive enough", we will seek compliments about our appearance from others. On the other hand, when we have a general feeling that we are "insufficient", "unworthy", "unlovable", "incomplete", or "not good enough" but we don't have a specific explanation for the feeling (i.e., "I feel unworthy because I have a low-paying job") then we seek appreciation, respect, admiration, love, and approval to make us feel "whole", "lovable", "worthy", "sufficient", and happy.

But just as we think that positive opinions from others will make us happy, we also believe that negative opinions will either make us suffer, make us feel "worse" about ourselves, or force us to remain unhappy. This is why we are almost constantly seeking love, approval, and appreciation from everyone, and why we are afraid of not getting it.

16. Am I absolutely sure that my guess about their thoughts, feelings, or intentions is true?

Since we look to others' opinions to improve our opinion of ourselves and make us happy, we are frequently trying to figure out what others are thinking about us. We can't actually know what others are thinking, but since we care so much about their opinions, we just guess what they're thinking and then unknowingly assume our guess to be true. Most of us tend to experience a large amount of anxiety, hurt, and disappointment just from these guesses about what others think of us.

One of the most common ways that we try to figure out what others are thinking is by asking ourselves, "What would I have to be thinking for me to act like that?" In other words, we look at the way *WE* think to figure out the way others think. We think, "Why would I have acted that way? What would cause me to act that way? What would my intentions have to be for me to act like that (or say that)?" *Once we figure out what we would be thinking if we were in their shoes, we believe that is what they are thinking because we unknowingly assume that other people think in the same way that we think.* This may seem to be a reasonable strategy, but it rarely works, because other people often think differently from the way we do and often value different things.

Suppose your boyfriend calls you every couple of days. You may think to yourself, "If I were in his place and loved my girlfriend, I would want to talk to her every day. Therefore, he *must* not love me". You may express your love by telling your partner, "I love you", being affectionate, calling often, always choosing to spend time with him over friends, buying gifts, or doing chores for him. So when your partner doesn't do one of these things, you may make a leap of logic and think, "If he loved me, he would do [that thing]. He *must* not love me". Then you feel upset because you can't have what you want (your partner's love), or you feel angry because you think it is "bad" that your partner doesn't love you. We feel these emotions and many others as if we know other people's thoughts, even though we have no idea whether our guess about their thoughts is true. Your partner could love you just as much as you love him, but just express his love differently from the way you do.

We make these sorts of leaps of logic in all types of situations. If our co-worker doesn't offer to help us, we may think, "When I like someone, I offer to help them. She *must* not like me". However, some people may not think it is appropriate to help a co-worker even if they like the person. If our date or friend shows up late to meet us, we may think, "If I care about a person, I always make sure to be punctual and not keep them waiting. He *must* not care about me". But even though *we* might only show up late if we don't care about a person, others may have a hard time being punctual for everyone and for even the most important of events. If our boss says "thank you" once a week, we might think, "When I appreciate someone, I always let them know by saying 'thank you'. He *must* not appreciate me". Others, though, may not have been trained to say "thank you" routinely, even when they feel appreciative of someone. What's more, if they don't care a lot about receiving clear expressions of appreciation, approval, or love from other people, then they may not think it is important to express those sentiments to others, may not remember to give these expressions to others, and may be completely unaware that the people in their life don't feel appreciated, approved of, or loved.

Asking ourselves the question, "What would I need to be thinking for me to choose to act that way?" is clearly not an accurate way to determine others' intentions or opinions about us. Once we recognize that a different interpretation is possible, then we can recognize that we really don't know whether our interpretation is true. When this recognition occurs, we lose our reason to be upset. Therefore, the suffering that our thought had been causing fades away.

The Questions: What are the facts and what is my interpretation of the facts? Have I interpreted the facts based on what I would be thinking if I acted that way? Am I sure that they express their feelings or choose their actions in the same way as I do? Is it possible that he doesn't express his love, approval, or appreciation in the way I am looking for it because he doesn't feel the need to receive love, approval, or appreciation in that way? Am I sure that they are aware of the emotional effect their words or actions have on me? Can I think of some other possible ways to interpret this situation? If so, can I be absolutely sure that my guess about their thoughts, feeling, or intentions is true?

17.   Am I sure that I want to continue believing that love and approval will make me happy?

Since almost all of us have been trained to believe that love and approval will make us happy, whole, and content, our pursuit of happiness through love and approval has become so strong that it tends to dictate much of our life. But despite its hold over us, many of us don't realize how intently we are pursuing love and approval from our partners, our friends, our parents, our children, and even strangers. Also, the vast majority of us don't realize how much we are doing to try to get love and approval. Let's now look at some of the ways in which this pursuit tends to take up our time and energy, makes us do things we don't want to do, creates our anxiety, and really makes us suffer.

While almost all of us do many of the following things, your immediate reaction to some of them may be, "I definitely don't do that". If you have this reaction, please try to be open to looking at your life honestly in order to see how you might actually be doing each of the following things. Also, the next time you are interacting with others, try to be aware of whether you are doing any of these things. Keep in mind that we can't change the way we think until we admit what we are thinking.

•   When we believe that love and approval will make us happy, and believe that we don't have it, this makes us believe that our life isn't "good enough" the way it is, causing us to feel as if something is missing from our life.

•   Once we decide that we want someone to love us, we generally spend a lot of time and energy searching for someone to love us. This search creates restlessness and dissatisfaction.

•   We decide what we want others to think about us based on either what we want to think about ourselves or what we think will get others to love us. We may think, "He wants someone who is smart", "She wants someone who is mature", "He wants me to be fun", or we may think, "I want him to think I'm interesting", "I want her to think I'm special".

We plan what to say, how to look, and how to act when we are with others in order to make ourselves appear in whatever way we want them to think about us. We pick out our clothes based on what look we think will impress others or get their love. We may plan what to talk about, what stories or accomplishments to mention, or what jokes to tell, all as a relatively unconscious strategy to get the opinion we want from others.

•   In interactions with others, we tend to change ourselves to be whoever we think will get others' love and approval (manipulating them for it). We might act as if we don't care about them even if we do, because we think that's what they want. We might pretend to be interested in certain topics even if we aren't. We might pretend to like certain food, events, or hobbies even if we don't. We might act enthusiastic even if we are normally more subdued. We might even lie or exaggerate to try to win them over.

•   During interactions with others, we often try to guess what others are thinking in order to see if we are doing a "good" job of impressing them and to see if we need to alter our strategy. This may include what we say, what we do, or just how we use any of our body signals. We may think, "Why isn't he looking at me – is he uninterested?", "He didn't laugh at my joke – does he think I'm boring?", "He doesn't seem happy to be talking to me – should I laugh louder or stop smiling?", or "Should I act more sexual or more reserved?"

•   While we are with others, we may have fear, anxiety, and uncertainty because we don't know what comment or action will get us the "best" response (approval), and we are afraid that whatever we say or do will get a "bad" response (disapproval). We might not dance because we fear what people will think. We may not be willing to speak in front of people because we fear their opinions.

• After interactions with others, we can spend a decent amount of time trying to figure out what they thought about us, what we did well, and where we messed up. We might think, "Did I impress him?", "Did she like me?", "Does he still love me?", "She didn't like it when I said that", or "I should have done that instead". This is an attempt to evaluate whether we got their love and approval, and to see what strategies (comments and actions) worked and what didn't. This way, next time, we can make sure that we say and do the things that will win their love and approval.

• To get approval from our parents (or because we fear their disapproval), we choose jobs we don't enjoy, stay in relationships we don't want to be in, wear clothes that don't appeal to us, or choose to live in a place that isn't interesting to us.

• If we think that we didn't get someone's love or approval, we often feel frustrated, angry, hurt, or sad. We may think, "There must be something wrong with me", "What did I do wrong?", or "Why doesn't he approve of me?"

• We are so focused on how to get love from others, and whether we're getting it, that we rarely actually give love to others. When the truth is that loving others is what fulfills us.

• In conversations, we care so much about saying something that will make others love us that we very often don't bother listening to them. We think about what we're going to say next while others are speaking. We might be waiting to make a clever point that will make them think we're smart. We might be waiting for the moment to tell a story that will show them we're fun. Or we might choose not to wait and just interrupt others with some comment that attempts to show people we are "better" than they are in one way or another (trying to one-up them). Others' words don't have much value to us when our primary concern is getting love and approval. Since almost all of us really just want someone to truly listen to us (whether we realize or not), this habit actually makes it harder for others to love us.

• In our relationships, we cook and clean when we don't want to, miss out on events we want to go to, eat foods we don't like, and go to events we don't want to go to. It may seem as though we choose to act selflessly just to make our partner happy, but if we allow ourselves to look honestly at the situation, then it is possible to recognize that at the root of it, we are actually sacrificing our time, energy, and enjoyment as a trade-off for the love and appreciation we think we will get from others in return (or because we fear that we will lose their love and appreciation if we don't do these things).

• If we are in a relationship and we believe love from our partner is supposed to make us feel happy, but yet we aren't fulfilled, this often leads to a lot of suffering. It makes us feel resentment towards our partner because we believe it is their fault we aren't happy. It makes us believe there is something "wrong" with our relationship or that it isn't "good enough" the way it is, which makes us feel disappointed. We may think our relationship is "worse" than our friends' relationships and that everyone but us is happy in their relationships, causing us to feel "worse" about ourselves. We may think we are "bad" for thinking about being with other people (fantasizing about someone who we believe can make us happy).

All of this worrying, dishonesty, and suffering come from the one simple belief that others' love and approval will make us happy, and that without it, we will be unhappy. *We have unknowingly made the decision that all of our effort will help us to get love and approval from others, and that this love and approval will give us enough happiness to make all of our suffering worthwhile.* In other words, this belief causes us to give up our happiness for love and approval. Imagine how much more free and happy you would be if you didn't have to worry about others' opinions. Imagine how much more lovingly you could treat others if you weren't constantly concerned about getting love and approval from them.

The Questions: What have I been doing to get love and approval? What have I been doing to make sure nobody thinks of me in the way I don't want to be thought of? What have I been sacrificing for love and approval? Does all this create happiness, or does it create stress, worry, fear, hurt, and restlessness? Does all this make me treat others with love, or am I just using them as a means to make myself happy? Do I want to keep living like this or would I rather stop seeking love and approval? Am I sure that I want to continue believing that love and approval will make me happy?

18.   Can someone else's love and approval make me happy?

We go through life pursuing love, appreciation, and approval because we believe it will make us feel whole, secure, and happy. In an attempt to get this love, appreciation, and approval, we give up a lot of happiness in our life by worrying, pretending to be someone we're not, doing things we don't enjoy, and being dishonest. We unconsciously believe that these sacrifices are worthwhile because of the happiness we think we will get from receiving the love we want. But does this love really give us the happiness we have wanted?

If you are able to recognize that love and approval don't have the ability to make you happy, whole, and secure, then you can stop sacrificing your happiness for them, stop worrying about what others think, stop feeling as if something is missing from your life, stop pretending to be someone you're not, stop feeling resentment towards your partner because he didn't make you happy, and stop feeling that your relationship is "bad" or "worse" than others'. But before we look at why love and approval can't fulfill us, let's look at how it gives us some momentary happiness.

When someone compliments us, or shows their appreciation, this can help to give us a positive thought about ourselves, which provides us with some pleasure, comfort, or security. When we find someone who we believe will love us and make us happy in the future, we can be filled with excitement (what we often call "love"). When someone proves to us through either their words or their actions (like a proposal) that they love us, we feel a huge relief that we don't have to keep searching for someone to love us, we don't have to fear that we will never find someone to love us, and we don't have to feel as if something is missing from our life because we don't have someone to love us. But all of this is momentary happiness—it doesn't last.

No matter how much someone else loves us, we don't directly feel their love; we only feel our thoughts about their love, or our love for them. To demonstrate this, imagine you are in a relationship in which you love your partner and they love you. You believe that you feel your partner's love very strongly. Then imagine that your best friend tells you that she is sure your partner has been cheating on you, and you believe her. Would you continue to feel your partner's love? Almost certainly not. You would experience anger, hurt, or sadness instead. Two weeks later, imagine that you find out that your best friend was wrong, and your partner hadn't cheated on you. Your partner actually loved you the same amount during those two weeks as he did throughout the entire relationship. If your partner still loved you, why didn't you feel his love during those two weeks? Quite simply because your thoughts about him and his love for you changed. These thoughts were what created your feeling of being loved, not his love.

Our emotions are created by our own thoughts. When we look for others' love and approval to make us happy, we are actually looking for others to change our thoughts from negative to positive. Here are some reasons why others' love and approval doesn't have the ability to give us the happiness we want.

•   If we firmly believe, "I am not lovable" (or any other negative thought), then we often can't be convinced that we are lovable (or loved) no matter how many times someone tells us or shows us that they love us. If someone shows us approval about some aspect of our life, but we don't approve of this aspect of our life, then their approval isn't likely to change our opinion. Nobody has the power to change our thoughts if we believe them strongly enough.

•   Even if our partner, our friends, our parents, or anyone else can convince us to think more positively about ourselves, we will still have many other insecurities, complaints about our situation, anxieties, and judgments about others, as well as any anger, sadness, or guilt we were already experiencing. By nature, in order to think something is "great", we have to believe other things are "bad". All of these thoughts will continue to prevent us from feeling fulfilled and complete.

•   As we saw in chapter 3, positive thoughts don't create a very strong happiness. Remember how much more fulfilled you feel in the moment that you get what you want than in the moment that you think about the "good" thing that you have.

• Once someone tells us that they love us, we can't just sit back and relax. We believe their love is the key to our happiness, so we want to make sure we keep it. We may frequently worry about maintaining their love and may do things we don't enjoy because we fear that we will lose their love. This fear and worry prevents us from feeling happy.

• If you are away from someone who loves you, and you don't hear from them or talk to them, do you feel their love? We feel loved when we think, "He loves me". This thought generally doesn't just show up on its own. If it does, the thought usually doesn't have much power. We normally need our lover to remind us that they love us or prove to us that they love us in order for this thought to enter our mind and have power. This may require a call from our lover, an email, a card, the words "I love you", some sacrifice made for you, a favor, or just a loving look. If they don't frequently remind us of their love, or prove their love, we generally don't feel it, no matter how much they love us. Someone can tell us (or show us) they love us only so much. The vast majority of our days will be filled with moments when we don't feel their love because we aren't being reminded to think about how they love us.

• Since receiving love and approval from our partner doesn't have the power to fulfill us, we don't just keep seeking more from our partner, but we also seek love and approval from our friends, our co-workers, our bosses, our parents, and even strangers. This seeking will continue to make us worry about others' opinions, and will prevent us from feeling free to be ourselves and do what we want because we will fear what others think.

• If we are seeking love and approval to be happy, then we are actually seeking someone to make us happy. In other words, we are looking for someone who we can use to make us happy. This is why we tend to think that receiving love means having someone to fill our needs (or wants). If we are using someone to make us happy, then we aren't really loving them. We just love how they help make us feel. When this is how we relate to love, we tend to think things like "if she loved me, she would change for me". What this really means is, "I want you to change so I can be happy". But what we are missing here is that if we truly love someone for who they are, then we wouldn't try to change them. If we weren't just using our partner to make us happy, then we wouldn't keep trying to change them just to make ourselves happy. The bottom line is that if we don't truly love someone, then we don't feel this love or the fulfillment that comes with it.

When we pursue happiness by seeking love and approval, we never stop seeking more of it because it is never enough to fulfill us or bring us peace. Since other people cannot change all of our negative thoughts to positive ones, we need to question the truth of our negative thoughts if we want to be happy. If we don't believe the thoughts which make us feel unappreciated, insufficient, or unlovable, then we will be completely happy regardless of whether or not others love us.

If we stop believing that love and approval from others will make us happy, then we can stop feeling as if something is missing from our lives, we can stop seeking love and approval from others, we can stop worrying about what others think of us, and we can stop sacrificing our own happiness just to get approval from others. In addition, without this belief, we can stop using others just to get love and approval, which allows us to start having truly loving and fulfilling relationships with the people in our lives.

The Questions:

a) Am I sure that someone else has the power to change my deeply held beliefs about myself? Am I absolutely sure that someone else can convince me that I am worthy or lovable if I have been believing that I am unworthy or unlovable for my whole life? Even if someone could help me think more positively about myself, is it true that more positive thoughts about myself would fulfill me and bring me peace? Is it true that someone else's love and approval can eliminate all of my insecurities, anxieties, anger, sadness, shame, sense of incompleteness, and judgments about myself and others? If someone's love or approval seems to make me happier, wouldn't I then begin to worry about losing their love or approval? If someone loves me, would I still feel this love when I am not with my lover, or when they are not doing or saying anything to remind me of their love? If I get someone to love me, isn't it true that the vast majority of my time will consist of moments where I am not getting reminders and reassurances of their love? Will getting someone to love me make me stop worrying about what my parents, friends, co-workers, and bosses think about me? Why do I want to find someone to love me? If I am looking for someone to love me because I believe it will make me happy, then can I admit that my love for them will be based on how they make me feel? If my love is conditional upon how my lover makes me feel, then can I admit that this "love" won't be very fulfilling or consistent?

b) If I can admit that love and approval can't fulfill me, then is it really worth sacrificing my happiness just to try to get someone's love and approval? If love and approval don't have the ability to make people fulfilled, then is it true that my life isn't "good enough" just because I don't have love and approval? If nobody has the power to change all the negative thoughts in my head, then is it really true that my lover is to blame for the thoughts which prevent me from feeling loved, whole, and happy? If a relationship in and of itself doesn't have the ability to make people fulfilled, then is it true that there is something "wrong" with my relationship or that my relationship is "worse" than others' just because I am not happy?

19.   Am I sure that pretending to be someone I'm not, in order to try to get love and approval, helps me to become happier? Am I sure that they would reject me if they knew the "real" me?

We tend to operate under the assumption that we know what others will love and approve of. We might think, "My parents will only approve of me if I make a lot of money", "My friends will only love me if they think I'm fun", "He will only want me if I act sexy", "She will only like me if she thinks I'm tough", "He will only want to be with me if I he thinks I have the same interests as he does". We act as if we know what will make others love us, when this is really just a guess.

The thought "they will only love me if I _____" doesn't cause problems in and of itself. If we think that others will only love us if we are exactly how we are, then this thought clearly wouldn't create any suffering. However, the issue is that we very often think that others will not love and approve of the "real" us. We think they'll reject us if we just be ourselves. This still wouldn't be a big deal if we were able to be honest with ourselves and others, regardless of whether we think others will love us or not. However, since we want others' love and approval so much, this belief often forces us to pretend to be whoever we think will win love and approval. If we aren't able to admit that love and approval can't make us happy, there is another way to get ourselves to stop pretending to be someone we're not – recognize that this pretending doesn't help us to become happier.

•   As we have now seen, the process of trying to win people's love causes a lot of suffering. We have to do things we don't like, spend effort to be someone we're not, think about what to do and say, and worry about whether others are thinking the right things about us.

• The major question is, "Do I actually know what they will love and approve of?" We may think, "He will love me if I act outgoing", but he may actually want someone shy. We may think, "She wants someone who is successful", but if we act as if we are really successful, she may feel "worse" about herself. We may think, "He will be interested in me if he thinks I'm mature", but he may want someone to act silly with. We may think, "She will love me if I pretend to have the same interests", but she may want someone who has their own set of different interests. We can't possibly know for sure what will make someone love and approve of us.

• We tend to automatically believe, "I am not good enough how I am; they would reject me if they knew the real me" or "They won't love me if I act like myself". But this is a huge assumption. When we don't approve of some aspect of ourselves, we tend to believe others won't approve of it or love it either. However, the truth is that we cannot know for sure whether others will love these attributes or whether these attributes will be irrelevant to them. We may be ashamed of our job, our income, or our body, or we may be ashamed that we are shy, that we aren't very smart, or that we don't have an interest in news and politics, but some people may love the attributes we are ashamed of, and some people couldn't care less whether we have them or not. Others may love us for being exactly as we are.

If we already have someone's love, we often don't do what feels right and honest to us because we fear that we will lose the love we have. We might think, "If I don't sacrifice for him and fill his needs, then he won't love me" or "If I don't do this for her, she won't want to be my friend". But can we really know for sure that this is true? If someone truly loves us, then they will want us to do what feels right and natural for us. If being ourselves and doing what feels honest to us cause us to lose someone else's love, then we never actually had it. The only way that someone won't love us for choosing to do what feels honest is if they are only using us to try to fill their own needs and to try to make themselves happy. It's certainly no fun to be in this kind of friendship or relationship.

We try to mold ourselves into whatever we think others will love, all because we believe others will reject the real us. But it is actually much easier for others to love us if we act like ourselves, regardless of what we are like. Almost all of us want to be around people who are comfortable being themselves, who act honestly, who are at ease, who don't seem to be trying to impress us, and who don't need anything from us. We like being around these types of people because they make it easy for us to be ourselves and feel comfortable.

• If we pretend to be someone we're not and wind up winning others' love and approval, it likely won't mean much to us because we know they love the pretend character we created, and not the "real" us.

We would also need to keep pretending to be whoever they love in order to keep their love. Acting how it feels true for us to act is likely to make them angry since that is not what they signed up for. Living like this clearly isn't very enjoyable.

• By the same token, if we pretend to be someone we're not, and they reject us, we will never know if they actually would have loved the "real" us.

• The funny thing about this is that we only want others' love and approval in order to make ourselves happy, yet the process we go through to get this love is a large part of what makes us unhappy. If we weren't so busy thinking about how to get love from others, it would be much easier to love others. When we love others, we experience the joy we have been trying to get from receiving love. If we allow ourselves to just be ourselves, to be honest, and to do what feels natural in any moment, we are already happy. When we aren't trying to be someone we're not, we can just relax and do whatever it is we want to do. This is the peace and contentment we hoped we would get from love and approval.

When we truly realize that we don't know what will make others love us, we can stop pretending to be someone we're not, because we can acknowledge that we don't really know whether our efforts will actually make them love us more. If we can admit that others might love and approve of us for being exactly as we are, then this may help us to stop pretending to be someone we're not. When we recognize that acting and speaking according to what feels natural and honest provides us with the happiness we have always wanted, then we may be able to stop acting dishonestly just because we hope that it might help get us some love.

The Questions: Do I really know with absolute certainty what they would love and approve of? Is it at all possible they will love and approve of me if I just do and say what feels right and natural in any moment? Isn't it true that we tend to love others who feel comfortable and at ease with themselves? Does pretending to be who I think they will love create anxiety, worry, and suffering, or does it make me happy? Is it worth being dishonest or pretending to be someone I'm not, considering that even if I get their love, I'll know they aren't actually loving *me*? If I win someone's love by pretending to be someone I'm not, then won't it be unenjoyable to try to maintain the false image of myself that I created? Is it worth pretending to be someone I'm not, considering the possibility that they could actually love the "real" me and the risk that they might not love the "pretend" me? If all it takes to be happy is to simply act according to what feels honest and natural, then does it make sense to pretend to be someone I'm not just because I think it might help get me some love?

20.   Am I sure that their opinion about me is true?

When someone says something positive about us (e.g., appreciation or approval), we generally experience some happiness or comfort and then believe the other person created it. When someone insults us, we often feel sad, angry, or ashamed, and then we believe that that person created our emotion. But is that true?

If you think, "I am terrible at my job", and then a stranger (who you know has never seen any of your work) tells you, "You're great at your job", is this likely to affect you? It is unlikely. On the other hand, if your boss told you, "You're great at your job", would this affect you? For most of us, this would yield at least a little bit of pleasure. So what's the difference between these two situations? Two people told us the same thing, they both had the same opinion about us, but yet only one of these opinions emotionally affected us. The reason only one of the comments emotionally affected us is that we only believed one of them. Since the stranger had never seen our work, we didn't believe his opinion. If we don't believe someone else's opinion, that opinion cannot emotionally affect us. Since our boss has seen us work, we will probably believe his opinion about us, which will improve our opinion of ourselves, and then create the corresponding feeling of pleasure.

What this shows us is that other people don't have the power to emotionally affect us. Others' words and opinions do not create our emotions. Our emotions are only created by our thoughts about ourselves. *If we don't believe someone else's opinion, then it won't have the power to change our opinion of ourselves, and therefore won't emotionally affect us.* The only way that someone else's insult or compliment can impact us is if we believe that what they say about us is true.

Let's look at another example of how this plays out in our lives. Please take a moment to imagine a stranger whose opinion you are highly unlikely to trust (e.g. a homeless person, politician, or teenager). If you think, "I am worthy of love", and then this random untrustworthy stranger on the street tells you, "You're unworthy of love", would their opinion emotionally impact you? It might annoy you a little, but it almost certainly wouldn't affect your opinion of yourself or create any serious emotional impact, because you are unlikely to believe this person's opinion to be trustworthy. But if your boyfriend or girlfriend of a few years were to tell you, "You're unworthy of love", do you think that would emotionally affect you? You are likely to feel hurt. In this situation, you are likely to believe that your partner's opinion is true maybe because their love played a large part in helping you to believe, "I am worthy of love" in the first place, or because you think their opinion is credible since you've spent a lot of time with them. Once you believe their opinion to be true, that would shift your opinion of yourself towards unworthiness. And when your opinion of yourself worsens, you experience the feeling of being hurt.

It's not your partner who created this hurt; it's not even their opinion that created it. If the opinion, "You're unworthy of love", directly created your feeling of hurt, then the stranger's opinion would have had the same emotional impact on you as your partner's opinion. Your hurt was created simply by your belief – your thought – that their opinion is true.

If you were to walk into a store that sells knives, buy a knife, and then cut yourself with it, would you blame the pain on the store, the knife, or yourself? We almost certainly wouldn't blame our pain on the store or the knife because we were the ones who bought the knife and then used it to cut ourselves. In the same way, if someone else tells us their negative opinion about us, the person is the store, and their opinion is the knife. Neither the person (the store) nor the opinion (the knife) has the power to hurt us. We hurt ourselves when we take their opinion (the knife), and then believe this opinion to be true (the action of cutting ourselves).

Others' opinions themselves do not have the power to emotionally affect us. When we believe someone's opinion to be true, it simply changes our thoughts about ourselves. When our thoughts about ourselves worsen, we feel hurt and we suffer. If we don't want to be emotionally affected by other people's opinions of us, all we need to do is recognize that we don't actually know whether someone's opinion about us is true. It would seem obvious that we can't know whether someone's opinion is true, but we very easily lose sight of this as we go through life.

If our partner insults us or breaks up with us, we tend to think that there's something "wrong" with us. If our boss insults us or fires us, we are likely to believe that we aren't "good enough". If our parents disapprove of us, we might believe that we're unworthy or insufficient. In other words, when someone else believes that we aren't "perfect", we often believe them. To understand the flaw in this logic, let's look at a quick analogy. Imagine you are with your four-year-old son as he plays one of his games at home. He has several wooden shapes that he is trying to place in matching holes on a wooden board. Now imagine that your son picks up a square shape and tries to put it in a triangle-shaped hole, and then says to you, "Daddy, the square isn't good enough for this hole". What would you say to him? Probably something like, "Sweetie, just because the square doesn't fit, it doesn't mean that the square isn't good enough or that there is something wrong with it".

The same is true with all of our relationships in life. If someone breaks up with us, fires us, or disapproves of us, that simply means we don't fit *their* definition of "perfect". To go back to the analogy, this means we don't fit in the shape of *their* hole. Just because we don't fit one person's definition of "perfect", it doesn't mean we aren't "good enough", or that there is something "wrong" with us.

We can't be "not good enough" and there can't be something "wrong" with us because there is no such thing as "good enough" or "wrong". Each of us has completely different definitions of what we think is "good" and "bad", "right" and "wrong", "helpful" and "harmful", "beautiful" and "ugly". What one guy finds unattractive, another one may find attractive. What one girl thinks is annoying, another girl may love. What one boss finds unhelpful, another boss may find helpful. What one boss believes is a "bad" trait, another boss may value. What one mom thinks is a ridiculous career choice, another mom may be proud of. What one dad may think is a disappointing house, another dad may be proud of.

Is one person's definition of "right", "good", or "attractive" somehow more correct or more true than others' definitions? If someone thinks one of our characteristics is "bad" or "not good enough", this just means we fit *that person's concept* of those words. It doesn't mean *we are* these concepts.

What this means is that nobody can hurt you. Only you can hurt you. You don't feel hurt because someone stops loving you or rejects you, you feel hurt because of what you think that means about you. When you believe someone else's opinion about you to be true, you suffer. This means you don't have to get everyone in your life to think you're "great" in order to be happy. All you have to do to stop suffering is just question whether you know that someone else's opinion about you is true.

The Questions: Am I sure that their opinion about me is true? Could someone else have a different perspective than theirs? If so, can I really be sure that their perspective is true? Am I sure that something about me isn't "good enough", or is it just that I happen to fit their specific definition of this word? Is it true that just because I care about this person, their opinion is somehow more valid than other people's opinions? Can I think of any reasons or examples as to why the opposite of their opinion might be true? If so, then can I know with absolute certainty that their opinion about me is true?

21. Do I believe what I want them to think about me?

Please take a moment to locate your answer to the questions "what do I want them to think about me? Who do I want to think it?" Or you can take a moment to answer these questions now. Whatever we want someone else to think about us, that is actually just how we want to think about ourselves. Others' opinions don't emotionally affect us, as we've seen. We just want others to think positively about us in order to help convince us to think more positively about ourselves, which makes us happier. For example, we would want someone to tell us, "You're pretty", or "You're a good person" because we want to think of ourselves as "pretty" and as a "good" person. We want someone to love us and approve of us in order to help us love and approve of ourselves.

Rather than sacrifice our time, energy, and enjoyment trying to get everyone to think what we want about ourselves just so that we can think what we want about ourselves, we can skip the middleman. We can just ask ourselves the question, "Do I believe what I want them to think about me?" Please take a moment to answer this for yourself right now.

If you already believe what you want them to think about you, then you can have the happiness you want right now. You don't need to wait for their positive opinion, because you already believe, "I am lovable", "I am pretty", "I am a success", or whatever thought applies for you. *For example, if you have been trying to get your father to tell you, "You are a success", all that this compliment can do for you is to help you believe, "I am a success".* If you ask yourself, "Do I believe I am a success?" and the answer is "yes", then you can tell yourself, "I am a success", and you will feel the same happiness you expected to feel if your father told you "you are a success".

If you just stop for a second and recognize that you already believe what you want someone else to think about you, then you get the same feeling that you would get if someone were to give you the compliment or approval you wanted. You already have the approval and appreciation you have been searching so hard for. All you need to do to feel it is to acknowledge it. Please take a moment to give yourself the love, approval, or compliment you have been seeking.

Did you feel the relief or pleasure from acknowledging some "positive" attribute about yourself? If this exercise didn't bring you some relief or pleasure, it is likely because you don't truly believe the positive thought about yourself. When we seek positive opinions from others, it's generally because we don't actually believe what we want them to think about us.

For example, we would want our father to tell us, "You are a success", because we don't believe that we are successful. We would want his positive opinion just to help change our thoughts of "I am a failure" or "I am not a success", and convince us that we are successful. If we want someone to think that we are attractive, funny, smart, or a "good" mom, or if we want someone to love us, it is often because we believe that we are not attractive, funny, smart, a "good" mom, or worthy of love. We are looking for positive opinions from others (love and approval) to convince us to stop believing our negative thoughts about ourselves, or to improve our thoughts about ourselves.

As we have already seen, this strategy of looking for love and approval from others to improve our thoughts about ourselves and make ourselves happy takes an incredible amount of time and energy, creates a lot of suffering, and doesn't actually have the ability to make us feel fulfilled. If we don't love ourselves or approve of ourselves, then it's very difficult for someone else to change that opinion.

Rather than go through all that trouble, there is a much easier way to be happy about ourselves. Any time we find ourselves seeking a positive opinion from someone else, we can stop and ask ourselves if we believe the opinion we want them to have. If we do believe it, we can just tell ourselves, "I already believe I am great" or whatever opinion you want. If we don't believe it, then all we need to do is question the truth of our negative thought about ourselves. When we truly love and approve of ourselves, we no longer have any reason to seek love and approval from others.

The Questions:

a) What do I want people to think about me? Isn't it true that their positive opinion only emotionally affects me if I believe it? Isn't it true that all their positive opinion can do is help to make my opinion of myself more positive? Do I believe what I want them to think about me? If so, then can't I just be happy right now because I already have the positive opinion about myself that I want? How does it feel when I tell myself the positive opinion that I wanted them to have about me?

b) If I don't believe what I want them to think about me, then wouldn't it be very difficult for them to improve my own opinion of myself, especially if I have believed it for a long time? Does it make sense to spend my time and energy trying to get the opinion I want from someone when their love and approval doesn't have the ability to make me feel fulfilled? Wouldn't it be easier to just disbelieve the negative thoughts I have about myself?

22.   Do I believe what I don't want them to think about me?

Please take a moment to locate your answer to the question "what am I scared they will think of me?" Or you can take a moment to answer this question now.

If somebody's negative opinion can hurt your emotional state, then you will fear their negative opinion. If somebody's negative opinion can't hurt your emotional state, then you won't have any reason to worry about their opinion. If you don't want to worry about whether someone has a negative opinion about you, then there are two ways to ensure that others' opinion can't hurt your emotional state. The first way is to discover that you don't believe their possible negative opinion, and the second way is to recognize that you already have the same negative opinion.

If you don't believe someone's negative opinion, then it won't worsen your opinion of yourself, and it therefore won't affect your emotional state. Similarly, if you admit that you already believe the negative opinion you fear that others will have, then their opinion can't worsen your opinion of yourself, and it therefore won't affect your emotional state. If a negative opinion won't affect your emotional state, then you don't have anything to fear. In other words, you would have nothing to worry about.

Rather than living in fear that others will reject us and doing things we don't enjoy because we fear that others will disapprove, there is a much easier way to be happy. You can take the shortcut by taking a moment right now to ask yourself, "Do I believe what I don't want them to think about me?"

For example, if you are worried about whether other people think that you are fat, then you can ask yourself, "Do I believe that I am fat?" If the answer is "No", and you truly don't believe that you are fat, then it doesn't matter what other people think because it won't worsen your opinion of yourself. If somebody thought that you were fat, you would just think that they are confused or not in touch with reality, and you therefore wouldn't take their opinion seriously. You could say to yourself, "I am not fat, so anyone who thinks otherwise must be crazy".

If you don't believe the opinion you fear, then please take a moment right now to acknowledge this to yourself. You may say, "I am a wonderful mother, and I don't believe anyone who thinks otherwise", "I approve of myself, so my father must be confused if he doesn't approve of me", or "I love myself, so it doesn't matter whether they love me".

If this doesn't provide you with relief or peace, then this likely means that on some level you do believe the opinion you fear or you could relatively easily believe it. Normally, when we have anxiety about what others are thinking, it is because we unknowingly believe what we fear others will think about us. For example, if you spend time worrying about whether others will think you're selfish, it is usually because you believe that you're selfish. At first glance, this idea very often seems untrue. This is because we are often completely unaware of the negative beliefs we have about ourselves. When we first admit a negative belief we have about ourselves, it can cause us to feel hurt, sad, or ashamed. Since we don't want to feel this way, we unconsciously do everything in our power to avoid admitting that we have these beliefs. We try to deny that we have them, pretend we don't have them, and convince ourselves that we don't have them.

In this way, if we truly believe, "I am a bad parent", we would try not to admit it to ourselves, we would pretend we don't believe it, and we would try to show everyone else how "great" a parent we are in an attempt convince ourselves that we are a "great" parent. We would be afraid that others would think we're a "bad" parent because any comment from others could reaffirm our own belief about ourselves, forcing us to acknowledge that we believe, "I am a bad parent". Admitting this would then cause us to feel hurt or sad. This dynamic often causes us to worry about how we are acting and to constantly monitor what we think others are thinking about us.

But if we just admit the negative belief we have about ourselves, we have taken a big step towards freedom. If we admit, "I do believe I am a bad parent", we will likely feel hurt at first, but then we would finally be able to question whether this thought is true or take the initiative to change how we are acting. If we are able to disbelieve our negative thought about ourselves, then we have also disbelieved the negative thought that we fear others will have of us, leaving us with no reason to worry about others' opinions.

Even if we can't disbelieve our negative thought, we will still have lost our reason to worry, because we will no longer need to hide our negative belief about ourselves from ourselves. If you really believe, "I am a bad parent", and you fully acknowledge that you believe it, then what emotional effect would it have on you if someone tells you that you are a "bad" parent? Since you already believe this, their comment wouldn't affect your opinion of yourself, and therefore wouldn't emotionally affect you. If others' negative opinions can't emotionally affect you, you have nothing to fear, and therefore no reason to worry about their opinions.

Let's go back to our initial example. If you are worried that others will think that you are fat, then you can ask yourself, "Do I believe that I am fat?" If the answer is "Yes", then you can admit to yourself right now "I believe that I am fat". Once you admit this, then instead of worrying about whether other people think you are fat, you would just think that it makes sense for everyone to think that you are fat. You would think that people would have to be blind or confused if they didn't think that you are fat. Since you just assume everyone thinks that you are fat, there is no need to worry about whether others do or don't think that you are fat. You may think it is "bad" to be fat, which might make you feel ashamed, but at least you don't have to worry, fear, or constantly monitor whether other people might be thinking that you are fat.

Instead of hiding your negative beliefs about yourself (insecurities) and then worrying about whether others will see what you see, you can just expose yourself to yourself. You can face what you don't want others to see. If you face these insecurities about yourself and admit, "I do believe what I'm scared they will think about me", then you can finally stop worrying about what others think. Not only that, but you can then question whether your negative beliefs are true, and finally stop believing the thoughts that make you feel insufficient.

The Questions:

a) What do I fear they will think about me? Isn't it true that their negative opinion can only emotionally affect me if I believe their opinion about me? Do I believe what I don't want them to think about me? If I really don't believe their possible negative opinion about me, then wouldn't their opinion be irrelevant? How does it feel when I tell myself, "I don't care what they think about me because I actually don't believe what I was afraid they would think"?

b) If I do believe their possible negative opinion about me, can I be completely sure that this thought I have about myself is true? If I can admit that I do believe their possible negative opinion about me, then isn't it true that their possible negative opinion about me wouldn't actually affect my opinion of myself (since I have already acknowledge that I believe it), and therefore wouldn't emotionally affect me? If their possible negative opinion about me wouldn't emotionally affect me, then isn't it true that I have nothing to fear?

Chapter Twelve

Questions to Disbelieve Your Judgments about Others

All of us have moments when we judge or insult other people. When we think about someone in a negative way, we are often thinking that they did something "bad" or said something "bad" or that something about them is "bad". We might think, "she's ugly", "he's selfish", "she's a bad mom", "he is too competitive", "she is ignorant", or "he is boring". When we think these thoughts about others, it is usually because we have an incentive to make these judgments. When we judge something about someone else to be "bad", we are almost always believing that they are "worse" than we are in that specific way or just "worse" than we are in general. We usually aren't aware of it, but this makes us believe we are "better" than they are in that specific way or just "better" in general. This belief slightly improves our self-image, which creates a little happy high or pleasure for ourselves.

Our opinion of ourselves, or all the adjectives we use to describe ourselves, are all relative to our opinion of other people. The concept of nice doesn't exist without the concept of mean. Smart doesn't exist without stupid. In order to view ourselves as smart and nice, we have to think of some people as stupid and mean. For example, if we see a man yelling at his child, we may think, "He is a bad parent". This makes us feel as if we are a "better" parent than he is or just "better" than he is in general. To improve any aspect of our self-image, we can judge others to be "worse" than we are in that area. If we want to think of ourselves as really funny, we can judge others to be boring and not funny. Then we get to feel as if we are funnier. We are incentivized to think negatively about others because it makes us think of ourselves in a more positive light. Our most frequent judgments of others are often based on the aspects of ourselves that we care about most. If we most commonly judge others as "stupid", it is because being "smart" is a major part of our identity.

However, our negative judgments about others come at a cost. On the subtlest level, our negative thoughts make us feel separate from others. Most obviously, our judgments create anger, disappointment, and frustration. When these feelings are more intense, they can often turn into hatred, abusive words, or hurtful actions. But perhaps most fundamentally, our judgments about others really prevent us from loving others. When we disbelieve our judgments about others, we are left in peace, feeling love for others and treating others with love.

23.   Is it true that they are "worse" than I am? Have I done what I judge them for doing?

Most of the time, when we judge someone else to be "bad" because of their actions, we are believing that they are "worse" than we are. However, the truth is, we have usually done whatever it is that we judge them for doing. We may have done the same "bad" thing to them as they did to us, or we may have done it to others, done it to ourselves, or done something very similar in the past.

Whenever we judge someone else to be "bad" because of their "bad" actions, we can look at our own lives and try to find an example of when we acted in the same way or in a similar way. If we judge someone to be "worse" than we are, then remembering a time when we acted in a similar way may make us recognize that the person we judged isn't actually "worse" than we are. This recognition usually ends our belief that they are "bad", or stops us from giving attention to our judgment for the following four reasons.

•   If we think, "I am good", and realize that they are not "worse" than we are, then we stop believing that they are "bad" just because they did something "bad". Since we have done the same "bad" thing in the past, we then consider them to be "normal" or even "good". If we think, "I am smart (good)", and see someone make a "stupid" mistake, then we might think, "He's stupid". But if we remember a time when we did something similarly "stupid", this may make us realize, "He isn't worse than I am" and therefore, "he probably isn't stupid; it's normal to make mistakes".

It is very common for us to think things like "if he cared about me, he would be more affectionate with me even though he doesn't like to be affectionate" or "if he loved me, he would go to the theatre with me even though he hates the theatre". We are essentially saying, "He is bad because he isn't willing to sacrifice for me". However, we don't seem to recognize that by asking someone else to sacrifice what they want, we are saying, "I am not willing to sacrifice what I want".

We may think our boyfriend is inconsiderate or selfish because he isn't willing to miss a friend's party to spend time with us. If we ask ourselves, "Am I ever inconsiderate to him?" we can see that we are being inconsiderate right now by asking him to miss his friend's party just to spend time with us. We may think it is selfish that our husband won't clean the dishes for us. If we ask ourselves, "Do I ever act selfishly towards him?" we can see that it might be selfish for us to try to get him to do the dishes even though he doesn't want to, or it might be selfish that we try to make him feel guilty about it just so that he will do what we want.

Once we recognize that we also are sometimes not willing to sacrifice what we want, sometimes inconsiderate, and sometimes selfish, then we may realize that we treat him just as he treats us. This recognition can help us to understand that his treatment of us does not make him "bad" in any way.

• If we recognize that we have acted based on the same intentions as the person we judge, we may realize that they aren't "worse" than we are. Just as we often commit the same "bad" actions as the people we judge, we also tend to commit different actions based on the same intentions. This may seem different, but, if two people each intend to shoot someone, would you consider them both to be "bad" even if only one person succeeds and the other one misses? Generally, we would believe that they are equally "bad" because they both had the same intentions even though their actions or the ensuing consequences were different.

Often when we judge other people to be "bad", their "bad" actions are based on the intention of making someone else suffer for what they believe to be a "bad" action (i.e., punishment). For example, if our husband yells at us for misplacing the TV remote, then he is essentially choosing the "bad" action of yelling as punishment for what he believes to be the "bad" action of misplacing the TV remote. When this happens, we may then judge our husband to be "mean" for yelling at us. It may seem that his action was to yell at us for misplacing a TV remote, but if we look at it from a more fundamental level, he was really just punishing us for what he believed to be a "bad" action. Therefore, instead of asking ourselves, "Have I ever yelled at someone for misplacing a TV remote?", we can ask ourselves, "Have I ever chosen to punish someone for what I believed to be a bad action?"

We may not have committed the same "bad" action as the person we are judging (here, yelling), or we may not have punished someone in response to the same "bad" action (here, misplaced remote), but we have almost certainly chosen to punish others for "bad" actions in the past. For example, maybe our husband forgot our birthday and we responded with insults, an "attitude", or other ways of withholding our love.

Our punishments may have been less extreme, but our intention was still to make someone suffer (even if it is just trying to prevent their happiness) for what we believed to be a "bad" action. Therefore, it is possible to recognize that someone who punishes others in different ways, or for different reasons, is not "worse" than we are. We too have done things with the intention of creating suffering for others (punishing). This doesn't mean we are both "bad"; we have all been taught to believe many concepts of "bad" and have been taught to believe that others cause us to suffer, so therefore it is "normal" that we all punish others.

- Once we stop thinking someone else is "worse" than we are, we no longer have an incentive to give attention to our judgments about them. We may not realize it, but we give attention to judgments about others because it makes us feel better about ourselves. When we stop thinking someone else is "worse" than we are, the judgment generally disappears on its own because the judgment no longer helps to improve our self-image, and we don't want to think of ourselves as "bad".

Imagine that you consider yourself to be a "good" parent, and you see another father at your child's school yelling at his child. When you see this, you instantly judge the man to be a "bad" parent for yelling at his child. This unconsciously makes you feel a little better about your own parenting. But if you then think back to a time when you yelled at your child, you will recognize that the other man may not be a "worse" parent than you. If you keep judging the other man to be a "bad" parent for yelling at his child, you are essentially judging yourself to be a "bad" parent because you have done the same thing. Since it doesn't feel nice to judge yourself, your judgment about the other man will often turn into, "I guess he isn't so mean; that's normal; I've done it also".

• If we realize that we weren't aware that we were performing the same "bad" action as the person we judge did, we may realize that they too may not have been aware of their actions. If they weren't aware of their "bad" action, and we weren't aware that we were doing the same thing, then it is difficult to keep blaming them for their actions. For example, if we are mad at our husband because we think he doesn't appreciate us, we can ask ourselves, "Have I not appreciated him at some point? Do I always think to show him appreciation?" We may realize that we often don't show him appreciation. We may have been completely unaware that we weren't showing him appreciation because we were too busy thinking about whether we were getting appreciated. Then we can recognize, "If I wasn't aware of whether I was appreciating him, then maybe he isn't aware that he isn't showing me appreciation". If we discover that we both weren't aware that we weren't showing much appreciation, then we can stop blaming each other for not giving much appreciation.

In summary, when we are able to recognize that we have acted in similar ways as the person we are judging we are usually able to see that the person we are judging is not "worse" than we are. Once this happens, we tend to stop believing that the person we are judging is "bad" for doing whatever they did. Then, instead of feeling anger, resentment, or disappointment towards others, what remains is love and acceptance.

If the question "have I done what I judge them for doing?" makes you aware of a "bad" action you didn't know you were doing, then you may wind up with a new judgment about yourself. If this happens, you can use the other questions in this book to disbelieve your new judgment. Alternatively, if you truly believe your actions have been unloving or hurtful, then you may want to change your actions.

Be aware that once you see that you act in the same "bad" ways as the person you judge does, you could be tempted to believe some version of "why should I treat them with love if they don't treat me with love" or "if she doesn't listen to me, I'm not going to waste my time listening to her". If this happens, just ask yourself, "Do I want to wait for everyone in the world to treat me with love before I can treat them with love, or do I want to lead the way and act how I want to see others act?"

If you decide that you want to change your actions, then you can make a conscious effort to discover what thoughts you are thinking right before (or during) your unwanted actions. These are the thoughts that tend to motivate your unwanted actions. If you can disbelieve these thoughts, you lose the motivation behind your unwanted actions, and you are therefore much less likely to act in these ways. When we don't believe the thoughts that drive our unloving actions, we naturally act with love.

The Questions:

a) What am I judging someone for doing? What person have I decided is "bad" because of their words or actions? Have I treated them, myself, or anyone else in a similar way (or based on similar intentions)? Have I, too, punished someone (intended to cause suffering or prevent happiness) for doing something "bad"? If we have both done the same "bad" thing, or done different things based on the same intention, then is it true that the other person is "worse" than I am? If I am "good" or "normal", and they are not "worse" than I am, then is it true that they are "bad"?

b) Was I aware that I was doing the same "bad" thing? Is it possible that he isn't aware that he is doing something "bad"? Wouldn't it be almost impossible for either of us to change any of our unloving or "bad" actions if we don't even realize we are doing them? Can I really blame him for doing something "bad" when we both do that same "bad" thing because we are unaware of it?

c) Do I want to wait for everyone else to treat me with love before I can treat them with love, or do I want to lead the way and be the loving person that I want others to be? What thoughts am I thinking right before or during my unwanted actions? Can I be sure these thoughts are true?

24. Am I sure my judgment about them is correct?

Most of us want to know what's going on around us because it gives us pleasure to think "I know", and because not knowing can seem scary or uncomfortable. Because of this, we often put people into categories as soon as possible. But since we often don't have all the information we need to put people into a category, we just guess. We interpret who others are based on a few actions or words, clothing, interests, and general appearance. We don't wait to make a judgment until we know more about a person, because we want to be in the realm of knowing right away.

In this way, when someone does one seemingly selfish, mean, irresponsible, stupid, or disrespectful thing, we decide this action represents who they are. Even after witnessing only one action, we can think, "He *is* selfish" or "She *is* irresponsible". We clearly don't know everything they have ever done, but that doesn't stop us from forming a conclusion (a judgment) about who they are.

Since we actually don't know whether the person is "selfish" or "irresponsible", this is really just a guess, an interpretation based on extremely limited information.

We may even interpret who someone is based on a few words or even just their outfit. For example, we may deem someone to be uneducated or dangerous solely based on the way they speak or the clothes they wear. Then we react to our interpretation, not the facts, and treat them accordingly. If we acknowledge that our interpretation (judgment) of them may not be true, then we can admit, "I don't know whether he is bad". This eliminates our emotional reaction and allows us to treat them with more love.

In addition to this, once we have formed a conclusion about someone and judge them to be a certain way, we often choose to interpret all of their future actions in a way that supports our previous conclusion about them. We do this in order to maintain our belief "I know, I am right" and because we don't want to admit, "I don't know" or "I was wrong to make that judgment".

If we judge someone to be mean, we are likely to interpret much of what they do to be mean. If we previously judged one of our co-workers to be mean, then we see him talking with friends and laughing, we are likely to interpret it as, "He must be making fun of someone". Whereas if our original judgment was that he was nice, we would likely think, "He is always making people laugh". This desire to believe "I know, I am right" perpetuates our opinions about others and rarely allows our opinion of others to change.

But as soon as we acknowledge that our interpretation (judgment) may not be true, we stop feeling the anger and disappointment towards others that our judgments have been causing, thereby allowing us to treat others with love.

The Questions: What are the facts and what is my interpretation? Do I really have all of the information I need about this person in order to make this judgment? Have I decided on this judgment (interpretation) because it confirms something I already believed to be true? How would I interpret them if I previously believed the opposite judgment? Can I think of any reasons or examples as to why the opposite of my judgment might be true? If so, can I know for sure that my original judgment is true?

25. Have I chosen to judge them just to take my attention off something "bad" about myself?

When our opinion of ourselves worsens, we feel hurt. But we only feel this hurt when we actually give attention to the "worse" thoughts about ourselves. Since the feeling of hurt can be very painful and hard to experience, we have formed a number of tactics to avoid this feeling. One of our main strategies to prevent ourselves from feeling hurt is to create a judgment about someone else in order to take our attention off the possible "worsening" of our opinion of ourselves. This strategy allows us to avoid feeling hurt and helps us to feel "good" for the moment, but this isn't enough. Our judgments about others often wind up creating anger, they prevent us from loving, and we can feel "bad" about ourselves for judging others. In addition, just because we don't admit that we have a negative thought about ourselves, it doesn't mean that the thought isn't there. This new "worse" negative thought about ourselves remains, creating suffering for us in unconscious ways (e.g., worrying about whether others will find out about us).

If our thoughts about anyone's words or actions cause us to feel hurt, we often instantly label some aspect of the other person as "bad" and get angry at them. For example, if our partner says, "You really don't look good in that outfit", we may instantly experience anger by thinking, "You are stupid and inconsiderate; why would you say that?" Our anger and judgment take our attention off the hurt we would feel from thinking, "I am not attractive".

If our boss gives us a "bad" performance review on our latest project, we might instantly begin to think, "He is stupid, he doesn't know what he is talking about", or "It is my co-worker's fault for making me include that useless information". Instead of allowing ourselves to think, "I am bad at my job", and experience the worsening of our self-image, we shift the blame onto others. This causes us to experience anger towards them. We form judgments about others so that we don't have to admit, "I didn't do a good job".

Often when we are angry at someone or judging someone, we are actually just attempting to take our attention away from a negative thought we have about ourselves. This is especially true when something happens that can potentially worsen our opinion of ourselves. If there is ever a chance that we are to blame for something "bad", instead of looking to see whether that is possible, we try to shift our attention away from ourselves and blame someone else.

For example, if someone gets angry at us for something, we tend to instantly get angry back at them because we don't want to discover that maybe we did something "bad" or that maybe they are right about us. If our child gets in trouble at school, we may instantly blame our partner for their troublemaking because we are afraid to look at ourselves and possibly discover that we are partially to blame. If someone who is really "attractive" and "great" at their job starts working where we work, we may decide to instantly judge them to be "bad" in one way or another, just so we don't have think of ourselves as "worse" than they are.

Once we notice our judgment about someone else, we can stop and ask ourselves, "Am I trying to avoid admitting a negative thought about myself?" If we allow ourselves to acknowledge the "bad" thought we have about ourselves or to admit that we are at least partially to blame, then we can also recognize that our judgment about the other person has been created solely as a means to take our attention off this thought about ourselves. Once we acknowledge the "bad" thought we didn't want to see about ourselves, we no longer have an incentive to keep judging others, and we gain the opportunity either to question our negative thought about ourselves or to improve whatever we believe is negative. As long as we try to pretend that the negative thought about ourselves isn't there, we can't question it or address it. The negative thought will just continue to create subtle unconscious emotions or issues for us, and we will keep being incentivized to judge others. Without our incentive to judge others, the judgment either disappears on its own, or it allows us to look at our judgment more objectively.

To continue with the example above, once we admit, "I think I'm bad at my job", we lose our incentive to make excuses for why the "bad" performance review wasn't our fault. This enables us to more honestly assess whether we know that our boss is actually stupid or whether our "bad" performance review was really our co-worker's fault. In addition, we can then question whether we are actually "bad" at our job, and maybe we can begin to look at what we can do to improve our performance.

The Questions: Have I chosen to judge them just to take my attention off something "bad" about myself? What is the negative thought I have about myself that I have been trying to avoid and don't want to admit to myself? Is it possible that I am at least partially to blame? Is it possible that they are right about me? If I can acknowledge the negative thought I have about myself, then does it help me in any way to keep believing my judgment about them? – Am I absolutely sure my negative thought about myself is true? If I believe it is true, what thoughts cause me to act in these "bad" ways, or what can I do to improve what is "bad"?

Chapter Thirteen

Questions to Disbelieve Your Judgments about Yourself

Our identity, our self-image, is made up of our thoughts about ourselves. It contains our opinions about our personality, appearance, intellect, job, relationship status, past experiences, and anything else. We might think, "I am a funny, caring, attractive, smart, and happily married marketing manager who has achieved a lot" That would be our self-image. For all of the factors that create our identity, we have a concept about what is "perfect". When we form an opinion of ourselves, we are comparing the way we act and live to each of our ideas of "perfect", then deciding where we fit in. If we consider it "perfect" to be married, successful, and thin, and we aren't, then we would consider ourselves to be "bad" for being single, unsuccessful, and overweight. We tend to almost always believe we aren't "good enough" in a variety of different ways because it is almost impossible to match up to our idea of "perfect" for everything. This is a major part of why we feel insufficient or incomplete.

Once we have formed a self-image, we begin to see life through the lens of our self-image. For everything we see in life, we tend to have thoughts about it. Our thoughts about what we see and experience are based on our perspective and interpretation. With everything that we come across in life, it is possible to think about it in a positive or negative way. Once we have decided that we are "bad" in some way, everything that we experience in life tends to reaffirm our belief, confirming that we are "bad". We judge ourselves to be "bad" over and over again because we unknowingly choose to keep perceiving and interpreting the facts of life in a way that backs up our previous conclusion. Once we have formed our self-image around having certain characteristics (e.g., boring, unattractive), we don't look to interpret the facts in our life in a way that could help us to see that the opposite characteristic could be true, because we want to be "right" and we want to maintain our identity.

Our minds often want to avoid being "wrong" at all costs, because we have an unconscious idea that it is "bad" to be "wrong" and it is "good" to be "right". In addition, regardless of whether our identity is positive or negative, we are often unknowingly scared of losing it. If our identity is negative, it would seem counterintuitive for us to want to remain with a negative identity, but this is often the case because we like to stick with what is familiar and what we know. In this way, when our self-image is negative or we believe, "I am bad" in any way, we constantly interpret life in a way that backs up our belief and constantly remind ourselves that we are "bad".

26.   Have I decided on my interpretation because it confirms what I already believed about myself?

When we believe that we are unlovable, ugly, stupid, boring, or "not good enough" or have any other negative self-image description, we are almost always looking for proof. If our friend doesn't call us back, we may think, "She *doesn't* care about me". If we see our boyfriend look at another woman, we may think, "He *doesn't* think I'm sexy". If our boss tells us he wants us to make a few changes to our client presentation, we may think, "He *thinks* I am stupid". If our boyfriend tells us, "I love you", we may interpret it as a lie and think, "He *doesn't* love me". If our parents compliment our sister more than us, we may think, "My parents *don't* approve of me".

What we think in each of these situations is actually just our interpretation, not fact. Yet we tend to unknowingly believe these interpretations to be true and factual. The truth is that we don't know what the other people are thinking. But while we may be unaware of it, we often choose specific interpretations to believe because they prove what we think we already know about ourselves. For each of these situations, an entirely different, more positive interpretation is possible.

If we believed that we are wonderful, smart, lovable, pretty, and completely "good enough", then our interpretation of these scenarios would be completely different. If our friend doesn't call us back, we may think, "She must be really busy, I'm sure she will call later". If our boyfriend looks at other women, we might think, "That's normal, all guys do". If our boss tells us he wants us to make a few changes to our client presentation, we may think, "I am lucky to have a boss that cares enough about me to suggest improvements to my presentation". If our boyfriend tells us he loves us, we would take his word for it. If our parents compliment us less than our sister, we might think, "I guess they think I am confident enough that I don't need as many compliments as her".

We also try to interpret what events and outcomes mean about ourselves. If we have a negative self-image, almost any time something unwanted happens in our lives, such as rejection, we blame it on ourselves. We think that the "bad" outcome happened because we weren't "good enough" in some way. If we fail a test, we may interpret it to mean, "I *am* stupid". If our boyfriend breaks up with us, or we don't get a job offer, we may interpret it to mean, "I *am* not good enough for them". If we experience sadness, we may think it is because "I *am* weak". If someone walks past us in the street without looking at us, we may interpret it to mean, "I *am* not attractive enough". We see all these as facts, not as opinions or guesses. In each of these situations, we would react to our interpretation, not the facts. This is how we were trained. But we really can't know whether our interpretation is true, because it is always possible to have interpreted these facts in completely different ways. For example, we could think, "I didn't study enough", "I guess we weren't a good fit", "I was brave to open myself up despite the possibility of getting hurt", and "They must have a lot on their minds".

By interpreting circumstances in a way that backs up our negative beliefs about ourselves, we are perpetuating our negative self-image. Once we realize that other interpretations are possible and that our interpretation might not be true, we can stop believing the thoughts "they *think* I am not good enough" or "this outcome happened *because* I am not good enough". Then, all of a sudden, our shame is gone, and we are left feeling whole.

The Questions: What are the facts and what is my interpretation? Does my interpretation agree with what I previously thought? Have I decided on my interpretation because it confirms what I already believed about myself? Do I know with absolute certainty that this unwanted outcome happened because I am "not good enough"? How would I interpret this situation if I had a positive belief about myself? Can I think of some other possible ways to interpret this situation? If so, can I be absolutely certain that my original interpretation of the facts is true?

27.   Is it true that I am "worse" than they are? Do others do what I judge myself for doing?

We often judge ourselves to be "bad" because we believe we have done something "bad". But the concept of "bad" is relative. In order to think we are "bad", we must think we are "worse" than others. For example, if we act selfishly, we would judge ourselves to be "bad" only if we believe others are less selfish than we are. But if everyone does the same "bad" thing that we do, then we wouldn't consider ourselves to be "bad" for doing it. We would just consider ourselves to be "normal" because we are not "worse" than others. So if we think we are "bad" for doing something "bad", the real question is, "Do others do the same bad things as I do". Let's examine this.

When do we hurt others? When do we act in "bad" ways towards others? When do we treat others without respect and love? When do we not help others? We act and speak in these ways when we believe, "Someone is bad", when we believe, "Someone did something bad", when we believe, "Someone made me suffer", when we are angry in general, when we feel worthless, when we aren't aware of what we are thinking, when our minds are filled with negativity, when we are so concerned about making ourselves happy that we don't want to give our time, money, or energy to help make someone else happy, and when we are so unhappy that we would do anything (or hurt anyone) to make ourselves happy. Isn't this why you have acted in "bad" ways?

Are you the only one that has these thoughts and feelings? No. These thoughts exist in almost everyone's mind. We are all taught to believe concepts about what is "bad", and taught to believe that circumstances (including people) create suffering. Almost none of us have been taught to be aware of the thoughts that drive our actions and our emotions, nor have we been taught how to disbelieve these thoughts. Since we act and speak based on the thoughts that we have, and we all have the same thoughts, then we all must do similar things, or at least act based on the same intentions. Regardless of whether we have judged others, don't appreciate others, treated others disrespectfully, yelled at others, insulted others, or punished others in different ways, everyone else has almost surely done the same "bad" things.

It may seem as though others are more selfless than we are, but it only appears that way. If we don't feel "good enough", complete, or happy enough, then our goal in life is to make ourselves feel sufficient, complete, and happy enough. This is the same for all of us. We have no choice about that. However, we all have different strategies to make this happen. Some of us pursue goals of success, wealth, power, and physical "perfection" to make ourselves happy, while others pursue happiness by trying to think of themselves as "a good person", "caring", and "selfless". In other words, when people act unselfishly, it is almost always because they want to improve their opinion of themselves. They want to convince themselves that they are "selfless" and "caring" because they believe that doing so will make them happy (even though we generally don't realize this is why we are acting this way). Therefore, while it may seem that others are less selfish than we are, almost everyone is putting their own happiness first. Other people only act "selflessly" to make themselves happy. We all have the same goal, and therefore we are acting based on the same intentions. We just tend to have different ideas about how to achieve our goal or intention.

In addition, we often don't see when others do "bad" things. Just as other people often don't know when we have done something "bad" to ourselves or to others, we don't know when others do the same thing. But since we know the thoughts that cause our "bad" actions, and we know almost everyone has those thoughts, we also know that others must either do the same "bad" things as we do or act based on the same intentions. This means that we are not "worse" than others. Others are not "better" than we are. Most importantly, we are not "bad" just because we have done something that we believe to be "bad".

The Questions: What am I judging myself for doing? Don't I usually do "bad" things because I believe, "Someone is bad", "Someone did something bad", "Someone caused me to suffer", or because I am just focused on making myself happy? Doesn't almost everyone have these thoughts? If almost everyone has these thoughts, isn't it true that they all must act based on these thoughts? Doesn't that mean that almost everyone must do the same "bad" things as I do, or at least act based on the same intentions? If others have the same "bad" thoughts, which cause the same "bad" actions or intentions, is it really true that I am "worse" than others?

Chapter Fourteen

Questions to Disbelieve
Your Concept of Blame

Most of us are filled with ideas about what are the ideal ways to act, speak, feel, think, and live. We often desperately want to live in these ways, but no matter how hard we try, we just can't. Then, when we come up short, we judge ourselves for it, and wind up with sadness, shame, self-hatred, and guilt. In addition, when we see others behave in "bad" ways, we often feel disappointment, anger, or even hatred towards them. The reason we judge ourselves and others for "bad" actions, and feel these emotions, is almost solely because we believe that we are each to blame for the way we act, speak, feel, think, and live.

Imagine that a man is walking down the street, when a stranger approaches him from behind and puts a gun to his head saying, "If you don't rob the next woman that walks past us, I will shoot you". If the man robbed the next lady to walk past him, would you get angry at him for it? Even though you would probably consider the action of robbing the lady to be "bad", you almost certainly wouldn't get angry at the man for robbing her. Why not? You probably wouldn't get angry at the man because you believe he didn't have a choice, he wasn't in control of the situation. Since he didn't have control, you wouldn't blame him for his actions.

In the same way, when we don't blame ourselves or others for the way we act, then we don't feel any anger towards ourselves or others when we do something "bad". Without blame, we can continue to love ourselves and others even when we or they do something "bad".

It certainly seems blatantly obvious that we are to blame for our own actions. It may even seem ridiculous to suggest otherwise. However, despite how it may seem, the way we act and live is actually not our fault. No amount of discipline or effort is enough to think positively and act lovingly all the time. If you are truly willing to be open to this possibility, you may directly discover this for yourself in the following sections. And if you really discover this, life becomes filled with an incredible sense of freedom. You will have lost your reason to get angry at yourself and others.

So just because we don't have someone holding a gun to our heads, does that mean we are to blame for our actions? Let's see.

28. Can I blame myself for a "bad" action if I wasn't in full control over my choice of action?

If we are able to see that we and others aren't in full control of our actions, we may be able to stop blaming ourselves and others for some of the actions we deem to be "bad". Have you ever done anything you didn't want to do? It is doubtful that anyone can honestly answer "no". We may not want to smoke, yell at others, eat unhealthily, bite our nails, act selfishly, feel jealous, or treat others without love, yet we do these things anyway. We may want to go to the gym more, be nicer to people, spend time on a new hobby, appreciate our partner more, or give more attention to our children, yet we often can't. If we were in full control, wouldn't we always be able to do what we want to do?

There are three major reasons we don't have full control over our choice of actions.

a)   Do you have full control over the thoughts you think? It may seem as if we do. But if we controlled our thoughts, then we would almost certainly choose not to think negatively. We would want to be happy all the time and never worry, have anxiety, get angry, or be sad. Yet we frequently have negative thoughts about ourselves, others, and situations that cause us to experience a variety of different emotions that we don't want to have.

b)   Were you taught that thoughts cause your actions? We clearly know that we can choose our actions based on the thoughts we have, but most of us weren't taught to understand that thoughts determine almost all of our actions. Our immediate reactions to yell, give attitude to others, or get angry at others are all created by our thoughts about someone else's actions, even though they seem spontaneous and natural. We usually engage in our "bad" habits of smoking, drinking, eating unhealthily, and biting our nails because we are trying to escape thoughts that are making us unhappy, discontented, or restless. We act selfishly or are inconsiderate because as long as our thoughts are making us unhappy, we will almost certainly care more about making ourselves happy than about anything else. We may stay in jobs, relationships, or other situations we don't like because thoughts make us fear the unfamiliar. But since we weren't taught that thoughts cause our actions, we generally aren't aware of the thoughts that cause our actions. If we aren't aware of the thoughts that cause our actions, we can't address these thoughts, and therefore often can't change our behavior.

c)   Were you taught that you could question whether your thoughts are true? Almost none of us were raised by parents or teachers who taught us that the thoughts in our mind could be questioned and disbelieved. If we can't disbelieve the thoughts in our minds, then we often can't change the unwanted thoughts in our minds that cause our unwanted actions.

Since we don't have full control over the thoughts that arise in our minds, we generally aren't aware of the thoughts that cause our actions, and we weren't taught how to question our thoughts, that means we often don't have control over our choice of actions. We are stuck acting on the thoughts that arise in our minds because we aren't aware of the thoughts we have, and we don't know of any way to change or eliminate these thoughts, since we weren't taught how to question them. This is why we often do things we don't want to do. *If we had full control over our words and actions, we quite simply wouldn't choose to do things that we believe are "bad", we wouldn't hate others, we wouldn't hurt others, we would always do what we want to do, and we would treat ourselves and others with love. Since we don't have full control over our "bad" actions, we can stop blaming ourselves for them.*

If we realize that we aren't always in full control over our actions, it is possible to recognize that others too don't have full control over their actions. This phenomenon isn't unique to any one of us. We are not the only ones who do things we don't want to do. We are all in the same situation. If we can acknowledge that others may not have been in control over whether they committed their "bad" action, then it is possible to stop blaming them for the action they committed. We may not consider them to be "bad" just because they did something "bad". We may not continue to feel anger towards them. Then, instead of blame, compassion may arise for them because we know how it feels to do something "bad" when we really don't want to. *We can forgive ourselves and others for our and their actions because we now understand that we don't always have control over which thoughts enter our mind, we generally aren't aware of the thoughts that are causing our actions, and we have never learned how to change or eliminate the thoughts that we are thinking.*

Since it can be difficult to forgive others, if you feel resistance to losing your blame, please go to Chapter 17 and read, "I want to keep blaming others for my suffering".

The Questions:

a) Have I ever done something I really didn't want to do? Have I ever tried to stop doing something but I just couldn't? If I were in full control over all of my actions, then wouldn't I always be able to do everything I wanted to do?

b) Do I control the thoughts that arise in my mind? If so, then wouldn't I choose to never think negative thoughts and experience unwanted emotions? Was I taught as a child to understand that thoughts almost always determine my words and actions? Am I always aware of the thoughts that determine my words and actions? Was I taught by my parents and teachers that thoughts can be questioned and disbelieved?

c) If my thoughts determine my actions, but yet I don't have full control over the thoughts that arise in my mind, I wasn't taught to be aware of my thoughts, and I wasn't taught how to question my thoughts, then can I admit that I don't have full control over my actions? If I am not in full control over my actions (and words), then is it true that I am to blame for my actions? If I am not to blame for my "bad" actions, then is it true that I am "bad" for committing a "bad" action?

d) If I am not in full control over my words and actions, then isn't it likely that others are not in full control of theirs either? If others aren't in full control over their words and actions, then is it true that they are to blame for their words and actions? If they are not to blame for their "bad" actions, then is it true that they are "bad" for committing them?

29.   Is it possible that I would act in the same way if I were them? Is it possible that they would act in the same way if they were me?

When we judge someone to be "bad" because of something "bad" they did, we are almost always believing that they are "worse" than we are for acting the way they did. But what if we were able to recognize that we could have acted in the same way if we were them? It is difficult to keep blaming someone for their action once we admit that we would have acted in the same way.

For example, let's say you're in a gas station convenience store buying some milk, when all of a sudden a man comes in with a gun to rob the place. When he leaves, after your initial fear, you are likely to feel anger towards him because you believe that what he did was "bad". But what if it had gone a little differently, and the man with the gun had robbed the store while saying, "My daughter needs surgery to survive and I need the money to help her". Would you still feel the same amount of anger towards him? In both scenarios, the same "bad" action took place, but yet your anger is likely to be much weaker or diminished completely in the second scenario. This is simply because you now have the thought in your head "it is possible that I would have done the same thing if I were him".

In order to help us realize that we could have acted in the same way as the person we have judged, we can simply engage in a role-reversal exercise. There are two different ways to do this.

The first way is to think about what is most important to the person we judge, rather than what is most important to us. Recognize that we act according to our own best interests. For example, if our wife wants to go out with her friends and asks us to come home from work early to watch the children, we may get angry at her because we think work is more important than socializing. But if we look at it from her shoes (her point of view), we might see that she thinks that a rare event with friends is more important than an extra two hours of work. If we can admit that we might act in the same way as our wife if we were her, then we would likely stop considering her to be "selfish" or "bad" in some other way.

The second way to approach role reversal is to imagine that we are the person we judge and that we have lived through all of their life experiences. It is particularly important to give attention to early life experiences. Essentially, the question becomes, "If I had lived through their life experiences, and I had been raised in a similar way, might I have acted in the same way?" For example, we may judge our husband to be "bad" for not being expressive or affectionate or for not showing us enough love and appreciation. Then we get angry at him because he acts this way. But if we had grown up with his parents and with his early life experiences, is it possible that we would act in the same way he does? If we can acknowledge that we might act in the same way as our husband, if we had the same life experiences as him, then we will probably recognize that he is not "worse" than we are for acting the way he does.

Once we understand that the person we judge is not "worse" than we are for acting the way they do, we may stop considering them to be "bad" because of their actions, and we may stop blaming them for their actions. When we stop blaming someone for their actions, we lose our anger towards them.

Just as we can do this exercise when someone else does something "bad", we can also do this when we judge our own actions to be "bad". We can ask ourselves, "Could others have done the same thing as I did if they were in my shoes or had lived my life?" This can help us to understand that we aren't "bad" or "worse" than others just because of the things we do.

The Questions: What would be most important to me if I were them? Don't I usually act according to my own best interests? If so, then isn't it possible that I would have acted in the same way if I were them? If I had the same life experiences as they had, and had been raised in the same way, might I have acted in the same way they did? If I could have acted in the same way, then is it true that they are "worse" than I am for acting the way they did? If I could have done the same thing, then is it true that they are really to blame them for their actions? – Could others have done the same thing as I did if they were in my shoes or had lived my life? If so, then is it true that I am "worse" than others for acting how I did?

30.   Is it true that an emotional experience can signify that a person is "weak", "stupid", or "bad" in some way?

Many of us tend to believe that we are "bad" in some way because of the emotions we experience. In order to believe this, we must believe that the emotion we have is "bad", our emotional experience is "worse" than others', and that we are responsible (i.e., to blame) for our emotions. However, if we discover that any of these assumptions isn't true, then we can stop judging ourselves and others for the emotions we have. Now let's take a look at whether these assumptions are true.

a)   We tend to think that emotions such as sadness, anger, frustration, anxiety, confusion, jealousy, fear, guilt, and hopelessness are "bad". These emotions may not feel pleasant, but is it true that these emotions are "bad"? Our emotions themselves are just feelings, physical sensations, which are completely neutral. No feeling is inherently or factually "bad". We all just have different thoughts about our emotions, labeling them as "good" or "bad", "productive" or "unproductive", "courageous to experience" or "weak to experience", "a sign that we are open and in touch with ourselves" or "a sign that we are a mess". To decide, "My emotion is bad", is to believe that our thought is true, when we really don't know whether it is.

b)   Thoughts create emotions when they are believed. Do you control the thoughts you think and believe? If you controlled what thoughts you think, then wouldn't you choose to never think negatively? If you controlled what thoughts you believe, then wouldn't you choose to never believe the thoughts that create your unwanted emotions? If we had full control over the thoughts we think and believe, we wouldn't choose to think negatively or to believe our negative thoughts. Since we aren't in full control over our thoughts, we don't have control over the emotions they create. If we don't have control over our emotions, then we aren't to blame for them. If sadness comes over you, but you aren't to blame for it, then the sadness doesn't signify anything about you.

Imagine that you are walking down the street, when all of a sudden, a guy sneaks up behind you, punches you in the back, and then runs away. Would you consider yourself to be "weak", "stupid", or "bad" in some way for experiencing the ensuing pain? Almost certainly not. Even though you may consider the feeling of pain to be "bad", you still wouldn't conclude that you are "bad" for experiencing it. Since you understand that you had no control over this feeling of pain, you wouldn't blame yourself for this feeling. The same is true of our emotions.

Almost all of us were raised to blame circumstances for our suffering. We weren't taught that thoughts create our emotions, and we weren't taught that thoughts could be questioned and disbelieved. Since we weren't taught how to avoid our unwanted emotions, we certainly aren't to blame for experiencing them.

If you are forced into a fencing match with an expert, and he stabs you with his blade, would you feel "bad" about yourself for experiencing the ensuing pain? Almost certainly not. We wouldn't feel "bad" about ourselves for experiencing this pain because we were never taught how to fence. In other words, if we were never given the tools to avoid getting stabbed by a blade, then we wouldn't blame ourselves for the pain we feel from getting stabbed. The same is true of our emotions. We were forced into life without being given the tools to avoid our unwanted emotions.

Even if we consider our emotion to be "bad", the emotion doesn't make us "bad", because we don't have control over whether we experience it, and we aren't to blame for it. Therefore, our emotions don't signify anything about who we are.

c)   When we look at our friends, the people around us, and the people on TV, many of them have smiles on their faces. We see these smiles, and we just assume that they are happy and content. But a smile doesn't mean that someone is happy. We tend to think others are happy, even when they're not, because we mostly see people when they are engaged in distractions. We are all happy when we're engaged in distractions (e.g., being entertained). This is also why many people could believe we are really happy even if we're not. We tend to think everyone else is happy except us. But in reality, everyone tends to think this.

Just as we don't have control over our thoughts and weren't taught to question our thoughts, others also don't have control over their thoughts and weren't taught to question their thoughts. Since we all believe many concepts of "bad" and believe that circumstances create happiness and suffering, we all often experience unwanted emotions. There is nothing "wrong" with us for experiencing them, and we are not "worse" than others for experiencing them. Experiencing anger, sadness, stress, and fear isn't unique to any one of us. Feeling discontent, unworthiness, and a sense that something is missing isn't a personal issue. It is an experience that we all share because we all have very little choice but to believe the same types of thoughts. Since none of us have known that thoughts cause our unwanted emotions or have known how to question our thoughts, we all go through life with the same feelings and emotions.

d)   Now that we have been given the tool of questioning thoughts, we finally have some control over whether we can identify the thoughts that create our emotions and whether we can disbelieve them. But we still don't have full control over whether we want to engage with this process, whether we remember to, whether we can identify the thoughts that create our emotions, or whether we can disbelieve these thoughts.

If we are able to recognize that we don't know whether our emotion is "bad", that everyone else is likely to experience the same emotions as we do, or that we aren't to blame for our emotions, then we can stop believing that we are somehow "weak", "stupid", or "bad" in some way because of the emotions we experience. This allows us to be at peace with ourselves regardless of our emotional state.

In addition, if we can see that our emotions don't signify anything about us, then we may also be able to recognize that others' emotions also don't signify anything about them. We can stop judging people for being angry or sad or for just having an "attitude". Instead, compassion may arise for the people we see with these emotions, allowing us to treat others with love, regardless of their emotional state.

The Questions:

a) Is my emotion inherently and factually "bad" or does "bad" only exist as a thought in my mind? Can I think of a few reasons as to why my emotion might be "good" to experience? Am I absolutely sure that my emotion is "bad"?

b) Do I control which thoughts arise in my mind? Do I control which thoughts I believe? If so, then wouldn't I choose to never think negative thoughts and experience unwanted emotions? If I haven't been in control of which thoughts I think and which thoughts I believe, then is it true that I am to blame for the emotions these thoughts create? Did I grow up being taught that thoughts create emotions, and that these thoughts can be questioned and disbelieved? If I wasn't taught to question my thoughts, then is it true that I am responsible for the emotions my thoughts create?

c) Do others control which thoughts arise in their minds, and therefore what emotions they have? If others also believe concepts of "bad", believe that circumstances create suffering, and don't know how to question their thoughts, then mustn't they suffer just as I do? If everyone else experiences unwanted emotions too, then is it true that I am "worse" than others?

d) Do I have full control over whether I can identify the thoughts that create my emotions? Do I have full control over whether I can disbelieve a thought? If I am not to blame for any of the factors that create my emotions, then is it true that my emotion somehow signifies that I am "weak", "stupid", or "bad" in some way?

31. Am I absolutely certain that I could have done something different considering the thoughts I had and believed at the moment of choice?

When we think that we have done something "bad", have caused a "bad" outcome, or didn't do enough to stop a "bad" outcome, we tend to feel guilty or "bad" about it. Part of the reason we get angry at ourselves is because we believe, "I could have done something different". However, it is important to understand that our words and actions are chosen based on the thoughts that we have and believe at the moment of choice. Therefore, when we claim, "I could have done something different", we are actually believing "I could have had and believed different thoughts in the moment of choice". But that is not possible.

If we chose a specific action, it can only be because our thoughts made us believe this action was our "best" option in the moment of choice. Our thoughts made us believe that the consequences of this action were "better" than those of the alternative action. Any time we think we would have done something different in the past, it can only be because the thoughts that we have and believe in this moment are different from the thoughts we had and believed in the moment when we chose our actions. In other words, we are choosing an action in the past based on our thoughts in this moment, and essentially saying, "Based on the thoughts I have now, I would have done something different".

But, if our thoughts about our possible choices of action are different in this moment than they were in the moment of choice, something must have happened during the elapsed time to change our thoughts about the situation. For example, we may now know that our actions produced an undesirable outcome, we might have different interests now, or we might care about different things now. But any changes to our thoughts about our options couldn't have happened without the elapsed time. Without the elapsed time, our thoughts wouldn't have changed, and we therefore couldn't have valued our options differently from the way we did in the moment of choice.

For example, we often think we could have done something different than we did because we now know what the outcome is. But how could we have had the thoughts we do now before we were made aware of the outcome? Therefore, how could we have made a different choice of action?

The nice thing about this is that if we couldn't have done anything differently than we did, then we can stop feeling guilty or angry at ourselves for our choice of action.

While we couldn't have done anything different from what we did, we *can* choose to do something different the next time we are in a similar situation. In order to do this, we need to figure out what thoughts caused us to act the way we did, see whether we still believe these thoughts, and then question whether these thoughts are true. If we disbelieve the thoughts that caused our actions, we are much more likely to act differently when we are in a similar situation in the future.

The Questions: Am I absolutely certain I could have done something different considering the thoughts I had and believed at the moment of choice? Am I sure that I could have had and believed different thoughts in the moment of choice? If I wish that I had chosen a different action, mustn't that be because I now have thoughts that are different from the thoughts I had at the moment of choice? Am I sure I could have acted differently considering that I didn't know what the effect of my actions would be at the moment of choice? If I now value my options differently, mustn't it be because something has happened in the elapsed time that has changed the way I view the situation? Am I absolutely sure that I could have acted differently in the past without this elapsed time to have changed my thoughts about the situation? – What thoughts caused me to act the way I did? Am I sure those thoughts are true?

Chapter Fifteen

Questions to Disbelieve Your Idea of How Things Should Be

Over the course of our lives we have learned many concepts about what are the "right" actions, words, and situations. The "right" way is very often referred to as "the way things should be" or "the way things should have been". Since we constantly compare life to our idea of the "right" way, it's very common for us to think or say, "Something shouldn't be the way it is", "Something shouldn't have happened the way it did", "Something different should have happened", or "Something should be different".

We tend to have many ideas about how people should act, what people should say, and what everyone's situation should be. Let's look at some of the concepts we have about what is the "right" way: "I should move out of my parents' house by 23", "I should have a steady job by 25", "I should be married by 30", "I should have children by 35", "I should be sad at a funeral", "I should be grateful", "I should be happy", "I should love my parents", "I should talk to my partner on the phone every day", "I should cook for my husband every night", "I should go to all my children's sports games", "I should love my children", "My children should love me", "I should be in good shape", "I should eat healthily", "He should respect me", "He should listen to me", "He should appreciate me", "She should be honest", "She should be nice", "She should say 'thank you'". All of these concepts basically make up our own set of rules for life.

As we know, when something in our life doesn't conform to how we think it should be, or when we don't do what we think we should do, then we often think, "I shouldn't have done that", or "My life shouldn't be like this". These thoughts then create our guilt, shame, sadness, feelings of unworthiness, and disappointment with ourselves. Of course, when someone else breaks one of our unwritten rules and doesn't act or live how we believe they should, then we get angry at them or feel disappointed with them.

"Should" thoughts create intense suffering

Our concepts of the "right" way or "the way things should be" are different from our other concepts of "best", "perfect", and "good". If the "best" action or outcome is a "10" on a scale of "1 to 10", then any other way can be considered anything from a "1" to "9". The "worse" it is, the lower the number on our scale, and the stronger our emotional response.

On the other hand, when we don't do the "right" thing, someone else doesn't do the "right" thing, our situation isn't "right", or an outcome isn't "right", then by nature, we must believe the circumstance is "wrong". The "right" way is a "10" on a scale of "1 to 10", and any other way is "wrong", which is a "1" on a scale of "1 to 10". There is nothing in between. Any time we think a certain action, comment, situation, or outcome is not "right", then we view it as "wrong", and this can create intense suffering. Therefore, when we think, "I shouldn't have done that", "He shouldn't do that to me", "I shouldn't be in this situation", "I shouldn't be like this", or "This shouldn't have happened", we tend to experience strong anger, sadness, or shame.

To take it a step further, sometimes, when we think, "Something shouldn't be the way it already is" or "Something should be different", we are really saying, "This wasn't supposed to happen" or "It isn't supposed to be this way". This means that we not only believe, "This is the *wrong* outcome", but also that "There was a *mistake*" or "There was some kind of *error* by the universe". We generally don't realize this is what we are believing, nor do we realize how strong a statement this is.

When we say, "Something shouldn't be the way it is" in this way, we are not saying, "I want it to be different", or "I wish it were different", we are saying, "The way it is (or was), is *wrong*, and it was a *mistake*". If someone told us, "Two plus two equals three", then we would say, "The answer shouldn't be three" or "The answer should be four". This doesn't mean, "I don't want the answer to be three". It means we believe, "Three is a *mistake*, you made an *error*, that was the *wrong* answer. Four is the *right* answer". In the same way, if we sign a contract with a painter to paint our house red, and he paints it blue, we will say, "You shouldn't have painted it blue, you weren't supposed to paint it blue. The house should be red". By this, we aren't saying, "I want it to be red", we mean, "You made a *mistake*, you did it *wrong*", or "A red house would be *right*".

Now that it is clear how the thought "it shouldn't be like this" can mean "this is a *mistake*", let's look at how this thought tends to create suffering for us. For example, if we just found out that our partner has been diagnosed with cancer, our emotional reaction will be based on what thoughts we have about it. If we think, "This is going to be really bad for her, I wish she didn't have to go through this", then we will likely experience sadness. However, if we think, "This shouldn't have happened to her! She is a generous and kind woman", then we are likely to feel anger and a sense of injustice in addition to our sadness from believing the situation is "bad" for her.

When we think, "This shouldn't have happened to her", we are essentially believing, "The universe has made some kind of *mistake*, this wasn't supposed to happen to her". We may think this event was a mistake because we believe our partner doesn't *deserve* to get cancer or just because we *expected* to live a comfortable life together. But regardless of why we believe, "Something shouldn't be the way it is", when we believe that the way things are in our life is a mistake, this thought often creates anger, a feeling of injustice, and confusion, in addition to whatever sadness we may be feeling from not wanting things to be the way they are.

When we act based on how we think we should, we suffer

Not only are our emotions caused by thoughts, but so are the vast majority of our actions and life decisions. Most of us unknowingly choose to live and act how we believe we should because we either believe it is the "right way", we don't want to suffer from thinking, "I shouldn't have done that" and "My life shouldn't be like this", we want others to approve of us, or we fear that others will disapprove of us if we don't live how we should.

When we live life according to what we think we should do, we are following our society's decision about what is the "right" thing to do. If what we think we should do also happens to be what feels true to us, then this doesn't create any suffering. But if we do what we think we should do even if it doesn't feel that we are being true to ourselves, then this often leads to a lot of unhappiness. If we choose our career, our partner, where to live, our actions, or our words based on what we think we should do, then we aren't being true to ourselves. We aren't living life in a way that aligns with what feels true and natural for us. Instead, we are living based on what we think is "right", what our culture has told us is "right". When we aren't acting how it feels natural for us to live, we are living life in conflict with ourselves. There is very little satisfaction in this type of life. Our life doesn't seem to flow naturally. Instead, it is often filled with internal conflict, friction, boredom, and a lot of tiring effort.

32.   Can I be absolutely sure that the way I think it should be is the "right" way, and not just *A* way?

Are all of our concepts about how we should act and live really the "right" way to act and live? If we take a step back, it is possible to see that all of our ideas about how we should act and live are really all just *A* way to act and live. No actions, words, or ways to live are inherently "right". Our actions, words, and situations are just our actions, words, and situations. End of story. But that's not where we stop. Each individual mind then believes a thought that says, "This is right, or "This is wrong", and "He shouldn't have done that", or "He should have done that". But these are just perspectives.

People act in all sorts of different ways and live in a wide variety of situations. Our concept about what is the "right" way was formed by our culture, economic status, and unique life experiences. People with different backgrounds can always disagree with our decision about how life should be. In some cultures, you should have children when you are young, while in other cultures, this would be considered a mistake or a "bad" decision. In some cultures, you should live with your parents, while in others you are considered a failure if you live with your parents. In some regions, women should cook for their husbands, yet in other regions this is considered to be demeaning or oppressive. In some cultures, people believe that you should have a high-paying, prestigious job, whereas in others you are considered to be confused if you value money and prestige over enjoyment and happiness.

When we begin to discover that there is no "right" way to live and act, then we can stop feeling ashamed about how we are, stop getting angry at others for how they are, and be free to do what feels right and true to us. We can take the job we enjoy over the job we think we should take, pick the girl we love instead of the girl we think we should date, we can do what we enjoy instead of doing what we think we should be doing. We can finally be ourselves. And that is a much easier and more liberating way to live life.

The Questions: Am I sure that there is a way people should act and live, or is this just a perspective? Could someone else disagree with how I believe I should act and live? If so, can I be completely sure this is how I should act or live? Is it true that there is a way people should act and live and that this is the "right" way, or is it possible that this way is just *A* way to act and live?

33. Is it true that something shouldn't be the way it is just because it doesn't match my expectations?

We tend to form assumptions about the future (expectations), and when the future doesn't go according to plan, we think, "This shouldn't have happened". We may think, "I am going to be married to this man for my whole life", "My child will grow up to be successful", "It is going to be sunny for my party tomorrow", "I will be married by the time I am 30", "I will make it to my appointment early", "My husband will clean the dishes tonight", or "My son will be home by midnight". We may think these statements are true and expect these future events to happen in these ways because it seems that we have great reasoning or strong evidence to support our statements. For example, we may think, "My husband vowed to stay married until death do us part, so I will be married to him my whole life", "My husband and I are both successful, so my child will be successful", "The weather forecast said no chance of rain, so it will be sunny for my party", "I am smart and attractive, so I will be married by the time I'm 30", "It normally takes 20 minutes to get to my appointment and I gave myself 30 minutes, so I will make it to my appointment early", "My husband promised me he would clean the dishes, so he will", and "The rules are that my son needs to be home by midnight, so he will".

But if the outcome doesn't turn out as we expected, we generally don't think, "I guess I was wrong". Rather, we often end up thinking, "He shouldn't have divorced me", "My child shouldn't be like this", "It shouldn't be raining", "I should be married by now", "It shouldn't have taken me an hour to get there", "He should have cleaned the dishes", and "He shouldn't have broken the curfew". These thoughts can then create anger, frustration, despair, or sadness.

When any outcome doesn't turn out as we expect, we often think, "This shouldn't have happened", "Things should be different", or "This wasn't supposed to happen". As previously stated, this means we are believing, "There has been a mistake, some kind of error, this is the wrong outcome". We think the universe made a mistake because life (reality) conflicted with our belief about how life would be. What actually happened (the facts) conflicted with what we thought would happen. *In other words, when life turns out differently from the way we expected it to, we think, "life should have gone according to my expectations".*

Any time we form an expectation, it is because we have a few pieces of evidence that lead us to believe that a certain outcome is likely. However, no matter how many pieces of evidence we have to suggest that a certain outcome will happen, there will always be other factors or variables that play a part in determining whether the expected outcome will actually happen.

Is a vow to be married until death the only factor involved in whether a couple stays married? Are successful parents the only factor in determining whether a child ends up successful? Does the weather forecaster know all of the factors involved in whether it will rain? Are intelligence and attractiveness the only factors that determine whether someone will get married by 30? Does knowing the normal duration of a trip take into account all of the factors that determine how long a trip will take? Is a promise from our husband the only factor that determines whether he will actually clean the dishes? Is a rule (curfew) the only factor that determines whether our son will be home by midnight? Clearly not. Couples get sick of each other, parenting without giving enough love and attention could have unwanted effects, a rain storm could come out of no-where, someone just may not find the right person to marry, an accident could cause a lot of traffic, our husband could change his mind or forget, and our child could choose to break the rules.

When we have an expectation, it is really just a guess about the future based on the limited information we have. If we wanted to bet on who would win a basketball game, we would analyze all the statistics available to us. If we chose Team A to win and they end up losing, our guess was wrong. We were wrong. The statistics don't take into consideration whether an important player has a "bad" game. If we then say Team B shouldn't have won, we are saying, "Life was wrong, my guess was right". Clearly, this is not the case. Our guess could not take into account all of the factors or variables involved in determining what the outcome would be.

Any time an outcome conflicts with our expectations, it is proof that there were factors or variables that we didn't consider. If we knew all of the factors that determined an outcome, we would always guess the outcome correctly. In fact, we wouldn't even be guessing. No matter how many factors we take into consideration, if an outcome conflicts with our expectation, there must have been other factors that we did not consider. If our logic and reasoning took into account all of the factors involved (and were unflawed), then life would have matched our expectation.

When we have an expectation, we are believing that we know the future despite the fact that it is only a guess. That is no big deal. But to then believe that "life should have gone according to my guess" is clearly not true and can create a lot of anger, frustration, self-pity, and confusion in our lives.

If we can just admit, "My guess (expectation) turned out to be wrong", then we are admitting, "It is not true that life shouldn't be the way it is". Once we see this, we instantly lose the anger, frustration, self-pity, and confusion that our "should" thought had been causing.

The Questions: What do I think shouldn't be the way it is (should be different)? Has life conflicted with my expectations (how I thought life would be)? What was my evidence to suggest life would turn out according to my expectations? Did my evidence take into account every factor and variable that would play a part in determining what would actually happen? Or, was my expectation just a guess about what would happen based on limited information (not knowing all the variables)? Considering that the outcome didn't turn out as I expected, is it more likely that the universe made an error, that this is the wrong outcome, and that life shouldn't be the way it is, or just that my guess was wrong? If life turned out differently from the way I expected, isn't it true that there must have been factors that I didn't consider as part of my guess (expectation)? Am I sure that the way life is (reality), is wrong, and that the universe made a mistake, because life should have gone according to my expectations?

34. If I know what is true and factual, then doesn't that mean any opposing thought must not be true?

When we believe, "Something shouldn't be the way it is", we aren't thinking, "I would like things to be different", we are claiming, "The way it is, is *wrong*". The way it is, is a fact, otherwise known as reality or what's true. If we claim, "The way it is, is wrong", we are unknowingly claiming, "What's true is wrong", or "Reality is wrong". We know what is true, but yet we believe a thought that says, "What is true is not true", or "What is true is a mistake". *But clearly, any thought that opposes what we know to be true and factual can only be untrue.* Please take a moment to fully digest that.

We would think it to be ridiculous if someone were to say, "Grass should be purple", "The sun shouldn't have come up this morning", "The sky shouldn't be blue", "Trees should grow sideways", "Dogs shouldn't bark", "Two plus two shouldn't equal four", or "Fire shouldn't burn paper". Don't all of these statements seem clearly illogical? Each of them would be very difficult to believe because each of them claims, "The way it is, is wrong". But, *the truth is that these statements are fundamentally the same as all of our normal "should" thoughts.*

For example, we may think, "People shouldn't lie", "I shouldn't still be in this job", "My child should be married by now", or "He shouldn't have yelled at me". But what's the truth? Do people lie? Are you still in this job? Is your child married? Did he yell at you? The truth is very clear. But even though *we know what the truth is*, we very often argue with it and claim, "It shouldn't be this way", which means we are believing, "The way it is, is wrong" or "the truth is wrong".

So what's the difference? Why do we believe our "should" thoughts? It is mostly because we don't realize that we are believing what is true to be "wrong". Since we don't realize that we are believing, "What is true, is wrong", we don't investigate our thought "Something shouldn't be the way it is". If someone came up to you and said, "I know that all grass is green, but grass should be purple", then the first question you would ask them would be, "What is your evidence?" But even if they show you a hundred great reasons why grass should be purple, those reasons can't be enough to prove, "Grass should be purple". If their reasons were sufficient, then grass would be purple. But since it's not, their statement "Grass should be purple" must not be true.

Since we don't realize what we are believing, when it comes to our own thoughts, we don't ask ourselves for evidence. It is therefore easy to keep unknowingly believing thoughts that claim, "Something shouldn't be the way it is", or "What's true is wrong". But now that we see what we are believing, we can simply ask ourselves the next logical question, "What evidence do I have to prove that the way things are is wrong?", "What is my evidence that the wrong outcome happened?" or "What is my evidence that someone acted in the wrong way?"

We may think that we have "great" reasons as to why "something shouldn't be the way it is" or "someone shouldn't have acted the way they did", but if we look at the situation more carefully, the real question is, "Can any reason really be sufficient to prove 'reality is wrong' or 'what's true is wrong'?"

For example, if we think, "My husband shouldn't be mean to me", then the first question we can ask ourselves is, "Is he mean to me?" If the answer is "yes" and he is mean, then what we are really believing is, "I know that he is mean, but he shouldn't be mean", which is the same as, "I know that all grass is green, but it shouldn't be green".

So then we ask ourselves, "How do I know that he shouldn't be mean? What evidence do I have to prove he shouldn't be mean?" Our answer may be, "I want him to be nice", "We would both be happier if he was nice", or "I am nice to him so I deserve to be treated nicely".

If "I want him to be nice" was a sufficient reason for him to be nice, then he would be nice. If the statement "we would both be happier if he was nice" was enough of a reason to make him act nicely towards us, then he would be nice to us. If "I am nice to him so I deserve to be treated nicely" was enough of a reason to make him treat us nicely, then he would treat us nicely.

But since he is not nice, clearly our reasons aren't sufficient to make it true that "he should be nice" or "he shouldn't be mean". It is not as though "he shouldn't be mean" and "it is wrong that he is mean", the truth is just that "he is mean" and "I don't want him to be mean".

Is it true that people should act how we want them to act? People act how they act. If we believe people "should act how I want them to act", we are guaranteed to suffer. *People often don't know how we believe they should act; it is not their job to act how we believe they should act; they may disagree with how we believe they should act; and they may not be able to act how we believe they should even if they really wanted to.* Just because we want people to act in a certain way, or we think that everyone would be happier if people acted in a certain way, that doesn't mean that people will or should act in these ways.

If we had a sufficient reason as to why life should be a certain way, then life would be that way. If life isn't the way we think it should be, then that can only be because our reasons aren't sufficient to make life that way. *The bottom line is, no matter how much evidence our thoughts can come up with to prove reality is wrong ("something shouldn't be the way it is"), we can't prove that what we know to be true is actually wrong or a mistake.* If we are just able to acknowledge this, and admit that it isn't it true that "something shouldn't be the way it is", then we can lose a large portion of our suffering in life.

The Questions: What do I think shouldn't be the way it is (should be different)? What is true and factual? If I know what is true and factual, then doesn't that mean any opposing thought must be untrue? If I can see, hear, and touch what is true, then doesn't any thought that claims, "The facts are wrong", have to be untrue? How do I know something shouldn't be the way it is? What is my evidence to prove that a situation, outcome, action, or other circumstance is wrong and shouldn't be the way it is or was? Can any evidence truly be sufficient to prove that the facts are wrong? Is it true that life should be a certain way (people should act in a certain way), or is this just how I want life to be? Is life how I want it to be? Is it true that life shouldn't be the way it is just because I don't want it to be this way?

Chapter Sixteen

Step 5: Question the Validity of Any Reason to Continue Suffering

Our minds often resist the present moment

When we start to engage with The 5 Steps to The Present Moment, our minds often resist this shift. We like to remain in familiar territory, even if the familiar is suffering. In order to prevent us from disbelieving our thoughts and becoming present, our minds often create an idea for why it "would be bad" to lose our emotion, or why some aspect of our life "would be worse" if we disbelieved one of our thoughts. Even though we know that the thought we are questioning has caused us to suffer, our minds can easily trick us into believing that suffering is "better" than the alternative. Often, the longer we have had a specific thought or emotion, the more resistance we have to giving it up because we have become more familiar with living with that thought or emotion. These "resistance thoughts", the ones that try to keep us suffering, can be very strong, and often very hidden and subtle.

For this reason, no matter how much we want to be happy, sometimes we will not want to disbelieve the thoughts that create our suffering. However, all of the reasons our minds provide to keep us from disbelieving our thoughts are all just more thoughts. This means that we can disbelieve our resistance thoughts in the same way we do all of our other thoughts. In this chapter and the next, there are 13 different questions/sections to help you stop believing the most common forms of resistance.

If you don't have any resistance to letting go of the thought or emotion that you have been questioning, then there is no need to read these chapters right now. However, it would still be useful to read through all of the sections at some point just so that you are familiar with the different resistance tricks that your mind may use in the future to try to keep you suffering.

On the other hand, if you have experienced some resistance, then instead of just reading through these two chapters, you can jump ahead to the questions that are relevant to you. The first two questions in this chapter can be applied to any resistance thought, the rest of the sections in this chapter are for disbelieving common reasons to keep specific emotions, and the sections in the next chapter are for disbelieving common reasons to not question your thoughts. You can choose to mentally answer the questions in each section or you may find it more helpful to write down your answers. Here is a list of the sections:

Chapter 16

1.   Is it true that life would be "worse" if I disbelieved the thought that creates my suffering?
2.   If my emotion is created by a thought, then how would I feel and act without this thought?
3.   "Anger and sadness help me to get what I want"
4.   "I am bad if I don't get sad"
5.   "I should feel guilty for what I did"
6.   "My anxiety and stress are helpful"
7.   "Worrying is helpful, responsible, and means I care"

Chapter 17

8.   "I want to keep blaming others for my suffering"

9.   "I don't want to admit 'I don't know' or 'I was wrong'"

10.   "If I don't see certain actions as bad, I will act in hurtful ways"

11.   "Disbelieving 'this should be different' or 'this is bad' will prevent me from acting towards positive change"

12.   "If I don't see my situation as bad, then this bad situation will remain the same and I will be settling" or "If I see that my goal can't make me happy, then I won't have any motivation to achieve it"

13.   "My 'should' thought helps me to act how I believe I should, which has a positive effect on my life and the lives of others"

1.   Is it true that life would be "worse" if I disbelieved the thought that creates my suffering?

If we are about to try to disbelieve our fantasy, our minds may stop us with the thought "I won't achieve my goal if I admit it won't make me happy". If we start to see that the thoughts that create our anxiety might not be true, our minds might tell us, "I won't put in effort towards my goal if I don't have anxiety". If we want to stop feeling angry at someone, our minds may prevent us from questioning our thoughts by telling us, "If I stop blaming him, I am letting him off the hook". If part of our identity is, "I am a woman who was treated badly by my parents", then we may have resistance to disbelieving the thought that our parents were "bad" and that they were to blame for our suffering because we are scared to lose our identity as the victim.

However, any idea that some aspect of our life "would be worse" if we disbelieve a thought is just an idea. If we never experienced living without the thought, how can we possibly know that some aspect of our life would be "worse" without the thought? It is pretty clear that we can't know. Our idea that something "would be worse" is created in our minds without any factual or experiential basis behind it. The idea is created out of nothing. Therefore, any time our minds say, "If you see this thought isn't true then ... something bad will happen", it is worth questioning whether that thought itself is true.

The Questions: Do I know with absolute certainty that some aspect of my life will be "worse", or something "bad" will happen, if I identify or disbelieve my thought? How can I know for sure that life would be "worse" or that something "bad" will happen without this thought, considering that I have no evidence, since I have never lived life without this thought? Am I absolutely sure that this thought prevents something "bad" from happening or helps me get what I want?

2.   If my emotion is created by a thought, then how would I feel and act without this thought?

There is no need to try to make the decision as to whether you want to apply The 5 Steps to every emotion or every thought you ever have in the future. There is no need to try to figure out how The 5 Steps apply to everyone and everything. There is no need to try to guess what all of the implications are of The 5 Steps. This is not about questioning all of our thoughts, beliefs, and opinions in life. It's not about drastically changing our life at all. The only relevant questions are those that apply to the thought that's taking our attention right now: "Does this thought create suffering for me? Do I want to keep suffering?" That's it.

Any other thought is just a guess about the future, a guess about cause and effect. If we disbelieve a thought that creates suffering for us right now, then we are happier right now. That's all there is to it. This is just about giving us the option to be happy instead of suffering in any moment that we want to be happy.

The Questions: Is it true that my thought won't create suffering as long as I don't admit that I have it? How do I feel when I think the thought? How do I treat myself and others when I believe this thought? How would I feel without the thought? How much freer and happier would I be in the situations where these thoughts normally arise? How much more lovingly could I treat others and look at others without this thought? How much easier would it be to avoid my "bad" habits without this thought? How much nicer would it be to just be happy now instead of having to put in all the time, money, and energy trying to make everything in life "perfect" in the hope that it might one day give me momentary happiness? If I know that the thought I am believing creates suffering, and I want happiness more than anything else, then wouldn't I want to disbelieve the thought? Do I want to be happy or do I want to suffer? Do I want to treat others with love or with hate?

3. "Anger and sadness help me to get what I want"

We may not want to disbelieve the thoughts that create our anger and sadness because we think these emotions help us to get what we want from others. When we were children and didn't get what we wanted, we would cry to get our parents to give it to us. Not only did crying often get us what we wanted, but it also got us love and attention. This created the unconscious belief in us that sadness can be used to manipulate others into giving us what we want. When our parents asked or told us nicely to stop playing or to clean our room, and we didn't listen, then they would choose to yell and get angry at us. Our parents' anger scared us into doing what they wanted us to do. This naturally taught us that anger will help us to get what we want from others.

We have taken these strategies we learned as children and brought them into our adult life. We use these emotions as tools to manipulate others to give us what we want. Anger provokes others to do what we want by making them feel guilty or by making them fear what we will think, say, or do to them. When we tell someone they have done something "bad", and they believe it, they may feel guilty about their actions, which can provoke them to change their actions. If we get angry at our wife for not picking up the children from school on time, she may feel guilty about her actions and try harder not to do it again. Others may do what we want because they fear that we might stop loving them or that we might verbally abuse them, leave them, or fire them.

In the same way, sadness can get others to do what we want because they do not want to see us sad or do not want to feel responsible for our sadness.

Both of these emotions, anger and sadness, can provide enough incentive to get others to do what we want. However, these strategies have overstayed their welcome. There are a few major reasons why it doesn't make sense to hold on to these emotions and not try to question them.

a)   We don't want to lose our anger and sadness because we believe they help us to get what we want from others. However, we only care about getting what we want from others because we believe doing so will make us happy. Therefore, we are actually saying, "I want to hold onto my anger/sadness because I think it will help me to become happy", or more succinctly, "anger/sadness will make me happy". This is clearly not the best strategy for happiness. If we question our thoughts, we will experience happiness right now instead of anger and sadness. It wouldn't make much sense not to question our thoughts just so that we can remain angry, which we think might help us to get what we want in the future, which we think might eventually bring us some momentary happiness. Instead of all this, we can take the shortcut and be happy right now by simply questioning the thoughts that create our anger and sadness.

b)   Anger and sadness are often not as effective as loving and nice behavior are in helping us get what we want from others, especially in the long-term. Anger may get someone to do what we want through creating fear or guilt, but since people don't want to feel afraid or guilty, this approach often makes people feel resentment towards us. The more we treat others with anger, the more resentment they will have towards us, and the more likely it is that they will treat us "badly" and not do what we want them to.

Similarly, acting sad may get others to do things for us, or get us love and attention, but it often does not give us the type of attention we want, and it often doesn't work in the long-term, because others will not want to be around us. Not only does nice behavior work more often, but the people around us will be happier and will and like us more, which will make them more likely to do what we want in the long-term (rather than just right now) and give us the love that we want.

c)   When we manipulate others into doing something they don't want to do, they resent us for it. If others do what we want instead of what they want, they expect to get something in return. This is the overwhelming dynamic of relationships: "I will give up something for you, but then I expect you to give up something for me". If we use anger or sadness to manipulate our partner into doing chores for us, missing work for us, giving up money for us, missing a big party, picking up the children, or coming to an event they don't want to come to, then they will think the relationship is unfair unless we sacrifice something for them in return. If we do nothing in return for our partner, their feeling of unfairness will grow. Our partner will think, "I have sacrificed for him, I have missed out on things I wanted to do, I gave my time for him, but he hasn't sacrificed anything for me. This isn't fair". This belief that our relationship is unfair creates a lot of resentment in relationships.

Manipulation is not an honest or a loving way to deal with the people we love, and it causes them to feel a lot of resentment. If we want something from someone and ask them nicely for it, but they don't want to do it, then we can either choose to respect their interests, or we can choose to put our own happiness above theirs and manipulate them to do what we want. Once we understand that our manipulation of others is based on pure selfishness, this can help us to stop using anger and sadness to manipulate others.

The Questions: Is the decision to keep my anger/sadness because I think it may help get me what I want, which might give me momentary happiness, the most effective way to make myself happy? Doesn't my anger help to create fear and guilt in others, which causes animosity towards me, and therefore makes it less likely for me to get what I want from others in the long-term? Does my sadness make others want to spend time with me and give me the type of attention that I want? When I manipulate others into doing something they don't want to do, don't they feel unhappy and resentful towards me? Do I want to put my happiness above others' happiness and manipulate people into doing what I want, or can I just allow others to do what makes them happy?

4. "I am bad if I don't get sad"

Even when we don't want to experience sadness, the idea of disbelieving the thoughts that create our sadness is often met with some resistance. We have been trained to believe that the amount of sadness we experience reflects how much we care about the victim of something "bad". When we feel sad for someone, it really seems as if we feel sad because we love the victim and we care about them. Therefore, when it comes to issues like death, injury, or sickness, we believe that sadness is the "right" response and that the intensity of our sadness signifies how much we care about the victim. Naturally, this makes us believe that not feeling sad would mean we don't care about the victim and that we are selfish, inconsiderate, or a "bad" person. This belief can prevent us from questioning the thoughts that create our sadness, and it can therefore prevent us from being happy and from being true to ourselves.

However, the amount of sadness we feel in reaction to death, injuries, sickness, or anything else actually has nothing to do with how much we care about the victim. Our degree of sadness only reflects how "bad" we believe the event or outcome is. If our son gets sick, he may be happy that he gets to miss school, but we may be sad because we think, "It is bad to be sick". If our friend breaks his leg in a car accident, he may be happy and relieved that he didn't get more severely injured, whereas we might be sad because we think, "It is terrible to have to deal with a broken leg". Does our son not care about himself? Does our friend not care about himself?

Clearly, both our son and our friend probably care quite a bit about themselves. If they care about themselves, but yet aren't sad about their situations, then it is clear that our sadness does not reflect how much we care about the victim. Regardless of whether the victim is sad or happy, we would only experience sadness if we believe a thought that says, "Their situation is bad", not because of a thought that says, "I care about them".

If we see someone fall on their face on the sidewalk, we will feel sad if we think, "That really sucks for them", whereas we might laugh if we didn't have this thought. Regardless of whether the person is a stranger or the love of our life, we can laugh or feel sad. We know that our sadness isn't a reflection of how much we love the victim, because we could feel sad for a stranger and laugh at someone we love when they fall. Sadness is not a sign that we care, but only a sign that we are believing a thought that says, "This is bad".

When there's a widespread belief that a certain event—like injury, sickness, or death—is "bad", it seems that everyone reacts with sadness. This leads us to believe that sadness is the "right" or "appropriate" response and that all other responses are "wrong" or "inappropriate". But just because most people react in one way doesn't mean that any other reaction is "worse". If we are happy when a family member is sick, then we are happy. End of story. Any decision that our happiness is "wrong" or "inappropriate" is just a perspective, a concept that only exists in our minds. It is not as though "being happy is wrong", we just have a thought about this happiness that claims, "It is wrong".

When someone in our life is sad about an event, we think that it is a nice gesture to show that we are sad for them, and we believe that this is the "right" thing to do. If we believe that it is "wrong", selfish, or inconsiderate to be happy in certain situations, then we may actually choose to continue suffering over being happy. But is it really selfish or inconsiderate to be happy in any situation? What is the actual effect of being sad around someone? Does our sadness really help anyone?

Let's examine a scenario in which our friend is sad because her boyfriend breaks up with her. If she believes, "Sadness means you care about me", then showing sadness to her might make her feel cared about, which may give her a little happiness.

However, there are a few other effects as well. If she is sad, this means she believes, "It is bad that he broke up with me". If we show her that we are sad about the event, we are essentially telling her, "I agree with you that this event is bad", which reaffirms her belief that "this event is bad", and therefore perpetuates her sadness. If she sees that we are sad for her, she might feel "bad" that she made us sad. In addition, our sadness can cause her opinion of herself to "worsen" because she may think, "They all feel bad for me and think I am a poor little victim". On balance, our sadness is not helpful to our friend. If we want to show our friend that we care about her, all we have to do is tell her that we care, listen to her, spend time with her, compliment her, and offer to help her in any way she needs. This allows us to be happy and helps our friend to become happy too.

It can certainly seem as if being happy when others are suffering is inconsiderate; however, acting selfishly or inconsiderately would be to act in a way that benefits ourselves while hurting others. However unnatural or "wrong" it may feel to be happy when others are suffering, it is important to recognize that our happiness does not negatively affect anyone else. On the contrary, if we can disbelieve the thoughts that make us unhappy, we are far more likely to be helping the victim to become happier. Therefore, there is truly nothing selfish or inconsiderate about being happy.

The Questions: Could I feel sad for someone even when they aren't sad about what happened to themselves? Wouldn't the victim care more about themselves than I care about them? Could I feel sad for someone I have never met? If I can feel sad for a victim I don't know, when that victim might not be sad about what happened to themselves, is sadness truly a reflection of how much a person cares about a victim? Can I be absolutely sure that a lack of sadness is "bad", "wrong", or "inappropriate"? Could someone else have a different perspective? Is it true that my sadness is helpful or that my happiness would be hurting someone? If not, then is it true that it is selfish or inconsiderate to feel happy?

5.   "I should feel guilty for what I did"

There is often a lot of resistance to questioning the thoughts that create our guilt. However, just as with all of our other emotions, there is no honest reason to keep feeling guilty. Here are a few of the main reasons why it isn't worthwhile to keep our guilt.

a)   We tend to look at guilt as if it is our punishment for the suffering we inflicted upon ourselves or someone else. If we think we did something "bad" or caused someone else to suffer, then it seems that it would be fair for us to experience guilt (suffer) in return. However, there are a few major flaws with this argument.

Our feeling of guilt is an uninvestigated assumption that what we did was "bad", the outcome was "bad", we are to blame for the "bad" outcome (and had full control), we are to blame for the victim's unwanted emotions (not their own thoughts), we deserve to be punished, punishing ourselves would make life more "fair", we know what the "fair" punishment is, and it is our job to enforce the "fair" punishment upon ourselves. Can we be absolutely certain of any of these assumptions, let alone all of them? These are some pretty difficult assumptions and decisions to make, but yet we make them and choose to feel guilty without giving it much thought at all.

b)   We tend to believe that "the more guilt I feel, the more I care about the victim". This belief actually makes us feel as if we are a "good" or "better" person for feeling guilty about what we did. If we didn't feel guilty, we may think, "Not only am I respon-sible for something bad, but I am a terrible person for not even feeling guilty about it". Feeling guilty is created by believing a thought that says, "The action or outcome was bad, and I am to blame". The amount of guilt we feel has nothing to do with how much we care about the victim.

If you are driving your child to school, and you get into a car accident that breaks your child's arm, would you feel guilty? It depends on your thoughts about what happened. If you believe, "The outcome was bad", and "I am to blame", then you would feel incredibly guilty. However, if you think, "The outcome was bad, but I wasn't to blame at all" because another driver cut you off out of nowhere, then you would feel no guilt. Similarly, if you think, "I am to blame for the accident, but I don't think the outcome was bad at all, I am so glad he wasn't hurt more", then you wouldn't feel guilty about it.

If the feeling of guilt reflected how much we cared about our child, then we would feel the same amount of guilt in each scenario. Each of these three scenarios has the same outcome, with the same love and care for our child, yet in two of them we feel no guilt. The only difference is a thought that says, "I am to blame" and a thought that says, "This outcome is bad". Therefore, guilt has nothing to do with how much we care about someone and everything to do with the thoughts we believe. Feeling no guilt after a seemingly "bad" action or outcome doesn't mean we don't care about the victim or that we are a "bad" person, it only means that we aren't believing thoughts that say, "This outcome is bad" and "I am to blame".

c)   We tend to think that feeling guilt will teach us not to do the same thing again. However, no matter how guilty we feel about our words or actions, guilt often doesn't help to prevent us from acting in the same "bad", hurtful, or unloving ways again. If we feel guilty, then our attention is on thoughts about how an action or outcome was "bad" and how we are to blame. The reason that guilt doesn't help to prevent us from acting the same way again is because these thoughts do not help us to see what caused us to act the way we did.

One of the most helpful things we can do when we do something "bad" or hurtful is to question why we did it. We can ask ourselves honestly, "What caused me to act the way I did? What was I thinking in that moment when I chose to act how I did? Why did my choice of actions seem like a good choice at the time?" Then we can question the validity of the thoughts that caused us to act in hurtful or unloving ways towards ourselves or others.

For example, if we yelled at our husband for not cleaning up after himself, then we might feel guilty about it afterward. Despite our guilt, we may yell at him over and over again every time he does this. If we ask ourselves, "What am I thinking when I yell at him?", we might recognize that we are thinking, "He doesn't respect me, he doesn't care about me; he would clean up after himself if he did". Once we see this thought, we might be able to recognize that our anger and actions towards our husband are reactions to these thoughts rather than to his actions. If we question these thoughts, we can notice that they are just interpretations that we don't know are true. As soon as we disbelieve these thoughts, our anger will subside, and we are much less likely to feel this anger when we are in the same situation again. Questioning the thoughts that cause our actions allows us to act differently if a similar scenario were to arise again in the future.

The Questions:

a) Am I absolutely certain that the action was "bad", the outcome was "bad", and I am to blame for it? Is it true that I am responsible for the thoughts that create others' emotions? Considering that our guilt doesn't help to change the past or help eliminate the victim's unwanted emotions, am I absolutely sure that I am making the situation more fair by punishing myself? Am I the decider of what is a fair punishment in this world? Am I truly the enforcer of fairness in this world?

b) Could I not feel guilty about hurting someone I love if I was thankful that the outcome wasn't "worse" or if I believed I wasn't to blame for it? If it is possible for me not to feel guilty about a "bad" outcome I created for someone I love, is it true that the amount of guilt I feel reflects how much I care about the victim? Is it true that I am "bad" for not feeling guilty, considering that my guilt doesn't help anyone and doesn't reflect whether I care about the victim?

c) Have I ever felt guilty about a "bad" action in the past but yet kept doing it over and over again? Does my guilt address the thoughts that caused me to act the way I did? Is it true that feeling guilty truly helps to prevent me from acting in the same "bad" way again?

d) What thoughts was I thinking (or trying to escape from) in the moment that I chose to commit my "bad" action? Can I be absolutely sure that these thoughts are true?

6.   "My anxiety and stress are helpful"

Many of us seem to believe, "Fear, anxiety, and stress help me to achieve my goals". This belief is generally created by the fact that we have often arrived at our goals when we have experienced anxiety along our pursuit. This has led us to believe that the anxiety helped. However, for most of us, this assumption has rarely been tested because we tend to have a very small frame of reference for performing actions towards goals without anxiety. It is true that fear *can* motivate us to take action. But, fear also has many counterproductive side effects, and the motivation it provides often isn't as strong as our motivation without fear. We have achieved outcomes we wanted in our life despite our stress, not because of it. Let's take a look at some of the reasons why anxiety is more hurtful than helpful.

a)   Anxiety prevents us from taking action towards our goals. We often choose to stay in situations we don't like, and we don't pursue our goals because we are afraid of not reaching our desired outcome. We withhold love from others, don't pursue dream jobs, don't move to our favorite destinations, don't enter competitions, and don't pursue the people we want to be with because we are afraid of failure. Fear prevents us from pursuing what we think will make us happy.

b)   Stress makes doing the work needed to achieve our goal very unenjoyable. It becomes much harder to work for long amounts of time when we aren't enjoying ourselves. Effort doesn't feel like effort when we enjoy what we are doing. Without stress, we are much happier and much more able to work for longer periods of time towards our goals.

c)   When we are experiencing anxiety, our attention is on thoughts of the future. This means our attention is not fully on this moment. Less attention on this moment means less energy given to this moment. Less energy given to our work in this moment makes us less efficient and worsens the quality of our work.

d)   It becomes difficult to be happy, enjoy ourselves, and have enthusiasm for life when we feel stress. In addition, stress causes our bodies to contract and feel tense, making us more irritable. When this is our experience, others don't want to be around us nearly as much. We bring them down and aren't enjoyable to be around. This hurts our chances of getting promotions and working well as a member of a team, and it often hurts others' opinions of us.

e)   It is very difficult to be creative and offer fresh insight when our attention is on thoughts of the future. Creativity arises from the space (silence) between thoughts and is therefore hard to come by when we are busy giving attention to the thoughts that are creating our anxiety.

f)   For some of us, our fear of failure prevents us from fully committing to a goal, from putting our full effort into a goal. If we give our complete effort and we still fail, then we have to admit, "I gave it my best, but I just wasn't good enough; I couldn't do it". This can make us feel hopeless, as if we are a failure, as though we aren't in control, and can really hurt our opinion of ourselves. Since we don't want to feel this way, some of us decide to never give our all towards our goals. This way, if we fail, we can claim it was because "I didn't try my hardest" or "I didn't really care about the outcome".

g)   We generally seem to care a lot about achieving our goals. Our goals of improving ourselves, finding someone to love us, or becoming successful are seen as incredibly important parts of our life. Achieving our goals (changing our circumstances) may even seem to be the most important thing in our life. Therefore, if you think that your anxiety helps you achieve your goal, you would naturally want to keep your anxiety. Because of this, it is important that you ask yourself a few questions about whatever goal makes you want to keep your anxiety or whatever goal is most important to you.

The first question is, "How do I expect to feel once I have achieved my goal?" For most of us, we expect to feel happy, peaceful, or whole when we finally achieve our goals. We may think that we will finally be able to relax. We may think that we will finally get love, respect, and approval from others (which we believe will bring us peace). We may think that we will finally be able to buy everything we want, which we expect will make us happy.

The second question is, "Why do I want to achieve my goal?" If we expect to feel happy or peaceful when we achieve our goal, then the reason we want to achieve our goal is because we believe it will make us feel how we want to feel. Although we generally don't realize it, we really just want to experience peace and happiness more than anything else, and we have unconsciously created our goals because we believe that achieving them will make us happy. Put differently, achieving our goals is just the means to get to our ultimate goal of being happy.

To make this more clear, let's look at a few simple examples. If you walk past an ice cream shop and begin to feel a big craving to eat some ice cream, why do you want to have the ice cream? It is not because we want ice cream, it is because we want the experience of pleasure that the taste of ice cream will give us. If you meet someone who is physically attractive to you, and you decide that you want to be with them, why do you want them? It is not because we really want the person, it is because we think that being with them will make us feel pleasure or happiness.

This is the same dynamic as with our goals. We may think that we genuinely want success, but we really just want to be happy, and we happen to think that success is the "best" way to make ourselves happy. We may think that we want wealth, but we really just want wealth because we think it can make us happy in one way or another. We may think that we want approval from our parents, but we really just want this approval because we think it will make us feel worthy and whole.

It seems as if we care a tremendous amount about achieving our goals, but if we look at the situation a little more closely, we can discover that achieving our goals (changing our circumstances) isn't really our ultimate goal in life. Our ultimate goal is just to be happy or peaceful, and we happen to believe that achieving our goal will help us to feel this way. Therefore, on the most fundamental level, when we claim, "Anxiety helps me achieve my goal", we are actually believing, "Anxiety helps me to become happy". If we recognize that our true goal is to be happy, then it wouldn't make sense to keep our anxiety just because we hope that it would help us to achieve our goal in the future, which we hope would make us happier. Choosing anxiety over happiness clearly doesn't make us happier.

The Questions: What "bad" outcome do I think will happen if I lose my anxiety? Am I absolutely sure that my anxiety is helpful at getting me what I want or preventing what I don't want from happening? Can I think of any reasons why not having anxiety might help me get what I want?

a) Is it possible that my fear of failure (anxiety) will prevent me from making any effort toward trying to achieve my goal (i.e., remaining in an undesirable job instead of pursuing my "dream" job)?

b) If I didn't have anxiety, wouldn't I enjoy my work towards achieving my goal much more, therefore enabling me to spend more time on it (i.e., it's hard to work when stressed)?

c) Wouldn't the quality and efficiency of my work improve if my full attention was given to what I was doing instead of to the thoughts that create my anxiety?

d) If I was happy (instead of stressed), wouldn't the people around me like me more, therefore helping me to get what I want (e.g., a new client or promotion)?

e) Isn't it easier to be creative and offer fresh insight when I am not giving attention to the thoughts that create my anxiety?

f) Doesn't my stress sometimes prevent me from giving my full effort toward my goals because I want to have an excuse if I fail?

g) How do I expect to feel when I achieve my goal? Why do I want to achieve my goal? Can I admit that I really just want to achieve my goal because I think it will make me feel the way I want to feel? Is it true that my anxiety or stress helps to make me happy?

7. "Worrying is helpful, responsible, and means I care"

Even when we really don't like worrying, our minds often come up with a few excuses to keep us from questioning the thoughts that create our worries:

a) "Worrying can help prevent, stop, or fix the scenario I am worrying about"
b) "Worrying will help prepare me for the worst case scenario"
c) "Worrying is the responsible thing to do"
d) "Worrying is a sign that I care. If I don't worry about someone, that means I don't care about them"
e) "Worrying can help me solve my problem"

Let's take a look at some of the reasons why worrying is much more hurtful than helpful.

a)   "Worrying can help prevent, stop, or fix the scenario I am worrying about". Worrying certainly does not help to prevent or stop future scenarios from happening.

> i)   How can thoughts prevent something from happening when we don't have control over whether it happens? When we are worrying, by nature, we are thinking and not acting. Thinking cannot prevent, stop, or fix a situation that hasn't yet happened.

> ii) Worrying about the future might indirectly increase the chances that the event will happen. If we are giving some of our attention to our worries about losing our job or our lover, then we are not giving our full energy to the job or lover. We might also hold back some of our effort or love because we fear that we will lose our job or lover. This can worsen the quality of our work, make us less enjoyable to be around, and prevent

the relationship from strengthening. This increases the likelihood that we will lose the job or lover.

b)   "Worrying will help prepare me for the worst case scenario". Worrying about a future scenario rarely helps to prepare us for it.

i) Most of our worrying is not planning. Creating a plan to avoid an unwanted outcome may be helpful. A plan would be a written-down list of things to do in order to avoid an unwanted outcome or to react to an unwanted outcome. Generally, our worries are just endless thoughts about what outcomes we don't want to happen, how "bad" they would be if they happened, how to avoid them, or what to do if they happen. These types of thoughts are rarely of any help. If we really want to make a plan, then it would be most helpful to set aside a 10-minute time slot in our day that is dedicated to creating this plan. This way, whenever we start worrying, we can just acknowledge that this is not the time for it, and we already have a time dedicated for it later.

ii) There is an incredibly slim chance that the scenario we think about will happen. Most of our hypotheticals aren't based in reality and are very unlikely to happen. Try to remember some of things you worried about in the past that never ended up happening. When we are in the midst of worrying, we tend to lose sight of the fact that the outcome we fear has a very low probability of happening.

iii) There are too many variables within any "bad" scenario for any pre-thought-out plan to fit in seamlessly. The probability that our feared situation will happen in the exact way we think it will is very slim. Therefore, it is incredibly unlikely that our plan would be able to impact the situation in our desired way. Within any scenario we fear, there is an infinite number of variables that can affect the situation. For example, if we worry that our child might get hurt, depending on what gets hurt, where they get hurt, who is around when they get hurt, and how badly they get hurt, our plan for how to handle it would be entirely different. It wouldn't make sense to plan for the hypothetical scenarios we fear, because we couldn't possibly form enough different plans to come up with "good" ways to fix each of them. Wouldn't we be much better at forming a plan to fix a situation once we know what the situation is?

iv) For example, we may have formed a plan that if our child falls at the playground then we will immediately rush them to the hospital. If our child does fall, there may be other parents around who are doctors and have first-aid kits in their cars that could help our child more quickly. If we automatically try to implement our preconceived plan, then we might not be noticing our surroundings and all of the unique variables in our situation. Automatically taking our child to the hospital instead of reacting on the spot by yelling, "Is anyone a doctor?", might end up hurting our child due to the added time before he receives treatment. We can't create the perfect plan to fix something when we don't know all of the variables. It is very difficult to plan for heroics and selflessness. When we think and plan before a "bad" event, we are often indecisive, selfish, and scared to act when the event happens. However, when we are faced with immediate, unforeseen challenging situations, this is when we hear tales of heroes. When we do not have the chance to think first, we risk our own lives for others and almost always seem to act selflessly. We would almost never be able to plan these types of actions.

c)   "Worrying is the responsible thing to do". Worrying is actually not responsible. When we worry, we take our attention off our responsibilities in this moment. This makes us less able to perform whatever task is needed in this moment because we are busy giving some of our energy and attention to thoughts of an imaginary future. If we are worried that our child might get hurt while we are with them as they are riding their bike or driving their car, then some of our attention will be on these thoughts and not on what our child is doing in the moment. This makes it more likely that we won't be present, aware, and available to notice when an accident is about to happen, and this makes it more likely that the accident will happen. Therefore, worrying is actually less responsible than leaving our attention on the present moment.

d)　　　"Worrying is a sign that I care. If I don't worry about someone, that means I don't care about them". Worrying is not a sign that we care about others. Worries are created by thinking about an outcome we believe "would be bad". Some people worry about those they love and some don't. Some people worry about people they don't even know and some don't. Caring about others does not require that we worry about them. We can love someone completely but never worry about them simply because we don't imagine future scenarios that we believe would be "bad". Not only that, but worrying about others makes it less possible for us to show others we care about them.

If we are busy worrying about someone we love while we are with them, then we actually aren't caring about them as much because: i) Our attention is partially on thoughts of a "bad" future, which means we are not completely listening to them and their concerns. ii) They may think we don't love them if they see that our attention isn't completely on them. iii) We may incite fear in them when they see through our words and facial expressions that we are worrying. iv) It is very difficult to fully engage in thinking about how to help them when we are busy worrying. v) It is unlikely that we will come up with creative solutions to help because we are too busy thinking (worrying).

e)   "Worrying can help me solve my problem". *When we spend time planning what we would do if something "bad" were to happen, we are essentially trying to solve a problem that doesn't exist.* The problems that we worry about are actually only thoughts about an imaginary future. Since we can invent an infinite number of future problems, we can spend our whole life trying to solve all of these imaginary problems. However, no matter how wonderful a solution we create, we can't solve these problems, because they don't actually exist.

For example, we may be lying in bed, when all of a sudden we start to worry that one of our co-workers will insult us tomorrow. So, in order to try to solve this problem, we spend time thinking about what we will say in response if they insult us.

But even if we were to create the "perfect" response, what would this solve right now? It can't solve any problem right now because there is no problem right now. We can't apply the "perfect" solution to our problem because our imaginary problem is in the future, and not happening right now. Since the "perfect" solution doesn't solve our problem, it doesn't make us feel any better. Of course, when we haven't solved our problem and we don't feel any better, we often keep trying to form more and more solutions to our problem. We do this because we hope that one of our solutions will actually solve our problem. Since the problem inherently can't be solved in our minds, we can spend an infinite amount of time trying to solve it.

Most of us spend a lot of time trying to solve problems that don't exist because we tend to think that our thoughts about "bad" events in the future are "real" problems. But if our problem is about a future event, then it hasn't yet happened, and therefore doesn't yet exist as anything other than a thought. If we don't want to spend our life solving problems that don't exist, all we need to is ask ourselves is, "Does this problem exist right now anywhere outside my own mind?"

The Questions:

a) What am I afraid will happen if I stop worrying? Is it true that my worrying (thinking without actions) has the power to prevent, stop, or fix the "bad" scenario that I'm thinking about? Is it possible that my worrying actually makes it more likely that the "bad" scenario will happen?

b) What are the chances that my worrying will help prepare me for the "bad" scenario, considering the low chance that the scenario would actually happen as well as all of the different possible variables within that scenario if it were to happen? How often has my previous worrying helped prepare me for a situation I encountered?

c) Is it true that worrying is the responsible thing to do, considering that worrying directs my attention to thoughts of the future and away from whatever is happening in this moment?

d) Is it true that worrying about someone means I care about them, considering that I can love someone and not worry about them, while I could worry about someone I don't love? Is it true that worrying shows I care, considering that I can't give my full attention to someone when I worry about them, and that I might incite fear in others if they sense that I am worried about them?

e) Does my problem exist right now anywhere other than in my own mind? If my problem doesn't exist, then is it possible for me to solve my problem? If not, then is it worth spending my time trying to solve an insolvable problem that doesn't even exist?

Question the Validity of Any Reason Not to Question Your Thoughts

When we are new to questioning our thoughts, our minds can create a variety of reasons why it would be "good" to keep our negative thoughts and why it would be "bad" for our life if we questioned them. This chapter contains explanations and questions to challenge a variety of our most common reasons to resist questioning our thoughts.

8. "I want to keep blaming others for my suffering"

For some of us, it can be very difficult to even allow ourselves to entertain the possibility that someone else might not be to blame for our suffering. In other words, we really want to keep blaming others for our suffering. So let's examine why we would want to hold on to our blame.

If we blame someone else for our suffering, what benefit do we get from it? Blaming our suffering on others can make us feel self-pity and as though we are a victim. It also creates anger towards whoever we believe is to blame. This anger can often be held on to for a long time, creating a lot of resentment. If we choose to act on that anger, then our blame can help to cause suffering for the person we blame. Our anger can affect the people around us (e.g., children, partners) inadvertently if they feel our anger in our interactions with them. Our resulting unhappiness can make us less enjoyable to be around, which may hurt our personal and professional relationships. In summary, blaming others for our suffering creates more suffering for ourselves and possibly more for others.

If we know that our blame creates suffering, why would we want to hold on to our blame? a) We want to punish others so that we can feel as if life is fair (hold people accountable); b) We want to teach people a lesson so that they don't do the same "bad" thing again; c) We don't want to admit that our own thoughts have created our unwanted emotions.

a)   When someone seems to make us suffer, some of us instantly, and often unconsciously, think that the "best" course of action is to get revenge. We may not realize it, but the idea of revenge, or punishment, is often based on the belief that these actions will make us feel better or give us relief. If someone seems to make us suffer in some way, then we spend a lot of time thinking about how what happened to us was unfair (how we didn't deserve it), then these thoughts would likely create feelings of anger, frustration, and possibly confusion. If we manage to create suffering for whoever we think is to blame for our suffering, the most we can get out of it is a new belief that the situation is now more fair than it was. If the thought, "This situation is unfair", was creating our anger and frustration, then making the situation "more fair" would likely reduce our anger and frustration. But punishing others as a means to make ourselves happy is far from the most effective strategy, because punishing others also causes us to suffer in a few different ways.

No matter what form of punishment we decide to inflict on someone, it is almost always designed to create suffering (or prevent happiness) for the apparent perpetrator of our suffering. Regardless of whether our punishment takes the form of verbal abuse, physical abuse, hurtful action, withholding of love or sex, or "attitude", we will simultaneously be creating suffering for ourselves. Treating people in a way that doesn't feel honest, caring, and loving makes us feel sad, angry, resentful, guilty, and "bad" about ourselves and can make us feel the hurt that we inflicted. This is especially true when we actually love the victim of our actions. In addition, the victim of our punishment may get angry at us and want revenge, which would perpetuate our suffering.

Beyond the hurt we feel from making others suffer, we often choose to punish others solely by being angry and giving "attitude" to the apparent perpetrator. But this is really only punishing ourselves. Others often don't feel our anger. We feel our anger. We are the ones getting punished by our anger towards someone else. By doing all of this, we are creating more suffering for ourselves and are therefore making our life seem even more unfair.

b) 	People decide on their words and actions based on thoughts. If we truly don't want someone to do the same "bad" thing again, then we need to help that person understand how their action was hurtful, help them to identify what thoughts motivated them to act the way they did, and then help them to question those thoughts so that they don't act on them again.

Do you ever engage in "bad" habits that you know are physically, emotionally, or monetarily harmful, but yet you keep doing them anyway? Despite our guilt, anger towards ourselves, and any other suffering, we still often aren't able to stop acting in the same way. Why isn't our suffering enough to help us learn our lesson and stop doing the same "bad" things? Quite simply, it is because we haven't addressed the cause of our actions, our thoughts. We have not discovered why we are doing what we're doing, so it is only natural that our suffering wouldn't help us to stop our "bad" habits. *Just as our own suffering often isn't enough to change our actions, punishing someone else (making others suffer) usually isn't enough to teach them how to change their actions.*

c)   When we have invested a lot of time and energy into blaming someone for our suffering, it can be very difficult to allow ourselves to see that our own thoughts have created our suffering, because this can make us feel "bad" about ourselves. But this only happens if we are shifting the blame of our suffering from others to ourselves. This isn't what we're doing here.

We have not caused our own suffering; believing our thoughts has caused our suffering. We are only to blame for our suffering if we are to blame for believing our thoughts. Do you have control over which thoughts you think? If you did, then wouldn't you choose to never think negatively? We don't have full control over which thoughts we think; we weren't taught that thoughts create emotions, and we weren't taught how to question our thoughts. Therefore, how can we possibly be to blame for the emotions our thoughts create? When we truly see that we aren't to blame for believing our thoughts, then we are off the hook, it's not our fault.

The beauty of this is that if you can acknowledge that no one else has been to blame for your suffering, then you are also acknowledging that no one has the power to make you suffer in the future. You are free. Nobody can make you suffer. You don't need to worry about what anyone else is doing or will do. The only thing that can hurt you or keep you from being at peace is believing your own thoughts.

The Questions:

a) If I get revenge or hold someone else accountable for my suffering, isn't it likely that I would feel more anger (suffering) or that I would feel "bad" about my actions? Who feels my anger when I blame someone else for my suffering?

b) Isn't it unlikely that punishing someone would be enough to get them to change their actions in the future, considering that punishments wouldn't help them to become aware of the thoughts that cause their actions or help them to disbelieve these thoughts?

c) Am I in full control over what thoughts enter my mind or what thoughts I believe? If not, then can I admit that I am not to blame for the thoughts that create my suffering?

9. "I don't want to admit 'I don't know' or 'I was wrong'"

Throughout our years in the formal education system, we are constantly taught that it is "good" to be right and to know the answer. We get complimented for being right, and we are rewarded by our teachers and society for knowing the right answers. Therefore, we have been conditioned to believe that it is "bad" to be wrong or not to know. This simple dynamic has had a profound impact on our lives.

Do you remember a time when you were in school and you raised your hand to correctly answer the teacher's question? How did it feel? It generally gave us a small feeling of pleasure because we got to think, "I know the answer, I am right". In the same way, any time we experience an emotion, we are essentially answering a question in our head and then believing our answer to be correct. For everything we encounter in life, we are asking ourselves some form of the question "is this good or bad?", "is he handsome or ugly?", "is she selfish or considerate?" Then, when we answer the question and think, "She *is* selfish", we are essentially believing, "I *know* that she is selfish, and I am *right* about it". Since we think it is "good" to be "right", when we make a judgment and think, "She is selfish", we get to experience a very subtle feeling of pleasure from believing, "I know, I am right". This feeling of pleasure is similar to the feeling we got when we raised our hand in class and correctly answered a question, as they are both the effect of slightly improving our opinion of ourselves.

Therefore, we may have resistance to disbelieving our thoughts because of this lingering unconscious belief that it is "bad" to not know the answer. We often unknowingly think it will worsen our opinion of ourselves to admit, "I don't know". We see this very clearly in the verbal arguments we encounter in which both people want to be "right" and neither is willing to admit that they are "wrong" or that they really don't know. The same thing happens with our relationship with our own thoughts. Once we believe a thought, we try to defend it because we are scared of being "wrong" or admitting that we don't know.

But is it really "bad" to admit, "I don't know"? What is the experience of going from "I know that this is bad" to recognizing, "I don't know whether this is bad"? When we believe, "She is selfish", we may feel a little high from believing, "I am right", but we also have to experience the anger, disappointment, frustration, or other suffering created by believing that she is selfish. On the other hand, when we admit, "I don't know" or "I was wrong to believe that", we experience peace and can treat others with love. The only cause of our suffering is simply believing our thoughts to be true.

Once we experience this peace, we can see that there is nothing "bad" about being wrong or not knowing. On the contrary, admitting, "I don't know", can be seen as wonderful because it instantly makes us feel happy. If we don't want to be unhappy, all we have to do is stop being "right". Which is more important to you, being "right" or being happy?

The Questions: Isn't it true that my unwanted emotion is created by believing my thought to be true ("I am right")? Considering that believing my thought makes me suffer, how would I feel if I stopped believing my thought to be true, if I admitted, "I was wrong" or "I don't know"? Am I absolutely certain that I would feel "worse" about myself if I were to acknowledge, "I was wrong", or "I don't know"? Which is more important to me, being "right" or being happy?

10. "If I don't see certain actions as bad, I will act in hurtful ways"

It is easy for us to think that we would act in harmful or hurtful ways if we stop believing many of our concepts of what is "bad". But what causes us to act in hurtful and unloving ways? We act hurtfully towards others when we believe that others are "bad", others have done something "bad", and others are to blame for our suffering. In addition, when we believe thoughts that declare we aren't "good enough" or our life isn't "good enough", then we become unhappy and can often be willing to hurt others (e.g., steal from someone) if we believe doing so would make ourselves happy. *In other words, it is actually our concepts of "bad" that cause our unloving words and actions.*

We don't need to ask ourselves, "Is this good or bad?" or "Is this right or wrong?" in order to act lovingly towards ourselves and others. If we don't believe our negative thoughts about ourselves, then we are already happy, and we therefore don't need to hurt others in order to get something that we think will make us happy. If we don't believe our negative thoughts about others, then we feel no hatred or anger towards them, which eliminates our reasons to hurt others. Without our judgments about others, we are left with love for others.

If we don't believe the thoughts that create our suffering, we are happy. If we are already happy, then we may not feel the need to spend a large portion of our money on entertainment, clothes, fancy cars, and other types of distractions and possessions that we would normally look to for happiness. What would we do with all of this extra money? Quite naturally, we often feel the urge to give it to others because we love them or because we see they need it more than we do. If we don't believe our negative thoughts, then we may not feel the need to spend all of our time and energy entertaining ourselves with activities we enjoy, since we are equally happy without engaging in these activities. We can then much more easily and lovingly give our time and energy to helping others.

When we are present, we already feel complete and worthy, so we can love others and help others without being motivated by selfish interests. We can give to others without any interest in getting something in return (e.g., love, appreciation, and approval). If we are already happy, we don't care about getting anything in return. We don't use others as a means to make ourselves happy.

One way to see how we act when we are present is to look at what people do when they are in quick life-or-death situations. We all hear stories in the news about acts of courage and selflessness that happen in quick life-or-death situations, where people do things such as jump onto train tracks to save people they don't know. This type of action tends to happen in these life-or-death situations be-cause there is no time for our minds to think and decide what to do. With no time to think or analyze what is "good" or "right", and no time for our minds to decide what is in our "best interest", we are forced to act from our intuition, and we wind up performing loving actions naturally. But, if we had the time to think first, it is unlikely that we would act in these unselfish ways because we might be taken over by fear, we might be too indecisive, or we might not be willing to risk our life to help someone we don't know. But from the present moment (from intuition), we are naturally inclined to act kindly, compassionately, and selflessly.

The Questions: When do I act in hurtful ways towards others? What thoughts am I thinking when I choose to act hurtfully? What is my emotional experience when I act hurtfully? If I were not to believe my judgments about others, wouldn't I no longer have a reason to treat others without love? If I were not to believe the thoughts that make me unhappy, wouldn't I no longer have a reason to act selfishly and without regard for others' well-being? Is it true that I need to tell myself, "this is the wrong action", or, "this is a bad action", in order to prevent myself from acting hurtfully towards others?

11. "Disbelieving 'this should be different' or 'this is bad' will prevent me from acting towards positive change"

It may seem as though disbelieving our thoughts about what is "bad" and how people should act would cause us to be indifferent towards the world and prevent us from making "positive" change. However, this is not the case at all. Even without our judgments about a situation, we can still feel compelled to act towards change. Complaints, anger, frustration, and sadness aren't necessary in order to be compelled to act. We generally don't realize this because it is not within our frame of reference. We can still be an activist with plenty of drive to make change in the world without the concept of "bad" or "wrong". It is just that the catalyst to create change comes from our intuition instead of from thought. Here are a few reasons why acting from the present moment can still allow us to act towards "positive" change in the world.

a)   If we want peace and love in this world, it has to start with ourselves. How can we help people to be loving and to stop hating when we are filled with anger and hate? How can we stop people from having conflicts with each other when our own minds are filled with conflicting thoughts? How can we get angry at people who punish others for what they see as "bad" actions when we are constantly punishing others for what we believe to be "bad" actions? How can people change their actions when they aren't aware of the thoughts that drive their actions and they don't know how to disbelieve their thoughts? How can we help people to change the way they act without addressing the cause of their actions (i.e., thoughts)? As long as we are believing our minds' judgments, we won't be completely peaceful and loving. If we want to make the world more peaceful and loving, we first need to discover this peace and happiness in our own lives.

b)   Often our activism comes from a place of righteous anger. This means we believe we are on the side of "good" fighting "evil", which naturally makes us feel "good" about ourselves. But what we are really doing is fighting a war. The same war as almost every other war. The war of "I am right and they are wrong".

Once we believe this concept "I am on the side of good, fighting evil", we are on a slippery slope that often leads to rationalizing "bad", dishonest, hurtful, or violent actions because we think they are justified in order to make the world "better". We think the ends justify the means. We may even believe we are "good" because we are willing to do something "bad" in order to make "good" in the world. For example, if we think someone is a "bad" influence on our community, and we want to make our community "better", then we may be willing to hurt that "bad" person for the "good" of the community. Even if we believe that hurting someone is a "bad" action, we can still think that we are "good" because we were the one willing to do something "bad" for the overall "good". But haven't many "bad" historical events happened because people thought certain "bad" actions would lead to some form of "good"?

We can't know for sure that we are on the side of "good" and that they are on the side of "bad" or "evil". And we can't know for sure what will make the world a "better" place. We also can't spread peace through anger. When we stop believing our judgments about what is "bad" and who is to blame, then our anger will subside and we can begin to act from love, with love, towards change.

c)   Trying to use thoughts in order to make decisions often leads to a lot of confusion or indecision because there are too many variables, too many pros and cons on both sides. When we are angry, it is even more difficult than normal to make decisions because our minds are generally unclear from being filled with so many negative thoughts. If our thoughts aren't believed, our choice of action then just presents itself to us in a very clear and easy way through our intuition. We can hear or feel our intuition in order to determine what to do rather than base our decisions on thoughts (perspectives). Our actions are then naturally less selfish, as our intuition is selfless in nature.

d)   Our catalyst for action towards change in this world generally arises either from our intuition or from thoughts and our natural desire to be happy. Our motivation for acting most often comes from believing an idea that something is "bad" or "not good enough". Once this happens, we often unknowingly decide to try to make the world "better" primarily because we believe that this is what will make us happy or peaceful. This could be because our negative thoughts about the world make us upset and we want to "fix" the world so that we can make ourselves happy. Or it could be because we unconsciously believe that "fixing" the world or helping others will improve our opinion of ourselves, which we think will bring us peace.

If we are able to disbelieve our judgments about what is "bad", we can experience peace right now. If our desire to change something in the world was initially motivated by our desire to be happy, and we are now happy, then we may no longer feel the urge to change the world.

However, if our drive to help bring about change in the world came from our intuition, then that drive for change will remain. In addition, if we never had the urge to make "positive" change, this drive may arise once we disbelieve our thoughts, because this allows us to love more and helps us to get in touch with our intuition. Of course, we don't view our course of action as making "positive" change, or helping to make the world "better", we are just following what feels true and natural for us to do.

e)　　　Completely new and creative solutions arise from intuition. Our thoughts are based on our genetics, our experiences, and what we have been taught. In other words, our thoughts refer to the past for information. Since thoughts are based on the past, they are not meant for offering new, fresh, or creative ideas. When we spend less time giving attention to our thoughts about who and what are "bad", there is more silence between our thoughts. In others words, there can be little breaks in our minds from our constant thinking. During these breaks, these gaps between thoughts, fresh creativity arises from the silence. Essentially, when we are present, creativity naturally arises.

f)　　　Others are more likely to follow our lead to act towards change when we come from a place of love rather than righteous anger. Would you rather spend time with and follow someone who was uplifting and filled with love or someone who was negative and filled with hatred? We generally tend to feel more inclined to spend time with people who are loving and kind rather than people who are angry and resentful. We naturally feel more inspired by love than hate because love gives us a feeling we enjoy and want.

The Questions:

a) How can I help people to act lovingly and stop hating when I am filled with anger and hate? How can I help people to stop having conflicts with each other when my own mind is filled with conflicting thoughts? How can I get angry at people who punish others for what they see as "bad" actions when I am constantly punishing others, as well as myself, for what I believe to be "bad" actions? How can people change their actions when they either aren't aware of the thoughts that drive their actions or don't know how to disbelieve their thoughts? How can I help people to change the way they act without addressing the cause of their actions (thoughts)? How can I help people to address the thoughts that cause their anger and unloving behavior when I haven't addressed these thoughts in my own mind?

b) Can I be absolutely sure that I am on the side of "good"? Can I be absolutely certain about what actions will best help to make the world "better"? Am I sure that my anger will best help to spread peace and love?

c) When I am angry, is my mind clear, or is it hectic, unclear, and filled with thoughts? Is it easier to make decisions from this place of anger, using my thoughts to weigh pros and cons, or is it easier to base my decisions on the clarity of my intuition? Are my actions more likely to be unselfish and loving when I am basing them on thoughts, or when I am basing them on my intuition?

d) If my urge to make "positive" change originated from my desire to be happy, then wouldn't I want to disbelieve the thoughts that are making me unhappy, since doing so would make me happy right now? If my urge to make "positive" change originated from my intuition, then wouldn't this urge remain, regardless of what thoughts I disbelieve?

e) Am I more likely to discover fresh and creative solutions when I am listening to thoughts (which are based on the past) or when I am present and able to feel my intuition?

f) Would I rather be around people who are angry or people who are loving? Are others more likely to follow my lead and be inspired by me when I am acting out of righteous anger or when I am acting out of love?

12. "If I don't see my situation as bad, then this bad situation will remain the same and I will be settling" or "If I see that my goal can't make me happy, then I won't have any motivation to achieve it"

It can seem as if disbelieving the thought "my situation is bad" or "achieving my goal will make me happy" would stop us from pursuing our goals or cause us to remain in our "bad" situation. In fact, sometimes our minds can scare us into not questioning our thoughts just by telling us that we will end up "settling" in our "bad" situation if we decide to question our thoughts. However, this is far from the truth.

An urge to change our situation or achieve a goal can come directly from our intuition or can arise because we want to make ourselves happy. If we disbelieve our thoughts, "my situation is bad" or "achieving my goal will make me happy", then whether we choose to remain in our situation or keep pursuing change depends on whether we are being driven by our intuition or by a desire to make ourselves happy.

a)   When our urge to change our situation (achieve a goal) comes from our intuition, then we almost certainly wouldn't lose our motivation to change our situation regardless of what thoughts we disbelieve. Our intuition lets us know what feels right and true to ourselves, and then guides us toward actions that are aligned with these feelings. Since our intuition's guidance has nothing to do with our thoughts or our unhappiness, disbelieving our thoughts about how our current situation is "bad" or becoming happy in our current situation both wouldn't affect our urge to change our situation. Even if we recognize that achieving our goal can't make us happy in and of itself, our intuitive urge or pull towards our goal won't be affected, because in this case our urge to pursue the goal was never motivated by promises of happiness.

For example, imagine that you are unhappy in your administrative job where you do computer data entry all day long. One day, after playing with some nieces and nephews of yours, you recognize that you love spending time with children. Imagine that this recognition came from your intuition and leads you to realize that you want to be a teacher. If you are able to identify and disbelieve the thoughts that are making you unhappy in your current administrative job, then you would be able to be peaceful at work. But, since your urge to become a teacher came from your intuition, and had nothing to do with your negative thoughts or unhappiness at work, you would still have the urge and full motivation to pursue being a teacher.

Similarly, disbelieving the thought "becoming a teacher will make me happy", wouldn't change your motivation to become a teacher because your decision to pursue teaching was based on your intuition or feeling that this is what you want to be doing, and not based on the idea that becoming a teacher would provide you with fulfillment.

b)   When we believe some version of, "My situation isn't good enough", "I shouldn't be in this situation", or "I would be happy if I was able to make this situation perfect", these thoughts make us unhappy in our current situation. Once these thoughts have made us unhappy, we are unknowingly motivated to try to change our situation or achieve a goal solely because we believe that these changes to our life will make us happy. If our motivation to change our situation or achieve a goal is solely based on our desire to be happy, and we are able to disbelieve the thoughts that have made us unhappy, then we may lose our interest in changing our situation or achieving our goal because we are now already happy.

This may sound discouraging, but if the only reason we wanted to change our situation or achieve a specific goal was to make ourselves happy (the ultimate goal), then we get to be happy now instead of waiting years as we try to achieve our goal (which doesn't actually have the ability to make us happy). This can't be considered "settling", because we are only choosing to remain in our situation because we are completely happy with the way it is.

If we aren't able to find peace and happiness in our current situation (because we aren't able disbelieve the thoughts that are making us unhappy), then our desire to change our situation will naturally remain, regardless of the where the urge comes from.

If we are pursuing a goal only because we want to be happy, and we recognize that our goal doesn't have the ability to make us happy, then we are likely to lose much of our motivation to achieve this goal. However, this recognition also has another major implication. When we stop pursuing what we think will make us happy in the future, we can start doing what we love. We can pursue what we are passionate about, what we enjoy, and what feels right to us, instead of doing what we think we should do. In other words, this recognition opens us up to pursuing something that more closely aligns with our intuition.

It is hard to imagine that staying in our "bad" situation wouldn't be "settling" only because we are unhappy in it right now. Take a moment right now to imagine how happy you would feel if you made your circumstances "perfect". Now imagine that you could be just as happy within your current situation. If you were as happy and peaceful as you want to be, then would you consider remaining in your current situation to be "settling"?

To make the distinction between these two types of motivation for change more clear, let's look at an example. If you think, "I shouldn't be in such a bad job", then you may feel ashamed or embarrassed about your job, and you would therefore want to change your job in order to try to make yourself happy. If you disbelieve your thoughts about your job, then you may actually end up loving your job and being happy in it. If this happens, then choosing to stay in your job can no longer be considered "settling". If questioning your thoughts doesn't make you happy in your job (because you can't identify or disbelieve the thoughts that are making you unhappy), then you would still look to change your job.

Similarly, if your original urge to leave your job came because you felt the job wasn't right for you (intuition), or you were being guided to a job you felt passionate about (intuition), then you would still want to leave your job and still feel motivated to pursue the new one even if you became happy in your job. These urges aren't created by thoughts, so they remain after our negative thoughts are disbelieved.

The Questions:

a) If my urge to change my situation or achieve my goal came from my intuition, then wouldn't this urge remain regardless of what thoughts I disbelieve? If my urge to change my situation or achieve my goal came from my desire to be happy, then wouldn't I want to disbelieve the thoughts that are making me unhappy, since that would make me happy right now? Wouldn't I only want to remain in my current situation if I ended up being happy in it? If I wind up happy in my current situation, then can I really consider it "settling" to remain in my current situation?

b) If I recognize that my goal can't make me happy, wouldn't this only affect my motivation to achieve my goal if I only cared about achieving my goal because I thought it would make me happy? If I recognize that my goal can't make me happy, isn't it possible that this will allow me to start pursuing what I am passionate about, what I enjoy, or what feels right to me?

13. "My 'should' thought helps me to act how I believe I should, which has a positive effect on my life and the lives of others"

When it comes to beliefs such as "I should eat healthy" or "I should be nice to people", it seems obvious that we should behave in these ways. Even if we see that these thoughts create suffering for ourselves, we still may not want to disbelieve them because we may think they are helpful. We tend to think these types of thoughts are helpful for two main reasons. First, we may think that acting how we believe we should will have "positive" effects on our lives and the lives of others. Second, we tend to believe that telling ourselves, "I should do..." is the best way to get ourselves to do whatever it is we think we should be doing. But if we look at the effect of these thoughts more closely, it becomes apparent that these thoughts actually create a lot of stress and shame in our lives, while at the same time they don't really help us to act in the ways we believe we should (especially over the long-term).

When we believe, "I should act this way", we are unknowingly believing that we know what action will be "best" for ourselves or others. But do we know what all of the effects of any action are? We can't possibly know what actions make ourselves or others happiest because there is no way to know what all of the effects of any action are. If we don't know what action will make ourselves or others happiest, then we can't really know that there is a way that we "should" act.

However, even if we did know what actions are "best", the thought, "I should do…" still isn't helpful to make ourselves or others happier.

Generally, our actions are decided based on the thoughts in our mind. More specifically, we decide on our actions based on what outcome is most important to us. Since our own happiness is almost always what's most important to us, we choose our actions based on whatever outcome we think will make us happiest.

If you walk into your kitchen and decide to eat a cookie instead of a carrot, it is likely because you are valuing the immediate pleasure from eating the cookie over the possible positive healthy effects (future happiness) from eating the carrot. If, in the moment that you choose the cookie, you think, "I should eat healthy" ("eating healthy is the right thing to do"), will this change your mind and make you put the cookie down? We have been taught to believe that the answer is "yes", but what is the real effect? When we tell ourselves, "I should eat healthy", this isn't likely to change our decision to eat the cookie because it doesn't change how we value our options. It doesn't make us value the future health effects more, and it doesn't make us value the immediate pleasure of eating the cookie any less. *In other words, "should" thoughts often aren't helpful at getting us to act how we believe we should because these thoughts don't change how we value our options.*

When we don't act how we believe we should, we can feel shame, guilt, or just down about ourselves. Because of this, sometimes "should" thoughts can motivate us to act how we believe we should by making us fear the feeling of shame that we think we will feel if we don't do what we should. If we are about to put a cookie in our mouth and then think, "I should eat healthy", the thought "if I eat this cookie, I am going to feel guilty about this later" may arise in our mind. Because we fear that we will feel guilty, we may decide to put the cookie down. It may seem as if the "should" thought helps us out in this situation, but living life with the fear that we will feel "bad" or guilty is thoroughly unenjoyable.

As long as we have ideas of how we should act, there will be times when we will act in ways that we believe we shouldn't. Since we don't have full control over the thoughts we think or the thoughts we believe, this is inevitable. As we all know, when we do something we believe we shouldn't, we feel "bad" about ourselves. This suffering actually has major implications on our actions. This is because most of the "bad" actions in life, the ones we think we shouldn't do, are caused by our own suffering. More specifically, we engage in harmful actions towards ourselves and others when we are trying to escape our suffering or because we are angry.

For example, many of us often go to unhealthy foods when we want relief from our discontent, when we want to feel better right now. The cookie is our escape. When we eat the cookie and then think, "I should be eating healthy", this often makes us feel shame, guilt, or just "bad" about ourselves. Once we feel less happy, our urge to go to the cookie strengthens because our urge to escape our unhappiness has now strengthened. As previously mentioned, the more unhappy we are, the stronger our urge is to escape our unhappiness. And "should" thoughts are a large source of our unhappiness. Therefore, "should" thoughts are, paradoxically, a major reason that we act in ways we believe we shouldn't.

Let's look at another example. If we aren't nice to people, this is likely because we are either believing thoughts that make us unhappy or we are believing thoughts that make us angry at others. If you are about to be mean to someone, and then you think, "But I should be nice to them", will this make you act nice to them? Let's look at the different scenarios.

Since the thought "I should be nice" doesn't make us any happier and doesn't address our anger towards the other person, it is unlikely that our "should" thought will be able to make us act nicely towards them. If this happens, we will now have the thought "I should have been nice", which is likely to make us feel "worse" about ourselves, which in turn makes us unhappier and therefore makes it harder to be nice to others in the future.

On the other hand, it is possible that telling ourselves, "I should be nice", may get us to act nicely towards someone. But if this thought doesn't address why we don't feel like being nice, then our nice behavior is fake. As many of us have likely come to realize, it doesn't feel great when we pretend to feel different from the way we actually feel. In addition, how do you feel when someone is just pretending to be nice to you? It usually isn't a very enjoyable experience. It may be more enjoyable than openly unkind behavior, but it is not nearly as enjoyable as being with someone who is genuinely kind to us. Therefore, even if the "should" thought gets us to act in a way we believe we should, it rarely has the "positive" effect on ourselves and others that we would hope it would.

In addition to all of this, *as long as we have ideas of how we believe we should act, we will also believe that others should act in these ways.* If we believe, "I should eat healthy", and "I should be nice", then we will also believe others should as well. Since others often don't act how we believe they should, this belief causes us to judge others and get angry at others. This anger clearly doesn't help make us happy, but this anger also makes it even harder to eat healthy, be nice to others, and act in all the other ways we believe we should.

We keep telling ourselves, "This is how I should act", because we believe these thoughts help us to act in ways we believe we should, which we believe will make ourselves and others happier. But ultimately we don't know what actions will be "best" for ourselves and others, these thoughts really don't help us act to how we believe we should, these thoughts often make us suffer, and our suffering in turn makes it more likely that we will act in ways we believe we shouldn't.

If we want to stop acting how we are acting, rather than telling ourselves, "I shouldn't act how I do", we just need to identify and disbelieve the thoughts that cause us to act in the ways that we don't like. If you want to eat healthier and be nicer to people, then you just need to identify and disbelieve the thoughts that cause you to eat unhealthy and treat people without kindness. The strange thing is, if we just stopped believing our "should" thoughts, we would feel much happier, which would likely make it much easier to act in many of the ways that we think we should.

The Questions:

a) Can I be absolutely certain of what action will make me or others happiest in the long run, considering that I can't know what all the effects of any action are? If not, then can I really be sure of what way I "should" act?

b) Does telling myself, "I should do ...", change the way I value the pros and cons of each of my options for what action to take? If I don't act how I believe I should, how do I feel? Is it enjoyable to live life being motivated to act in certain ways by the fear that I will experience shame or guilt if I don't act how I believe I should?

c) Isn't it true that my thoughts determine how I act, and thus whether I act how I believe I should? Do I have full control over what thoughts I think and believe? If not, then can I always act how I believe I should? How do I feel when I do something that I believe I shouldn't do? Isn't it true that I often engage in my harmful actions (unhealthy food, drugs, alcohol) because I want to escape my unwanted emotions? Isn't it true that I treat others in unloving ways when I am either feeling unhappy or believing negative thoughts about others? Does telling myself, "I should treat them with love", get rid of my negative thoughts about them or make me happier? Or is it more likely that my "should" thought will make me feel "bad" about myself? If my "should" thoughts often make me feel ashamed and unhappy, and I often act in ways that I believe I shouldn't because I want to escape my unwanted emotions, then isn't it true that my "should" thoughts also motivate me to act in ways that I believe I shouldn't?

d) If I believe that I should act in specific ways, isn't it true that I must also believe that others should act in these ways? Do others always act how I believe they should? Do my "should" thoughts help me to love others, or do they cause me to judge others and feel anger towards others?

e) If I don't like the way I am acting, and I would like to change my actions, wouldn't it be much easier to identify and disbelieve the thoughts that are driving my actions, rather than tell myself, "I shouldn't act in this way"?

Chapter Eighteen

Applying The 5 Steps to The Present Moment

When to question our thoughts

Throughout our lives, in any moment that we haven't felt happy, we have generally only had two different ways to try to make ourselves happy: 1) distract ourselves from our thoughts through entertainment; and 2) try to change whatever circumstance we believe is "bad" or "not good enough". But since we now know how to question our thoughts, we now have another option. Let's take a look at why we might want to choose our new option the next time we feel stressed, angry, or ashamed.

If we don't feel happy in a given moment, it is often quick and easy to make ourselves happy by meeting up with friends, putting on a movie, or enjoying some funny content on the internet. But the issue with this is that the suffering we are trying to escape from will be waiting for us when we are finished giving our attention to whatever distraction we are using. There is no harm in engaging in any of our forms of entertainment, but if we want to be happy without these distractions, then we eventually need to question the thoughts that are making us unhappy.

If we are angry, stressed, or ashamed, then we often try to change whatever circumstance we believe is to blame for our unwanted emotions in order to try to make ourselves happy. If we are stressed in our job, we may try to change our job. If we are ashamed about our living situation, then we may try to change where we live. If we are angry at our partner for how they are acting, we may try to change them. If we manage to change these circumstances, we may be happy at first. But since this strategy addresses only a small fraction of the thoughts that are making us unhappy, our happiness is almost certainly going to be brief.

If we are angry at our partner because of the way they act, it is because we are believing a thought that says, "It is bad that you… don't clean up around the house, don't compliment me, show up late to events". If we manage to change one of our partner's actions, such as their not cleaning up around the house, we are likely to be happier at first because we have now lost our thought "it is bad that you don't clean up around the house".

But it is only a matter of time before our partner acts in another way that makes us think, "It is bad that he is doing that", or "The way she is acting isn't good enough". We have too many ideas about what are the "perfect" actions, and when it would be "perfect" to perform them, for us to be able to make someone "perfect". Eventually, we may decide that "he doesn't call enough", "she hangs out with her friends too much", "he isn't affectionate enough", "he doesn't help out with the kids enough", or "she isn't a good enough provider". These new thoughts will continue to make us angry at our partner and make us feel disappointed about our relationship. Or, if we change to a new partner, we will judge our new partner just as we judged our last one.

If we are stressed in our job, it is because we are believing a thought that says, "It would be bad if … I get fired, I don't finish this on time, my boss doesn't like my work". If we unknowingly believe that our stress is directly caused by the circumstances within our job, then we may decide to change jobs in order to make ourselves happy. But no matter what our new job is, there will still be the possibility of getting fired, the possibility of not finishing our work on time, and the possibility that our boss won't like our work. Therefore, even if we change our job, our boss, or the type of work we do, our thoughts ("it would be bad if...") will continue to create stress for us.

If we are ashamed about our living situation, it is because we are believing a thought that says, "It is bad that I am living where I do", or "my life isn't good enough because I am living in this place". If we are able to afford a bigger and "better" living situation, then we are likely to be happier at first because we will have lost these unwanted thoughts that were creating our shame. However, it is only a matter of time before "something in my life isn't good enough" or "I am not good enough" arises through a different manifestation. We may continue to think, "I'm not attractive enough", "I'm not smart enough", "I'm not lovable enough", or "I'm not wealthy enough". We may soon have thoughts about how "my job isn't good enough", "my car isn't nice enough", "my kitchen isn't clean enough", or "my couches aren't nice enough". These thoughts will continue to make us feel insufficient and ashamed about ourselves or our life.

When we change our circumstances to make ourselves happy, we aren't happy for very long because the fundamental cause of our unhappiness isn't addressed. Getting what we want eliminates the thought "this is bad", but it is purely a "Band-Aid solution". We have too many beliefs about what is "perfect" and what is "bad". If we change one aspect of ourselves, of others, or of our circumstances from "bad" to "perfect", one thought will be eliminated, but there will still be a large supply of other circumstances that we will think aren't "good enough".

Rather than spending all of our time, money, and energy trying to make ourselves, our situation, and others fit our idea of "perfect" in every way, we can just take the shortcut and question whether our concepts of "perfect" and "bad" are really true. If we can disbelieve the thought that is making us feel angry, stressed, or ashamed right now, then we can feel peace right now. This is clearly a much quicker and easier way to experience peace.

Naturally, sometimes we may not be able to disbelieve the thought that is making you unhappy on our first attempt. If this happens, we can try again at a later point in time, or we can clearly still choose to change whatever circumstance we believe is "bad" in order to try to make ourselves happy.

Changing our habit

When we experience an unwanted emotion, our immediate reaction is to blame it on something about ourselves, others, or our situation. We have been trained our whole lives to blame emotions on circumstances, so it has become a very strong habit. Now that we know how to question our thoughts, we can begin to change this habit.

As we first start to question our thoughts, when we experience an unwanted emotion, it can often take a few hours or days before we remember to question our thoughts, and it can require some time and energy to engage with The 5 Steps. But, as we engage with the process of questioning thoughts more and more, we begin to remember to question our thoughts as soon as we feel discontent, and the actual process of disbelieving thoughts can be done mentally with little time or effort.

For example, if our partner says something seemingly disrespectful to us, we may instantly get angry and then yell back at our partner with unloving words. A few hours later, we may stop and remember to question the cause of our anger. Then we would sit down and engage with The 5 Steps to identify and disbelieve the thoughts that caused our anger. If we are able to disbelieve our thoughts, our anger towards our partner can dissolve, and we can apologize to them for our unloving words. But eventually, after this type of event happens a few times, as soon as anger arises, we can recognize it as a thought to be questioned, and we will be able to identify and question the truth of this thought mentally in that moment. This allows us to remain in peace, but it also helps us to treat our partner (or whoever else) lovingly instead of automatically reacting with anger.

As we become more accustomed to questioning our thoughts, our old habit of trying to change external circumstances to make ourselves happy becomes replaced with the new habit of questioning thoughts any time we aren't happy. We focus on our own reaction instead of what person, situation, or event we believe is to blame for our reaction. When we are able to immediately recognize that our emotional reaction has been created by thoughts, we are not only happier, but we are also able to adjust our actions to reflect what is true for us.

As we question our thoughts more, the process becomes much easier and much quicker, and ultimately becomes second nature. While it can take ten minutes to question a thought in the beginning, it eventually only takes a few seconds to disbelieve most of our thoughts. Even if we aren't able to disbelieve the thought that is creating our unwanted emotion, just acknowledging that our emotion has been created by a thought can take the blame off whatever we were blaming and stop us from feeling like a victim. Each time we see one of our thoughts, the nature of that thought becomes clearer and clearer, and we identify with that thought less and less (allowing ourselves to look at that thought more objectively). This usually reduces the power of our emotion and makes it easier and easier to disbelieve the thought.

As we question our thoughts more often, instead of reacting to our unwanted emotions with the thought "what needs to change for me to be happy?", we find ourselves naturally asking, "What thought am I believing in this moment?" Our unwanted emotions become a signal to us that we are believing a negative thought to be true. We see our emotions as just letting us know that it is time to question whether the thought we are telling ourselves is really true. Any time we have an unwanted emotion, we see it as an invitation to question our thoughts.

Take it one moment at a time

Once we become aware that our thoughts create our suffering, we may start to think that we have to disbelieve a lot of thoughts in order to be happy. But this isn't true. We may have many concepts of "perfect" and "bad", but not all of them are creating suffering for us at the same time in every moment. Our unwanted emotion in a particular moment is caused by whatever thought we are believing in that moment. If we want to be at peace right now, we just have to disbelieve the thought we are believing right now.

Imagine that you really don't like it when rain falls on you because it makes your hair and clothes wet. There is an endless supply of rain drops, and they may show up at any time to make you wet. Would you worry about trying to stop the rain from coming in the future? No, if it is not raining, there is no problem. If you see it start to rain, you just take out your umbrella, and your problem is solved.

Just as with the rain drops, we have many concepts of "bad" that may show up and be believed at any moment. Do you need to worry about trying to stop all of these concepts of "bad" from showing up in your mind in the future? No, we don't have to worry about disbelieving all of our concepts of "bad", or about making sure that we don't re-believe the same thoughts again, or about eliminating all of our future suffering, because we can always disbelieve a thought in the moment that it enters our attention (open the umbrella). Just as we do with the rain, we can address our thoughts when they come. It takes only a few seconds to a few minutes.

If we have disbelieved a thought in the past, and then we believe it again, it is very important that we question the truth of this thought again as opposed to telling ourselves, "I know this thought isn't true". Telling ourselves, "My thought isn't true", doesn't help us to discover that we don't know whether our thought is true. This may even create internal conflict because we are thinking, "My thought isn't true" while actually believing the thought to be true. For this process to be most helpful, we have to directly discover that our thought might not be true each time a thought arises.

Each time we disbelieve a thought, the suffering it created dissolves, leaving us in peace. We don't have to disbelieve all of our thoughts right now. The moment that a thought arises to create suffering is the moment when it is time to disbelieve our thought. All we need to do is focus on the thought that is creating suffering for us right now.

The value comes from applying this process, not from reading about it

For some of us, this book may have been difficult to engage with. But it is important to know that this isn't personal. This is a common experience because the content in this book is meant to expose the negative thoughts we didn't know we had or didn't want to see. Seeing these unwanted thoughts can bring many different emotions to the surface, and this can be very confronting. But, if we just continue to ignore and distract ourselves from the thoughts that make us unhappy, these thoughts will continue to run our lives and prevent us from feeling peace. If we don't admit that we feel incomplete or discontent, if we don't bring our issues to the surface, then we can't ever address these issues.

In other words, we can't change or become happy unless we first discover the unwanted thoughts that are creating our unhappiness. So when we discover a new unwanted thought or feeling, instead of viewing this discovery as "bad", we can see it as a step towards freedom. Once we admit that we don't feel free, whole, or happy, once we discover our unwanted thoughts, then we can begin the process of disbelieving our thoughts and becoming present.

If you want to experience the inherent peace, freedom, and wholeness of the present moment, then I invite you to apply The 5 Steps to your life. You can use this process when you are caught in the grip of anxiety, when you feel overwhelmed with worry, when you are feeling ashamed of yourself, or when you are filled with anger towards someone. The 5 Steps can also be there for you when you feel a subtle sense of discontent, loneliness, or incompleteness. And eventually the process can be used to question the thoughts that take your attention off the present moment, even when they don't appear to be creating any suffering.

As we disbelieve more and more of our thoughts, we become more and more happy and peaceful. Since we will have increasingly fewer concepts of "bad" that we believe, these thoughts will arise to create suffering for us much less often. This makes life much more enjoyable and makes all of our relationships much more fulfilling.

In order to help you engage with this process on your own, you can go to my website, www.liveinthemoment.org, where you can:

1)	Access the free interactive web app "The 5 Steps to The Present Moment". This web app will allow you to simply and easily go through The 5 Steps to disbelieve your thoughts.

2)	Check out my video blog. The blog contains an ever-increasing number of videos and written explanations for how to live in the moment, and for how to use these questions to lose each of your unwanted emotions.

3)	Setup an individual session with me, or view my schedule of public events.

Acknowledgments

First and foremost, thank you dad for being my personal guide at every step along this journey, for leading me towards meditation through your example, for helping me to get in touch with and trust my intuition, and for showing me when I was unknowingly believing thoughts. Thank you for making this journey much quicker and easier than it ever could have been without you. Thank you mom for all your love, support, and laughter. Thank you to all of the teachers who have played a role in helping me to get where I am now. Thank you Jonas Iverson for planting the seed for this book.

Thank you to my wonderful editors, Karen Wolfgang-Swanson and Anne Barthel, for helping me to bring much more clarity to this book. Thank you to everyone who provided me with feedback, including my sisters Margeaux and Samantha.

Thank you to OC&C Strategy Consultants for giving me my perfect job, and thereby helping me to see what I truly wanted in life. Thank you to the many children that I played with over the last couple of years for all of the laughter and insights. Thank you to all of you that have allowed me to help you disbelieve the thoughts that were keeping you from feeling free, whole, and happy.

Made in the USA
Middletown, DE
22 January 2019